Additional Praise for *The Lost Book of Moses*

"With the skill and awareness of a Conan Doyle we are taken on a journey by a master storyteller that turns a historical investigation into a detective yarn that's a page turner. . . . In [Chanan Tigay's] hands, obsession feeds the excitement. Narrative artistry magnifies it. And like so many investigative stories the answers were hiding all along in plain sight."   —**Lowell Bergman, winner of the Pulitzer Prize**

"Chanan Tigay takes a fascinating headfirst dive into a cadre of obsessives pursuing a lost treasure linked to one of the great, elusive, and possibly criminal figures of early biblical archaeology. Years of international detective work have produced a saga of faith and fraud set in the days when it seemed one ceramic shard or scrap of parchment just might change the world."

—**Matti Friedman, author of** *The Aleppo Codex: In Pursuit of One of the World's Most Coveted, Sacred, and Mysterious Books*

"An intriguing and wide-ranging tale. . . . Arresting. . . . Painstakingly reconstructed. . . . Touching and informative."   —*Kirkus Reviews* **(starred)**

"An enthralling historical mystery in the grand tradition of *The Devil in the White City* and *The Professor and the Madman*. Tigay unfolds a compelling narrative of passions, delusions, deceptions and death, an epic of frailties and faith worthy of the Old Testament itself. *The Lost Book of Moses* marks the auspicious debut of an assured researcher and gifted storyteller."

—**Jason Roberts, author of** *A Sense of the World: How a Blind Man Became History's Greatest Traveler*

"A wonderfully fluid, rich biography-cum-archeological mystery about an enigmatic, fascinating figure, previously lost to the vapors of time. In his global search for the truth about Moses Shapira's life and the ur-Bible he hoped would make his fortune, Tigay has sorted through mountains of scholarly material and transformed them into a riveting, lucid narrative."

—**Lis Harris, author of** *Holy Days: The World of a Hasidic Family*

"Tigay [traces] each step of this complex and curious story across Europe and through the Middle East. In the end, [he] offers a dynamic and satisfying account of a strange, remarkable man whose discovery could turn the world of biblical scholarship on its head."   —*Publishers Weekly*

THE
LOST BOOK
OF MOSES

THE HUNT FOR THE WORLD'S OLDEST BIBLE

CHANAN TIGAY

ecco

An Imprint of HarperCollins*Publishers*

HarperCollins books may be purchased for educational, business,
or sales promotional use. For information please e-mail the
Special Markets Department at SPsales@harpercollins.com.

FIRST EDITION

Library of Congress Cataloging-in-Publication Data has been applied for.

ISBN 978-0-06-220641-1

16 17 18 19 20   OV/RRD   10 9 8 7 6 5 4 3 2 1

FOR MY MOTHER AND FATHER

CONTENTS

DRAMATIS PERSONAE

NINETEENTH CENTURY

Moses Wilhelm Shapira: A Jerusalem manuscript and antiquities dealer

Mahmoud al Arakat: The sheikh in whose home Shapira first heard of the Deuteronomy scrolls

Salim al Kari: Shapira's factotum

Walter Besant: An English author and leader of the Palestine Exploration Fund

Edward Bond: The chief librarian of the British Museum

Yaqoub Caravacca: Hired by Ganneau to secure a squeeze of the Moabite Stone

Sabah Cawar: A Jerusalem teacher dispatched to Moab to negotiate for the Moabite Stone

Charles Clermont-Ganneau: A French archaeologist and Shapira's nemesis

Claude Conder: An officer of the British military and one of the first people to whom Shapira agreed to show his scrolls on arriving in London

Charles Tyrwhitt Drake: A Palestine Exploration Fund explorer

Fendi el Faiz: Sheikh of the Beni Sachr Bedouin and a Moabite Stone suitor

Christian David Ginsburg: The leading English Bible scholar charged with authenticating the Shapira scrolls for the British Museum

Jemil: One of three horsemen who attempted to make a squeeze copy of the Moabite Stone for Ganneau

Frederick Augustus Klein: Discoverer of the Moabite Stone

Philip Brookes Mason: An English physician and naturalist

Charles Nicholson: The English-Australian nobleman thought to have purchased the Shapira scrolls

Edward Henry Palmer: A Palestine Exploration Fund explorer and Cambridge Arabic professor

J. Heinrich Petermann: The Prussian consul in Jerusalem, 1868–1869

Bernard Quaritch: The London book dealer who bought Shapira's scrolls at a Sotheby's auction

Konstantin Schlottmann: The German scholar to whom Shapira first showed his scrolls

Myriam Harry (Maria Shapira): Shapira's daughter and a famous French author

Rosette Shapira: Shapira's wife

William Simpson: A sketch artist for the *Illustrated London News*

Hermann Strack: A German Orientalist and Shapira correspondent

Baron Thankmar von Münchhausen: Germany's imperial consul in Jerusalem, 1874–1881

Charles Warren: A British military man and Palestine Exploration Fund explorer

Charles Wilson: Led the British Royal Engineers in the Ordnance Survey of Jerusalem

Zattam: Klein's guide in Moab when he discovered the Moabite Stone

TWENTIETH AND TWENTY-FIRST CENTURIES

Mahmoud Alassi: Manager of preservation and restoration for the Louvre's Department of Near Eastern Antiquities

Anneke Barends: A Dutch history enthusiast

Paul Beringer: An Australian pastor

Elisabeth Fontan: The former chief curator for the Louvre's Department of Near Eastern Antiquities

Moshe Goshen-Gottstein: A Semitic philologist at the Hebrew University

Matthew Hamilton: An Australian Shapira researcher

Menahem Mansoor: The University of Wisconsin Semitics scholar who reopened the Shapira case

Oscar K. Rabinowicz: A journalist and educator unconvinced by Shapira's scrolls

Michael Ruprecht: The director of the archives at the Martin-Luther-University of Halle Wittenberg

Yoram Sabo: An Israeli documentary filmmaker

Annette Schwarz Scheuls: A living German relative of Shapira

Solomon Zeitlin: A professor of rabbinic literature at Dropsie College in Philadelphia who spoke out against the Dead Sea Scrolls.

ORGANIZATIONS

PEF: Palestine Exploration Fund

DMG: Deutsche Morgenländische Gesellschaft (German Oriental Society)

BNHAS: Burton-on-Trent Natural History and Archaeological Society

THE
LOST BOOK
OF MOSES

A FAMOUS CORPSE

THE NETHERLANDS

Sunday, March 9, 1884, began as a slow news day at police head-quarters in Rotterdam. At ten thirty, Catharina Johanna van Vliet arrived in a huff after her brother-in-law spent the morning call-ing her names. At one o'clock, two patrolmen attempted to detain a drunken German. With six o'clock came a break in the Case of Some Stolen Sausages: Officers A. van der Muelen and L. J. A. Hoogland had collared a suspect on the Westplein. The arrest came too late to save the sausages, but the constables' work was considered so exemplary that each was slated for a bonus.

It was right around this time that the station received a con-cerned dispatch from a seedy hotel called the Willemsbrug. Two days earlier, one of its guests had entered his room and locked the door—and hadn't been heard from since. Adjunct Inspector G. Put-man Cramer was sent to investigate. Arriving at No. 6 Boompjes Street, situated on a block of brick buildings that housed a bank, a life insurer, and a zinc merchant, Cramer approached the room in question and broke through the door.

He entered to a grisly scene. Slumped on the bed was the bloodied corpse of a middle-aged man, a bullet hole notched in his head. Beside the bed lay the man's suitcase. It was stuffed with manuscripts—some new, some ancient—written in English and Hebrew, among other languages. Nearby was a stack of business cards. Cramer slipped one from the pile and took down its inscription:

M. W. Shapira, Book Seller and Antiquarian
Agent of the British Museum
Jerusalem

That evening's police register logs the death, noting the name of the deceased but offering no indication that authorities knew they had a world-famous corpse on their hands—that months earlier this brilliant man had been a household name, meeting with England's prime minister and its intellectual elite, making daily appearances in European gossip columns, staying in fancy hotels as he prepared to become exceedingly rich. "The guest in question . . . appears to be named M. W. Shapira," the duty officer reported. "After having been viewed by Dr. C. H. Eshuijs he was taken to the morgue."

Just beneath this, the night's final entry: "There is nothing to report about garbage."

It took three days, but the press eventually figured out who the dead man was. A short item in the March 12 edition of the *Leidsch Dagblad* noted that "this is probably the person who became disreputable last year in England for his falsified manuscripts."

Not quite the epitaph M. W. Shapira had been hoping for.

EIGHT MONTHS EARLIER, when he arrived at the London doorstep of Sir Walter Besant, longtime secretary of the Palestine Exploration Fund, Moses Wilhelm Shapira—archaeological treasure hunter, antiquities maven, inveterate social climber, and, by that point, a man painfully down on his luck—believed that the contents of the stylish carpetbag he carried would help repair a once-solid reputation that had nearly been destroyed by scandal.

At home in Jerusalem, Shapira's wife and daughters awaited news of his mission. If all went according to plan, they would soon rank among the Holy City's wealthiest inhabitants, assuming a place in its social hierarchy that the fifty-four-year-old Shapira had been clawing for ever since he bolted Eastern Europe three decades earlier in search of his absent father and his fortune.

That July morning, Shapira—a little bit Indiana Jones, a little Jay Gatsby—had appeared at Besant's claiming to have in his possession an ancient manuscript that would "simply make students of the Bible and Hebrew scholars reconsider their ways." It was a bold claim, redolent of a magician's patter, and while Shapira's performance intrigued Besant, he also found the whole thing a little annoying. The Brit was entirely familiar with the bearded, bespectacled foreigner standing before him now: the previous year, Shapira had played a small, unsuccessful part in an attempt to rescue one of the Palestine Exploration Fund's orientalist explorers when the man, Edward Henry Palmer, was kidnapped by Bedouin brigands during a reconnaissance mission in Egypt. The fund had paid Shapira eight pounds and change for his efforts; Palmer had not fared so well. Soon after his capture the Bedouin had slaughtered him, tossing his body off a cliff to be feasted on by birds.

Besant also knew Shapira as one of the British Museum's most important purveyors of centuries-old Hebrew manuscripts. Over the prior six years, Shapira had collected a vast stockpile of these valuable books and scrolls from communities throughout the Middle East; some of them dated back as far as seven hundred years.

The museum had paid handsomely to add these manuscripts to its own collection, as had other such institutions around Europe—a fact that imbued Shapira's stagy pronouncement with the aura of authenticity.

Archaeology in the late nineteenth century was a popular pastime among Western elites, and, as Shapira approached Besant, the field was still emerging from the domain of gentlemanly adventure into one governed by tenets of science. The British were engaged in a drawn-out rivalry with Germany and France, not only for colonial dominance but for international prestige. Archaeological prowess—manifested by the display of looted relics in the gilded galleries of their national museums—offered an express passage to glory.

After its discovery by French soldiers near the mouth of the Nile, England had managed to secure what became known as the Rosetta Stone for the British Museum, opening the way for scholars to decipher Egyptian hieroglyphics. When an Anglican missionary found the Moabite Stone—its inscription offering the first confirmation of a biblical story outside the Bible itself—the French snatched it up, depositing the 2,700-year-old basalt monument in the Louvre for all the world to ogle. The Germans, however, had yet to acquire relics of such magnitude for their Royal Museum. Indeed, efforts to keep pace with their European adversaries had recently ended in humiliation.

That debacle began in 1872, when Shapira—himself an occasional Anglican missionary—came into possession of nearly two thousand ancient clay vessels and statuettes allegedly discovered in the biblical region of Moab, just east of the Dead Sea. Many of these items were engraved in an ancient script similar to the one found on the Moabite Stone, which told the story of King Mesha's blood-soaked rebellion against the Israelites. Others coarsely depicted nude women with genitalia that appeared to have been fashioned by the swing of a battle-ax. Eager for a big win after losing Mesha's stele to Paris, the Prussians had gone all in, purchasing Shapira's collection for twenty thousand thaler. Much as his sale of Hebrew manuscripts would boost the reputation of the British Museum, Shapira's pottery had buoyed Prussia. But when the artifacts were dismissed as clumsy forgeries, the fallout came as a great embarrassment to the Germans. Shapira had been laboring ever since to repair his reputation. Despite recent success as an agent to the Brits, he remained unable to entirely shake the taint of disgrace.

"The man was a good actor," Besant recalled some years later. "He was a man of handsome presence, tall, with fair hair and blue eyes; not the least like the ordinary Polish Jew, and with an air of modest honesty which carried one away."

Besant's reference to the religion of Shapira's birth raises questions about the true nature of his misgivings. Nor did Shapira's rendition of the events leading to his visit smooth Besant's hackles. Beyond claiming that his discovery would change the world's conception of the Bible, he would divulge nothing about the purpose of his visit. Unconvinced that the handsome man standing before him was anything more than a charlatan, Besant suggested that if Shapira was unwilling to disclose exactly what he was hiding in his bag, he should simply go away.

Faced with Besant's ultimatum, Shapira relented, uncorking a few details about his find. The scrolls, Besant would recall Shapira saying, contained a copy of Deuteronomy—the fifth and final of the Five Books of Moses, remarkable for its seminal role in formulating monotheism, but best known for what is embedded in chapter 5: the Ten Commandments. Only this was no common manuscript. This was the original thing. The closing book of the Torah, handwritten more than three thousand years earlier, at the very time the events it described were taking place.

"It was nothing less than a contemporary copy of the book of Deuteronomy written on parchment," Besant said. "A contemporary copy!"

Stunned, Besant asked if he could see it.

Shapira obliged, pulling from his bag a narrow strip of leather tattooed in ancient script. "It was written in fine black ink, as fresh after three thousand years as when it was laid on," Besant reported, "and in the Phoenician characters of the Moabite Stone."

This last bit hinted at the fragments' great antiquity and led Besant to assign the scrolls a date far earlier than any biblical manuscript then known to have existed. This ordinary day had just become quite extraordinary. If these leather slips truly constituted a contemporary copy of Deuteronomy, then Shapira could stop acting—he had just uncovered the oldest Bible on earth.

Gathering himself, Besant suggested that his guest "make this discovery known to the world." Shapira, still coy, was not yet ready to go public with his find. But after a subsequent meeting, Besant said, he agreed to show it to two people. One was C. D. Ginsburg, among the great Bible scholars of the day and an acknowledged expert on the Moabite Stone, whom Shapira had encountered more than a decade earlier in Jerusalem.

The second man Shapira agreed to see was Claude Conder, an officer of the British military whose survey work for the Palestine Exploration Fund (PEF) had helped lay the groundwork for a more scientific approach to archaeology in that region. Conder had worked in Moab and published on matters of the Bible's geography. (More recently, his name has been floated as a possible Jack the Ripper.)

A meeting was set, invitations were dispatched, and Shapira repaired to his room in the Cannon Street Hotel. There was nothing for him to do but wait.

INTERPRETING THE SUMMONS as an occasion to gather his friends, Ginsburg arrived the following night at the PEF's Adam Street headquarters along with "the whole of the British Museum" and "all the Hebrew scholars in London," Besant recalled. The scene was striking: a host of the country's top Hebrew and Bible savants, as they were known, assembled in a single room to await the unveiling of their visitor's secret haul. Even the hour was charged: Besant had called the meeting for the stroke of midnight.

Shapira, moreover, was said to be asking an astounding million pounds sterling for the strips—about $250 million today. By comparison, in the previous decade the Louvre had purchased the Moabite Stone for what now seemed a pittance of just 15,000 francs (about $60,000 now). But a million pounds? That figure made even these sober professors, PEF executives, and British Museum specialists straighten their well-earned scholarly stoops.

As they milled about, Besant would recount, excitement charged the room such as "is very seldom exhibited by scholars." Finally, like a conductor waiting to unleash his orchestra on a hushed symphony hall, Shapira sensed his moment had arrived. Reaching into his bag, he removed fifteen leather strips, dappled and blackened with age. Most were about seven inches long and three and a half inches wide. A few were somewhat smaller. Forgoing the reverence with which one would expect the owner of such valuable antiquities to behave, Shapira, ever the showman, took the darkened leathers and tossed them jauntily on the table.

These strips, Shapira announced, contained three copies of Deuteronomy, in which Moses delivered his valedictory speech to the

Children of Israel on the plains of Moab. But this was not the Deuteronomy these scholars knew. It was much shorter, and was rife with passages that were different—sometimes very different—from the traditional version. And here was the kicker: judging from the ancient Hebrew script, then also called Phoenician, the scrolls could have been written closer to the time of Moses than any other known manuscript.

The scholars immediately understood the enormous import of the discovery. Beyond their monetary value, the scrolls could take three thousand years of religious faith and turn them upside down. If they were real, the scrolls offered evidence that the Bible then used in synagogues and churches the world over was not the version handed by Moses to the Children of Israel just before they crossed into Canaan. Rather, the so-called Masoretic, or traditional, text with which the world was familiar was a newer and longer version, based on the one Shapira now displayed, but altered and edited by human hands over the course of centuries.

Shapira's arrival with this manuscript could not have been better timed. Britain was just then in the throes of a Bible craze, captivated by a cadre of Protestant theologians who questioned the divine authorship of the Bible. Applying critical theory to the Holy Book, a number of these prominent thinkers claimed that several books of the Old Testament had begun as shorter documents, added to by multiple authors over the years. As for the Torah, some scholars surmised that editors had gathered four separate texts and melded them into the official narrative. The very year Shapira came to London, Julius Wellhausen, father of this "documentary hypothesis," published his definitive volume on the matter, making his case so powerfully that it had snared the attention of British scholars and laymen alike.

Now here was Shapira and his swanky bag, and in it what appeared to be the original article, furnishing proof for some of these theories—and evidence that others of them were mistaken.

To many minds, the notion that the Torah as read in modern times was not, in fact, the same book God had originally dictated was a jarring, even blasphemous proposition. After all, such thinking implied that human beings had, at the very least, played a significant role in creating the Bible. And if that were the case, perhaps the Holy Book was not quite so holy. Perhaps its stories and its laws were not immutable. Perhaps questions could now be raised about which portions of the Bible were divine and which were not, and perhaps those deemed to have originated with man could now be ignored. The implications were profound—unfathomably so.

A few years earlier, the influential Scottish theologian William Robertson Smith had been tried for heresy when he wrote an encyclopedia article raising similar questions about the Bible's origins. Smith's trial had enthralled the British public and offered many an education in the critical approach to the Bible. Among eight counts originally leveled against him, the single charge that survived as the marathon case plodded forward took aim at Smith's theories on Deuteronomy, which he claimed was written long after the death of Moses. Wellhausen, too, believed this book was a late addition to the Torah—introduced sometime around 622 BCE.

But Shapira's scrolls, written in a form of the alphabet used two centuries before that, demonstrated that Deuteronomy *could* have originated with Moses—or at least that it was centuries older than Wellhausen and Smith argued. Whatever these scrolls said about the accuracy of the traditional text, the emotional impact of seeing, touching, and reading from an original copy of the Torah would have been electrifying. So, too, would be proving the critics wrong.

The scholars who had come to see Shapira's manuscript could hardly bridle their elation. "This is one of the few things which could not be a forgery or a fraud!" one professor cried out. Shapira reached back into his bag and brought forth several smaller Hebrew manuscript fragments, one of which, reported William Simpson, a sketch artist for the *Illustrated London News*, "was rolled up in a rude way and suggested from its shape and colour the un-smoked half of a gigantic cigar, which I suggested must have been left by Og King of Bashan." Next Shapira produced a few stone bottles inscribed in ancient Phoenician characters.

"I assumed that all these were authentic," Simpson recalled, betraying an early hint of skepticism about the scrolls, "and were meant to give an air of reality to the whole."

Simpson was right about one thing. The cigarlike fragment and the stone bottles were mere accessories. Shapira's fifteen leather strips were the stars of his show. As the scholars eyed them, though, they found it rather difficult to make any confident determination about their origin or content. In spite of Besant's recollections, the fragments were largely dark—very dark—and whatever writing was etched on their surface had been clouded by the years. Shapira claimed to be familiar with the problem. He'd faced the same issue five years earlier, he said, when a Bedouin felon had first delivered the scrolls on Jerusalem's desolate outskirts. Now, as the scholars puzzled over the mysterious manuscript, Shapira pulled yet another item from his bag, a bottle of spirits. He poured it on the old leathers, rubbing the liquid brusquely over their surface with a small brush. Suddenly, acted on by the alcohol, the writing emerged with greater clarity. The effect was wondrous—and shocking. Simpson described it as "a sight to make one shiver."

As the men examined the documents, one put a question to Shapira about the nature of the leather. Shapira reached for one of the strips, tore off a fragment about an inch in diameter, and held it out for him to examine.

"This he really did to a document he declared to be as old as 900 B.C.," Simpson recalled. "McMullen was standing beside me and I whispered in his ear, 'See there is a precious fragment worth at least £500 torn off.'" As Simpson's aside landed, someone knocked over the spirits, which spilled onto the manuscript.

It was dazzling theater, exciting and odd and a little bit dangerous. Over the course of years as the proprietor of an antiquities shop in Jerusalem, Shapira had developed a salesman's knack for closing a deal—and a riverboat gambler's stomach for risk. Still, it was baffling behavior from a man asking a million pounds for his find. Perhaps he felt the dramatic appeal of the gesture was greater than the damage it would cause. Or maybe he was so certain of his discovery's value that he felt nothing could diminish it.

Either way, the three-hour meeting was an unmitigated success. London's top specialists departed impressed and energized; the British Museum was now officially interested in obtaining the fragments; and Shapira's reputation was buttressed, completing a remarkable shift for the émigré who a decade earlier had been famous chiefly as the face of an archaeological scandal. News of his discovery would shortly leak to the press, making its way through Europe and across the Atlantic to the United States. For a short time in that exhilarating summer of 1883, Shapira would become, at last, world famous.

In the meantime, there was work to be done. The text had to be transcribed and translated, interpreted and assigned a date. The savants elected Ginsburg for the job and he hurried the scrolls to the British Museum to begin work at once. As the scholars filed out of the PEF headquarters that night, one particularly excitable fellow noted that Shapira's manuscript was "a remarkable illustration of the arts as known and practiced in the time of Moses."

Perhaps. But within eight months, another Moses—Moses Wilhelm Shapira—would be dead. His name would be sullied both in the halls of European power and at home in Jerusalem. His scrolls would be publicly shot down as forgeries. And then, as though ashamed to be seen, they would vanish.

1

FROM PHILADELPHIA TO JERUSALEM

I first heard the name Moses Wilhelm Shapira from my father, a rabbi and Bible scholar whose most important work to date is a six-hundred-page commentary on Deuteronomy, the very book that got Shapira into so much trouble. My father spent sixteen years honing his analysis and so, like Shapira, understands a good Deuteronomy obsession.

On a Friday night in 2010, I was sitting at my family's table finishing up dinner when he launched into the story of a bizarre Bible scroll that had been enveloped in scandal. This was not our standard table talk. True, Deuteronomy usually made an appearance. The Bible—and the languages spoken by the ancient Near Easterners who lived in close proximity to the Israelites—was a fixture of our life. When my dad withdrew cash from an ATM, he'd tell my mother he was getting *kaspu*. He used this Akkadian word for money so that any lurking thieves wouldn't get wise to his plans. The ruse worked; apparently very few of Philadelphia's crooks speak Akkadian.

Growing up, Friday night dinners were a time of copious food and chaotic revelry—my three brothers and I doing our best to make each other laugh, our parents struggling to maintain some sense of decorum. Our behavior was tempered, if only somewhat, by the presence of our frequent guests. When one would pose a question to my father, he would disappear from the table only to return hauling a large stack of books exhumed from his study. Seven hours later, his answer complete, dessert would be served.

On this particular Friday night, though, talk turned to a series of articles I had recently written about biblical frauds. A few days earlier a team of Chinese evangelicals had publicly touted their discovery of Noah's Ark, buried beneath the snows of Turkey's Mount Ararat. The find, if authentic, would have been mind-blowing—to see, touch, and smell the vessel that had saved humankind, together, two by two, with the entire animal kingdom, would have represented nothing short of a modern-day miracle. For believers especially, it would have offered proof that the Bible was not simply a compendium of instructive fables but rather a true account of world history.

But there was a problem: the discovery was a hoax. It had taken nearly five thousand years to unearth the "ark"—and just three days for the so-called discovery to be debunked. A couple of years earlier, a group of Kurdish laborers, hired by a local guide working with the Chinese expedition, had removed several large wooden beams from an old structure near the Black Sea and dragged them to a cave by the peak of Ararat, long thought by believers to have been the spot where Noah's Ark eventually washed up.

When I finished telling this story, my father chimed in with the tale of another biblical scandal. In 1883, he said, a Jerusalem antiquities merchant named Shapira had offered an ancient copy of Deuteronomy to the British Museum for one million pounds. That deal had blown up, the scrolls scorned as frauds. Shapira had died soon after, and his scrolls had disappeared.

The mystery was intoxicating—and it got better. Shapira's manuscripts, I would soon learn, were strikingly similar to another great desert find that had altered our understanding of the Bible's origins and changed the course of Near Eastern archaeology: the Dead Sea Scrolls. Shapira's Deuteronomy was said to have been discovered in a cave. So, too, were the Dead Sea Scrolls. Shapira's manuscripts were full of departures from the traditional biblical text. So, too, were the Dead Sea Scrolls. Shapira's strips were found by Bedouin wandering the desert near the Dead Sea. So, too, were the Dead Sea Scrolls. Indeed, their discovery six decades after Shapira's death had led some scholars to reopen the investigation of his oddball Deuteronomy, whose dismissal all those years earlier, they now believed, might have been tragically premature.

IN THE WINTER of 1947, three Ta'amireh shepherds were grazing goats along the mountainous rim that overlooks the Dead Sea. To pass the time, one of the shepherds tossed rocks toward the mouth of a nearby cave. His aim was good. One sailed right in, and the noise that came back surprised him. It was not the sharp snap of rock on rock, or the dull scratch of stone skidding along the cave's dirt floor. Instead, he heard pottery shattering. Two days later one of the Bedouin, Muhammad ad-Dibh, awoke before his comrades and returned to the cave. Inside, he came upon ten clay jars. Most were empty. Some, however, held something interesting: old leather scrolls wrapped in linen and black with age.

Ad-Dibh took his discovery to a Bethlehem antiquities dealer named Khalil Eskander, better known as Kando. Kando was impressed, and sent the shepherds back into the desert to look for more. When they returned, they had collected a total of seven scrolls. Kando bought four and, in short order, sold them to Mar Athanasius Samuel, archbishop of St. Mark's Syrian Orthodox monastery in Jerusalem. The Bedouin sold the remaining three scrolls to another Arab antiquities dealer in Bethlehem.

Meanwhile, Eliezer Sukenik, a respected archaeologist at the Hebrew University, learned of the scrolls' existence. The Arab–Israeli violence that would shortly culminate in the bloody War of Independence—known among Palestinians as the Catastrophe—rendered a trip to the dealer's place treacherous. But the lure of these ancient scrolls was too great for Sukenik. Risking injury, even death, he arranged a secret rendezvous with another antiquities dealer at the city's military zone, where rolls of coiled concertina wire lay like infernal tumbleweed in the street separating Jerusalem's Arabs and Jews. On the opposite side of a barbed-wire fence, the antiquities merchant displayed a fragment of the scrolls. Sukenik was captivated. Casting caution aside, he hustled to Bethlehem to get his first good look at what would soon become known worldwide as the Dead Sea Scrolls.

"My hands shook as I started to unwrap one of them," he wrote that day in his diary. "I read a few sentences. It was written in beautiful biblical Hebrew. The language was like that of the Psalms, but the text was unknown to me. I looked and looked, and I suddenly had the feeling that I was privileged by destiny to gaze upon a Hebrew scroll which had not been read for more than 2,000 years."

Sukenik purchased the three manuscripts—the Thanksgiving Scroll, the War Scroll, and a copy of Isaiah—and as violence spun out unabated, Mar Samuel secreted *his* four scrolls to the relative safety of New Jersey. There, on June 1, 1954, he placed an ad in the *Wall Street Journal:*

"The Four Dead Sea Scrolls"
Biblical Manuscripts dating back to at least 200 BC,
are for sale. This would be an ideal gift to an educational
or religious institution by an individual or group.

Sukenik acquired these scrolls, too, on behalf of the fledgling State of Israel, which built a special wing of its national museum to house them. They called it the Shrine of the Book.

Over the next several years, scholars and Bedouin searched in the heat of the Judean Desert, competing to find as many of these valuable scrolls as they could. What they found fell into two major categories. First were ancient copies of the twenty-four books that made up the Bible, older by some one thousand years than nearly all other known manuscripts. Suddenly scholars, believers, and others with even a tangential interest in scripture could see what the text of the Bible had looked like ten centuries earlier, and how it had developed in the intervening years.

The second category became known as sectarian literature—documents written by and for the sect of ancients who lived at Qumran, site of the discovery. In the days leading up to Christianity's birth, multiple Jewish factions emerged in the Holy Land. Judaism as we know it developed from a group known as the Pharisees. Other sects, like the Sadducees and the Essenes (who were later identified as the Qumran community), petered out after the Romans sacked the Second Temple in 70 CE. It was from this fluid milieu that Christianity evolved—and some thought the authors of the Dead Sea Scrolls were the very first Christians.

Much of the world sang hallelujahs. Major newspapers gave the discoveries front-page treatment. Magazine writers pondered the scrolls' origins and implications. But as in Shapira's day, there were doubters—and their arguments were similar to those eventually advanced about Shapira's scrolls. Prominent among the Dead Sea Scrolls' detractors was Dr. Solomon Zeitlin, a professor of rabbinic literature at Dropsie College in Philadelphia. Zeitlin took up his cause with gusto, publishing a series of long articles in a journal of which he happened to be the editor, insisting that the manuscripts were "not an important discovery, but possibly a hoax."

Part of the problem, Zeitlin said, was that the Dead Sea Scrolls used words that didn't find their way into the Hebrew language until centuries after many scholars were claiming the scrolls had been composed. Imagine finding a copy of the *Odyssey* in which Odysseus makes his marathon journey home aboard a "groovy" ship and you'll have a sense of what Zeitlin was arguing.

Beyond that, he took issue with the story of the scrolls' discovery—pointing out what he believed to be inconsistencies and criticizing one scholar for "accepting at face value the word of any Bedouin or Oriental merchant." What really happened, Zeitlin suggested, was that these Bedouin (or some other merchants) had gotten hold of manuscripts that had been removed from synagogues in Cairo, Hebron, or Jerusalem and planted them in the Qumran caves for theatrical effect.

Zeitlin was wrong. In the years after the scrolls were discovered, international scholars subjected them to rigorous analysis—from comparative literary, archaeological, and paleographical examinations to accelerator mass spectrometry techniques that did not yet exist in Shapira's day—and discovered that the scrolls were inarguably real, and immeasurably significant. As recently as the 1990s, scientific tests reconfirmed the scrolls' antiquity. Today no serious scholar doubts their authenticity.

I was hooked on Shapira that first night at dinner and started to investigate further. The more I learned, the more I began to share the suspicions of a small group of scholars who believed Shapira might have stumbled onto the first Dead Sea Scroll, seventy years before Muhammad ad-Dibh had clambered into that cave in Qumran. Had this once-impoverished immigrant, I wondered, made one of the most important archaeological finds of his generation, only to be pushed toward death by those who simply wouldn't allow themselves to believe it was real? Had the discovery of the Dead Sea Scrolls vindicated the disgraced Shapira? Would his scrolls, had they come to light *after* the Dead Sea Scrolls, have passed muster? Were they, in other words, painfully authentic?

One year after Shapira entered my life, I left my apartment in San Francisco and flew to Ben-Gurion International Airport, just outside Tel Aviv. From there I made the thirty-mile drive to Jerusalem in the little Hyundai Getz I'd rented. It's a beautiful route—snaking through the Ayalon Valley and crossing into the West Bank before the winding mountain ascent. In places the road is lined with the rusted husks of trucks that supplied Jerusalem's besieged Jewish community during the War of Independence. These vehicles point to Israel's obsession with the past but are among its newest relics. Today Israel, and especially Jerusalem, is the epicenter of biblical archaeology. From the Western Wall of the Holy Temple to the Bethesda Pool, in which Jesus reanimated a paralyzed man, to Nicanor of Alexandria's family tomb on the Mount Scopus campus of Hebrew University—anywhere one turns in the Holy City, it is virtually impossible to not run into an ancient site of major historical import, religious significance, or scholarly value.

I had come to Israel on assignment, to write about a unit of Bedouin Arabs who serve as trackers in Israel's military, putting their native mastery of the area's deserts to work hunting down arms smugglers, terrorists, and assorted other unwanted visitors.

Jewish soldiers describe these men as wizards of a sort, seers who, spotting a set of footprints sunk in the border sand, can determine how many people have infiltrated, how old they are, how much each weighs, whether they are men or women, and, in some cases, that one has a limp or is pregnant. Some infiltrators wear specially fitted shoes that slip on backward so it appears that they are leaving

Israel rather than entering. Trackers can spot this ruse with ease, much as they can detect when an infiltrator has fastened sheepskin to the soles of his feet in an effort to leave no discernible prints at all.

By the time I arrived, what was meant to be a lengthy embed had been reduced to a three-hour visit to the unit's base one Monday morning. Along the way, the military spokesman had offered a shifting litany of excuses—it was too dangerous; the unit's commanders didn't want reporters around; the Bedouin soldiers themselves feared their names and pictures would be splashed across newspaper pages, where unfriendly folks back home might suddenly notice what they did for a living. All of this, especially the last explanation, made sense to me. But I was not pleased.

After a disappointing visit to Biranit, a charmless military base along the border with Lebanon, I stopped at a gas station and bought an ice cream. Sitting there in the awful summer heat, chocolate dripping down the side of my hand, I quickly realized that, while the army could limit my access to enlisted soldiers, they could not control who else I spoke to. I began to set up meetings with former soldiers, activists, journalists, and government insiders, all of whom, I hoped, could offer some insight into life as an Arab in Israel's army.

These interviews landed me in Jerusalem's Old City, where I'd planned to interview a source who advised the Israeli government on Arab affairs. He'd asked if we could meet at Christ Church, whose placid stone courtyard he often used as an outdoor office. It was an odd request. Maybe he figured no one who mattered was likely to spot us talking there.

But that name—Christ Church—was immediately familiar. It was the seat of Jerusalem's Anglican bishopric and the cathedral in which Shapira had worshipped, been married, and baptized his daughters, Maria and Augusta. When this man asked to get together at Christ Church, I smiled at my good fortune.

I ARRIVED EARLY, hoping to find someone at the church conversant in the Shapira story, and approached the slim older woman sitting at the front desk.

"I'm doing some research about a man named Moses Wilhelm Shapira," I said. Then, before I could explain, the lady started talking.

"Oh, yes," she said in a light English accent. "He is a naughty boy, isn't he?"

I'd never before heard anyone refer to Shapira as naughty—or in the present tense. It was the first indication I had that I might not be the only one around who was obsessed with him. The second took place about six seconds later when she told me that archaeologists still stopped into the church occasionally to comb its underground tunnels and cisterns for Shapira's missing scrolls. She suggested I contact the church's rector, David Pileggi, to learn more.

Half an hour later, over coffee and orange soda on ice, my source on Arab affairs laid out his views about Israel's Bedouin population. As we spoke, a large man with dark, curly hair approached the table and greeted us warmly.

"David Pileggi," he said, taking my hand.

When I mentioned Shapira, I could almost hear his eyes rolling back toward his spine. "Why are you all so interested in Shapira?" he said.

I laughed awkwardly, unsure if he was serious or teasing. The Shapira story—with its overtones of mystery and religion and intrigue—was so utterly alluring to me that it was hard to imagine why anyone would not be enthusiastic. As it turned out, Pileggi's skepticism seemed to derive less from a lack of interest than from a mild annoyance at the stream of people who came in asking about Shapira. I'd hardly begun my search and hadn't yet been asked to defend my fascination, so I stammered through an explanation and he listened kindly. Then he suggested that I speak with someone else—

the Reverend Aaron Eime, a Christ Church deacon and manager of its Heritage Center.

I met Eime on Purim—when Jews don costumes and get drunk to mark their salvation from an ancient Persian plot to ethnically cleanse them. Much of Israel's population is not religiously observant, but this is a holiday most can embrace. I had to fight my way through throngs of sloshed Osama bin Laden look-alikes blowing foghorns and spraying silly string to arrive at my appointment on time.

Eime, a reedy man with longish hair who signed his emails, "In His service, Aaron," met me in the church library. Shapira once found employment in Christ Church's "book depository," and I wondered if this was the same room in which he had worked. It was cool and dark and abutted a chamber that held a large model of the Temple Mount, complete with movable pieces, assembled in the nineteenth century by the Jerusalem architect Conrad Schick. I'd prepared a list of questions and was hoping to spend the afternoon grilling my host—which Old City shop had been Shapira's? Did Shapira have any living relatives in Israel or elsewhere? Who were these archaeologists searching the church's tunnels? Like Pileggi, Eime patiently answered my questions, though he, too, seemed bemused. Someone showed up asking about Shapira every couple of weeks, he told me.

Eime described Shapira's involvement in Jerusalem's Anglican mission and the London Society for Promoting Christianity Among the Jews. He directed me to a shelf full of nineteenth-century journals—from *Jewish Missionary Intelligence* to the *Reports* of the London Society to the handwritten minutes of the church's leadership committee—from which I learned that Shapira had traveled as far as Tunisia and Yemen as the organization's "agent." But when my questions veered into the missing scrolls, his answers were invariably the same: "Yoram Sabo would know that."

Sabo was a talented filmmaker who had produced a movie about the Old City and, Eime told me, was now at work on a documentary about Shapira. This news was both welcome and distressing. On the one hand, it was a good lead—here was someone who might have the answers I was seeking. On the other, it occurred to me that Sabo must have been much further along in his project than I. It seemed unlikely that he would part freely with hard-earned intelligence—and if that proved true, it was equally doubtful that I would ever catch up.

Eime gave me Sabo's mobile number and I rushed outside to call. Standing at the intersection of David and Armenian Quarter Streets, which were paved in smooth beige stone—and, I would later learn, were situated just one minute by foot from the shop on Christian Street that had once belonged to Shapira—I dialed Sabo's number. When he picked up, I explained why I was calling.

"Good," he said. "Another Shapiramaniac."

So there was a name for my condition. We chatted another few minutes, Sabo telling me he'd been collecting every Shapira-related item he could get his hands on for thirty years—books, letters, newspapers, photographs.

"I'll either give you everything or I'll give you nothing," he said.

"I vote for everything," I said.

"I need to figure out if I can trust you."

"You can call my mother and ask," I said.

"And what will she tell me?" he said. "That you're a nice Jewish boy?"

"Yes," I said. "And a genius. And very sweet."

I could hear him thinking on the other end. Evidently he was as reluctant to part with information it had taken decades to gather as he was hesitant to send me on my way.

"It's like you're a stamp collector and you find someone else who collects stamps," he said. "You want to talk to him."

I let that hang there awhile, hoping he'd feel the need to break the silence with an invitation to meet.

"Where are you staying?" he asked at last.

We set up a meeting an hour later at a café in Jerusalem's German Colony that doubled as a movie theater. Sabo needed time to gather his materials. I spotted him before he came inside, as the armed security guard sitting by the entrance made a cursory pass through his bag. Sabo looked like an international art thief—the kind of guy you wouldn't be surprised to learn could handle himself in a knife fight.

As we sat down and ordered our coffees, something in Sabo's manner indicated that he was still grappling with whether or not to divulge any of what he'd discovered. He looked a lot like I imagined I would in twenty years—the short hair and beard, the jeans and glasses. The man bag. He seemed to be searching me for some clue to help determine whether I was a fellow traveler, a worthy adversary, or a competitor of whom he needed to be wary.

Moviegoers lined up to watch *The King's Speech*, and our waitress served our drinks from a tray. Sabo flipped open his bag, reached inside, and removed a thumb drive.

"So, you probably want to see this," he said.

Before handing it over, Sabo asked me a number of questions about myself and my intentions. I told him I was planning to write an article about Shapira. "About Shapira?" he asked. "Or about searching for the scrolls?"

I had not yet settled this question for myself. I knew that I wanted to immerse myself in the story, to learn everything I could about Shapira and the era in which he lived. But it felt almost embarrassing to say out loud that I was looking for the scrolls. Who, exactly, did I think I was? What skills did I possess that led me to believe I might be the one to solve this century-old mystery?

"Well," I said, "it's mostly about Shapira, but like everyone else, if in the course of my research I happen to find the scrolls . . ."

He smiled, perhaps because he saw in me some hint of himself as a younger man, just beginning his journey.

"Did you bring your laptop?" he asked.

I set the computer down on the wobbly table and Sabo inserted the drive. It held a PowerPoint presentation with more than 150 slides, telling the story of Shapira and his scrolls in some detail. It included photographs of the protagonists, many of whose names were still unfamiliar to me. Names like Besant and Ginsburg, Conder and Sutro. It included documents in a number of languages that Sabo had found in archives and purchased from international book dealers. It included clippings from newspapers published well over a century ago. In short, the drive contained the fruits of a thirty-year obsession, one Shapiramaniac's (perhaps *the* Shapiramaniac's) blueprint for a sweeping documentary film on the Shapira affair. Ninety percent of it was new to me. What's worse, he already knew how the film, to be called *Shapira and I*, would end: with him discovering the scrolls.

"There are six clues in the material about where the scrolls are," he explained. He spoke with the bravado of a general about to do battle with an inferior enemy. He said things like "When I find the scrolls . . ." Psychologically, he seemed already to have found them and had moved on to worrying about the impact the spotlight would have on his life. All that was left now was the busywork of tracking them down. And as soon as he finished raising the rest of the money for his film, Sabo told me, he would begin doing just that, following the Six Clues to their inevitable conclusion.

Until that moment, the notion of my searching for the scrolls had been an unformed idea, an egg waiting to be fertilized. Primarily I had been concerned with how best to tell the tale of Shapira's outsize life. Sabo's Six Clues were the fertilizer I now realized I'd been awaiting. Though I hadn't thought much about hunting for the scrolls myself, suddenly, faced with the real prospect that someone else might find them, I could imagine no other way forward. What would be the point in telling Shapira's story without solving the mystery that lay at its heart—were the scrolls real or fake? The problem was, I'd been working as a freelance reporter, had recently gotten married, and was hoping to have a kid sometime soon. A quick look at my latest bank statement would have made clear that an international hunt for ancient Bible scrolls was a very bad idea. But I was overcome with the idea of discovering what could be the original copy of Deuteronomy, a book my own father had devoted so much of his life to understanding. I thought of my parents' joy when I called to inform them of my discovery, the pride they might feel at knowing before anyone else did that the important manuscript still existed. If I was successful, this could be the most meaningful thing I'd ever done. Sabo didn't know it, but just like that, he had radically altered the trajectory of my nascent project—and my life. When I awoke that morning, I had not heard of Yoram Sabo. Now here he was, sitting across from me at a Jerusalem café and uttering two words—"Six Clues"—that would come to dominate my existence for the next four years.

I would not be the first to pursue Shapira. The mystery surrounding his life had lingered for more than a century, puzzled over by an obsessed few looking for answers. What each of these Shapiramaniacs had discovered instead was this: there was no possible way to know the truth about Shapira until someone, somewhere, uncovered the missing scrolls.

I once heard a medical scientist describe her joy at a competitor's discovery—after all, she said, a step forward in science was good for everyone. If Sabo had found the scrolls, the discovery might help confirm exactly how the Bible itself had been written, rewritten, and revised.

Of course, if *I* found the scrolls, the same discoveries would be in the offing. And I wanted to find them. Badly. Which, I suppose, is another way of saying I did not want someone else to find them. My great-grandmother used to tell my father that he could just as easily fall in love with a rich girl as a poor one. I felt something similar. If someone was going to find these scrolls, why couldn't it be me?

I should have been grateful for the kind way Sabo had shared his work with me. But he had a thirty-year head start, and unless I could convince him to hand over his clues the way he'd just plugged all that other information into my laptop, he was sure to win. Understandably, he had no intention of doing so. I sat there in the crowded Jerusalem café, nodding silently as Sabo spoke. Patrons filed out of the matinee. My search, it appeared, was over before it had begun.

Then Sabo offered me a lifeline.

"I considered having another person—not me—as the one we follow on camera," he said. He paused here and thought awhile. "I don't know. Maybe that could be you?"

I tried to play it cool—as though I, too, needed to parse a tricky proposal. Years earlier I had starred in an off-Broadway play and an independent feature film, and I mentioned this to Sabo to hint at what a stupendous performance I would turn in if I decided to take this on.

He said he'd think about it. I said I'd think about it. In the meantime we shook hands and wished each other good luck, though neither of us really meant it.

RATHER THAN INTERVIEW Bedouin soldiers that week, I sneaked off to Jordan. Maybe the first clue was hidden where this all began—near the cave where Shapira claimed his scrolls had been discovered. Beginning the day in East Jerusalem, I caught a service taxi in a dank alcove across from the Damascus Gate and rode to the Allenby Bridge, which links the West Bank and Jordan. Due to diplomatic exigencies stemming from the fact that I am an Israeli citizen, guards there refused me passage. I hired a car to drive me to northern Israel and, several hours later, crossed the border at Beit She'an. There I caught another cab south to Madeba, an eighty-mile drive on a narrow, poorly maintained road where potholes and bad drivers seemed to be competing to foreshorten my life. A smattering of small towns dotted the route, announced by short strips of decaying shops. At the curbside, men in kaffiyehs sold vegetables from white boxes. Trash littered the road. The landscape between these towns can be described in a single word: brown—though looking west over the border, one could see the rich green of Israeli farms nestled in the Jordan Valley. I arrived at the Mariam Hotel early in the evening and met Benjamin Porter and Bruce Routledge poolside for drinks. Along with two other archaeologists, Porter and Routledge direct the Dhiban Excavation and Development Project at the site where an Anglican missionary had found the Moabite Stone in 1868.

The next morning Porter and I set out for the rim of Wadi Mujib—biblical Arnon—the massive gorge where several Bedouin were supposed to have happened upon Shapira's scrolls. On the way Porter stopped at Dhiban to show me his dig. Some archaeological sites—the pyramids in Giza, Petra—are so grand, so evocative, that their import is unmistakable even to the untrained eye. Dhiban is not one of them. It's hard for a nonspecialist to understand much of the site's history as a Moabite settlement without a good imagination and an expert like Porter leading the way. What I remember most vividly is that when we stepped out of his car, he said, "You might want to grab a couple rocks in case the wild dogs show up."

We toured the site for about an hour as the sun stood taller and taller. Porter guided me to a makeshift tent to meet the man guarding the site. Salim al-Lemone may very well have been the oldest person in the world—his sun-leathered face crinkled like the scrolls I was hunting, a mustache betraying dwindling traces of its original darkness, and a bleach-white kaffiyeh exaggerating the narrowness of his head. He carried a wooden stick for walking on the rough terrain. And he was, it quickly became clear, nearly deaf. The idea that he could protect the site from looters was as improbable as the discovery of the Moabite Stone, which had been found just a few feet away.

Even in the recent past, archaeology in parts of the Middle East was largely divorced from Middle Easterners. Western academics would parachute in to excavate but did not interact with locals. Since 2004, Porter told me, he and his colleagues have been trying to involve the community in the area surrounding their dig—hiring them, teaching them, trying to understand how they see the sites where these foreigners are digging.

Al-Lemone had been hired with this noble goal in mind, and he'd been selected precisely because he was old. "We often think the children will respect an old man," Porter explained. "If an old man starts hitting you with a stick, you'll stop what you're doing."

But there's a flip side. "The older guys also won't listen to you," he said. "They sleep a lot and let goats trample and shit on the excavation."

Shortly after I left, al-Lemone was fired.

By the time we arrived at Wadi Mujib, the sun was so intense that it played tricks on the eyes: huge mountains seemed to bleed one into the next, creating the impression of a single monolith broken only by the occasional blue-green of a desert pool. But the shimmering sun could not hide a series of gaps in the face of the steep cliffs overlooking the canyon. These, Porter told me, were caves. He pointed toward Ara'ir, the town nearest the Shapira cave, and told me that the scrolls could have survived had sediment traveled down the mountainside and sealed the cave, protecting it from the damp outside. Other important manuscripts had been shielded in this way—including the Dead Sea Scrolls. Colluvial erosion, as this process is known, is responsible for caves opening and closing repeatedly over thousands of years. Open, their interiors are exposed to the elements. Closed, caves are an environment in which organic material can survive.

Given the heat and the lunar landscape that stretched out in all directions, it was hard to imagine that damp weather was ever an issue out here. In fact, said Porter, who wore a baseball cap, sunglasses, and a blue shirt with its collar turned up against the heat, the wadi is known for flash flooding from pounding storms that come out of nowhere and drench the river basin. Even so, he told me, if Shapira had faked the scrolls, this would have been a good place to claim they had been found.

"No one could double-check Shapira's work," he said. "It was the Wild West out here."

Early the next day, I headed down into the wadi itself. The taxi ride from Madeba was desolate, russet hills undulating from the car to the horizon, decorated periodically by a sturdy Bedouin tent made from burlap coffee sacks stamped PRODUCT OF EL SALVADOR. The last half hour was an unrelenting descent, steep and winding, until at last we stopped at the mouth of the wadi and parked. At 1,350 feet below sea level, we had reached what was nearly the lowest spot on earth.

At the entrance, I walked past the guard desk and the man sitting behind it said, "Is that what you're wearing?"

I looked down at what my brother calls my journalist costume: long army pants, a khaki button-down, and boots.

"Yes?" I said.

He shrugged and waved me through. A moment later I caught sight of my driver walking briskly by me in his sneakers and underwear. Almost as soon as we stepped into the wadi's approach, I understood.

Entry was through a narrow gorge, steep red-brown cliffs rising starkly on either side and climbing a hundred or more feet into the sky. As I headed in, a channel of green water two or three inches deep trickled out toward the Dead Sea. The gorge narrowed quickly, blocking out the sun. Pushing forward, I found myself high-stepping through water that was now a foot deep. The farther I walked, the deeper it became. After about three hundred yards, I was in water up to the collar of my very inappropriate shirt. I looked over at my driver, who was luxuriating in his boxers.

"Flood," he said. Then he smiled and swam ahead.

We hiked this way for two hours, scaling rocks and dodging waterfalls in the dark, flooded passageway. But it was all for nothing—the current became too rough and we had to turn around. Heading back, I recalled the scene in 2 Kings when the armies of Israel, Judah, and Edom joined forces to quell the Moabites. As troops circled the Dead Sea's southern tip, not far from where I walked, their water ran out. Panicked, they called in the prophet Elisha, who prophesied that dry pools would fill miraculously. Suddenly I appreciated how that might have occurred. I also understood what Shapira's critics had charged late in the nineteenth century: that the wadi was too damp for the scrolls to have survived.

Drenched, the driver and I rode back to Madeba in our underwear.

THOUGH MY TRIP had yielded nothing but these insights, I was energized. Over the next several months, I read everything I could about Shapira, in hopes I might somehow come across Sabo's clues. But I came to understand that they were well hidden, deeply embedded in forests of information spread across multiple continents. Finding them would require time, travel, and funding. And telling that story, alongside Shapira's, would take a book. I gathered my research and wrote up a proposal, which I sold to an editor in New York.

Then I returned to Israel where, over coffee and muesli at what had already begun to feel like our café, Sabo and I exchanged pleasantries before discussing cooperation. The benefits for me were clear. If Sabo divulged his clues, I could circumvent years of research. In return, I had begun to think that I might act as something like his field producer, traveling to track down his clues. I'd use whatever I discovered for my book, and Sabo then could drag his camera crew only to locations that I'd found fruitful, saving a great deal of time and money.

"The thing is," Sabo said now, "I also want to write a Shapira book."

He might be willing to work together, which is to say share the clues, he told me, if my book became a collaboration "by Chanan Tigay and Yoram Sabo." I was reluctant to make this concession—and reluctant to reject the benefits that would come with it. What's more, I wasn't sure how productively we could collaborate.

After finding the scrolls, Sabo had told me, his film would end with a poetic gesture. No one knew where Shapira's grave was. Sabo was going to find that, too. And when he did, he said, "I will put a rose on it."

I should probably note here that I detest confrontation of even the most minor variety. If I order soup and get a salad, the idea of sending it back provokes anxiety and bloating. My version of road rage never makes it out into the road. If Sabo and I worked together on the book—*my* book—would I be forced into such schmaltz just to keep the peace?

Turning down his offer of cooperation seemed vain and stupid. Accepting it would allow me to skip several steps and jump right into the Six Clues it had taken Sabo decades to find. I called my agent to ask about the logistics of adding a coauthor. She explained what it would entail to include a second person as signatory to my contract, and crystallized for me a host of potential complications that might ensue. In short, the answer was no.

I was relieved. I had never really wanted a partner on the project and felt free. I badly wanted to find the scrolls but was equally excited about the strange ride that lay ahead. If I wanted Sabo's Six Clues, I would have to find them myself.

AFTER SHAPIRA'S DEATH, his Deuteronomy scrolls were put up for sale at the venerable London auction house of Sotheby, Wilkinson & Hodge. In 1885, Bernard Quaritch, a successful bookseller, bought the scrolls and two years later lent them out for display at the Anglo-Jewish Historical Exhibition at the Royal Albert Hall. There, in an effort to promote interest in the history of England's Jews, organizers assembled an extensive showcase of ecclesiastical art, ritual objects, and valuable antiquities. Among exhibits arranged in two semicircular rooms, visitors were treated to an ancient ram's horn, blasted on the high holy days, monographs published by the Palestine Exploration Fund, and a large model of Jerusalem's Holy Temple. The show also included a world-class collection of Torah scrolls produced by Samaritans. This ancient sect believes it is descended from Israelites who remained behind when most of their kin were exiled by the Assyrians and Babylonians. Today its members still adhere to a version of the Torah markedly different from the traditional one.

Shapira would have liked the show, with its exploration of the nexus between European and Near Eastern Jews, the English pomp of the displays, and the focus on Samaritans, whose writing he had encountered in his own work. He had been dead three years by the time of the showcase, but Shapira lived on in his manuscripts, which graced the shelves of Europe's best collections, and the Deuteronomy fragments, which were still attracting notice in Room 2, one of several loans made by Quaritch to the exhibit's organizers.

The Anglo-Jewish Historical Exhibition, which did much to revitalize enthusiasm for Jewish history in the United Kingdom, was, as far as anyone knew, the last time Shapira's scrolls were ever seen in public. With the show's closing in the summer of 1887, their trail went absolutely cold.

A BIBLE AND A SPADE

Walter Besant was far better known for his prodigious literary output—he was perhaps England's most popular writer of his day—than for the nearly two decades he spent at the helm of the Palestine Exploration Fund. His autobiography, though ostensibly a work of history, strayed occasionally into the fanciful—and Besant's rendering of Shapira's sudden arrival in London was rife with errors.

Shapira was handsome, as reported, but was not, as Besant claimed, fair-haired—only a single photograph of him remains, and it depicts a man with short dusky hair parted gently to the side and a full dark beard. Besant's memoir, published in 1902, dates their fateful meeting to 1877, although in fact it took place six years later. In Besant's telling, Shapira, acting oddly, agreed to allow just those two men—Ginsburg and Claude Conder—access to his manuscript. This, too, is incorrect. Besant himself dispatched an invitation to William Simpson, the artist from the *Illustrated London News*. And that "fine black ink, as fresh after three thousand years as when it was laid on"? It was, as we have seen, nearly invisible without the clarifying aid of spirits.

Perhaps Besant's portrayal of Shapira as a cagey showman was meant to demonstrate that he had tabbed his visitor as an odd bird before the rest of the world caught on. Maybe, however, his errors were the result of a less sinister actor: time. It would come as no great revelation if, writing nineteen years after the fact, the aging Besant botched certain details.

History is a fickle thing—as are those who record it. This is why men like Shapira exist. Antiquities dealers, archaeologists, and other connoisseurs who trade in hard evidence of the ancient past thrive because humans, by nature, are proof seekers. Faith goes far, but without tangible evidence for one's beliefs (the nails of the True Cross, the Shroud of Turin, Noah's Ark), a great chasm emerges that can flood with doubt. These history merchants provide links to glorious pasts, commoditizing authenticity. Sometimes they do one better and offer confirmation for deeply held convictions. In searching for Shapira's scrolls, I suppose I was looking for something similar.

Besant's history, in any case, was defective. And the suggestion that Shapira's downfall began the day he arrived in London, or shortly thereafter, when excited savants appointed Ginsburg to examine the scrolls—that's not quite right, either.

In fact, one could start the story nearly thirty years earlier, in 1856, when Shapira first arrived in Jerusalem—twenty-six years old, stateless, and alone.

Born in 1830 in Kamenets-Podolsk—a town that at times has been part of Lithuania, Poland, or Russia—Shapira was reared in a province famous as the birthplace of Hasidic Judaism, a mystical sect characterized by its adherents' fealty to charismatic rabbis and a spiritual approach to religious observance. Though Jews' access to land in Kamenets was limited by law, as a whole the southern part of the Pale of Settlement was a hub of Jewish life and learning, replete with *heders* (Jewish elementary schools), *batei midrash* (study houses), yeshivas, and synagogues. Kamenets offered a young man ample reason to leave, but it was an ideal training ground for someone whose life would revolve around Hebrew manuscripts.

Sometime in the mid-1850s, Shapira and his grandfather departed for Palestine in search of Shapira's father, who some years earlier had left the family home to live out the millennial dream of Jews in exile: "Next year in Jerusalem." It was an arduous expedition, the first of many on which Shapira would ultimately embark, and it took him from Ukraine to Bucharest before at last he reached Jerusalem, then a stinking backwater of the sick-man Ottoman Empire. Shapira's grandfather died along the way, and while this loss was doubtless traumatic for the lonely nomad, he did find something to soothe his pain: Jesus Christ.

During a five-month sojourn in Romania, Shapira would later write, "my relationship with missionaries there convinced me of the truth of the Gospels, and I was received into the Christian fold by holy baptism." It is tempting to play armchair psychologist: in the aftermath of his grandfather's death, Shapira, in his mid-twenties, was suddenly alone in the world—drifting in a nation not his own, en route to a country he knew largely from books, to find a father who had left him behind for the biblical Holy Land. What better time to seek a new patriarch? Especially one whose teachings called out to the least among us.

But there is also this: it was a grim time in the Holy City. Disease was rampant, work scarce, and tension among—and within—religions constant. With a total population of just fifteen to eighteen thousand, putrid animal carcasses littering the streets, and the threat of cholera lurking, Jerusalem's singles scene could not have been inspiring.

And to be Jewish in Shapira's Jerusalem was a particularly unattractive proposition. The city's Jews were impoverished, their streets and alleyways filthy. Residing very near the bottom of the socioeconomic totem pole, Jerusalem's Jewish population was reliant on the *halukah*, charity from foreign coreligionists, just to fill their stomachs. Protestants, meanwhile, thrived, enjoying access to money from Europe and support from their mother churches. Which is to say that if you were a young Jewish man making his way, lonely and penniless, to Jerusalem in 1855, Christianity offered significant opportunities, both spiritual and monetary. Shapira found, and embraced, those prospects.

As a new Christian, he couldn't associate with the Jews—they despised apostates. Their attitude toward the city's Christians was summed up by the nickname they bestowed on Christian Street, the noisy thoroughfare on which Shapira would eventually open his antiquities shop: they called it Treyf Street, using the Yiddish word marking certain foods as forbidden. Converts were subjected to even graver scorn.

The city's rabbis took a dim view of most contact with the Protestant community, whose motives were often rooted in the desire to lure Jews toward the good news of Christ. The rabbis resented the Protestant bishopric's standing cash reward for converts, and its wielding of medical treatment as an inducement to embrace Christ. Before big names from abroad like Baron Edmond de Rothschild and Sir Moses Montefiore erected Jewish hospitals, the best health care available in Jerusalem was to be found in places such as the English Hospital, established in 1844 by the London Society for Promoting Christianity Among the Jews. As is evident from its name, the organization was not strictly concerned with medical care, and the hospital seemed interested in saving lives primarily as an avenue to saving souls. Shapira spent his first few years in Jerusalem working with various arms of the society.

"The bitter hatred entertained by the rabbis toward a living Christianity, and, in particular, towards the missionaries, makes it almost impossible for the latter to speak to the Jews about the concerns of their souls," wrote C. W. M. van de Velde, a Dutch cartographer who toured Jerusalem in the middle of the nineteenth century.

> *On this account the London society has very wisely attached to its agency at Jerusalem a medical institution in the form of a hospital, in which gratuitous attendance is given to sick Jews. The haughty heart, when broken by the disease of the body, is willing to listen to the voice of Divine compassion, especially when the lips of those from whom the voice proceeds are in correspondence with the benevolent hand of human sympathy and tenderness.*

This is one interpretation of what happened inside that hospital's wards. Another, promoted by Jerusalem's rabbis, held that such missionary efforts simply preyed upon society's weakest—poor, sick Jews desperate for aid, whatever its origins and conditions. Rather than subject themselves to such proselytizing, many Jews preferred simply to gamble on their immune systems. So vehement was the rabbis' opposition to the society's missionizing that they began excommunicating those who worked or sought treatment in the facility. In 1846, one poor Jewish woman had the singular misfortune of drawing her final breath in the English Hospital. The city's rabbis refused to allow her burial in a Jewish cemetery, and over the next several days her body was shuttled through the streets of Jerusalem as missionaries sought a suitable cemetery. A "mob" of a hundred Jews blockaded their graveyard. Another plot turned out to be *waqf*, sacred to Muslims. While the deceased's final resting place was being sorted, the English Hospital remained a flashpoint: its butcher was cornered and beaten. A private security team barred access to the building. The mission's doctor claimed that the rabbis had ordered a hit on him.

This all reminds me of a joke.

A young couple visits a rabbi shortly before their wedding. They ask whether or not they will be permitted to dance together after the ceremony and the rabbi tells them that's impossible: men and women dancing together is, of course, strictly forbidden.

"But what about sex?" the young man asks. "Can we do that?"

"Sex? Of course sex," the rabbi says. "It's a mitzvah."

"Lying down?" the young woman asks sheepishly.

"Sure, sure," the rabbi says. "A mitzvah."

"On the kitchen table?" the groom asks.

"Food and sex?" the rabbi says. "Double mitzvah!"

"Standing up?" the young man asks.

Here the rabbi explodes. "No! Never standing up!"

"But why?" the girl asks.

"Because standing up," the rabbi says, "could lead to dancing."

One gets the sense that Jerusalem's rabbis viewed convalescence in the English Hospital in much the same way the joke's rabbi approached coed dancing: the proximate gateway to the sin was as frightening to them as the sin itself. The rabbis became as scared of seeking medical help from Christians as they already were of their people being "willing to listen to the voice of Divine compassion."

The Protestants, for their part, didn't give the rabbis much reason to think otherwise. They were, after all, trying to capture souls at their hospital and such efforts, God forbid, sometimes led to dancing.

THE OTTOMANS DID not officially recognize the Protestant faith and so it held no purchase in Jerusalem at the outset of the nineteenth century. In spite of this, Protestants ultimately became the city's most active Christians, founding not only the hospital but schools, hostels, and cultural institutions. In 1848 the London Society for Promoting

Christianity Among the Jews completed construction on their pièce de résistance, Christ Church, the "first large modern structure to be built in modern Jerusalem," according to the great historian of the city Yehoshua Ben-Arieh. The church, built at a cost of some twenty thousand pounds, served not only as the seat of the Anglican bishop and the center of Protestant life in Jerusalem but also, until the onset of World War I, as the British Consulate. The building's mission was reflected in its very design. Though constructed in the shape of a cross, its chapel was devoid of crucifixes and heavy on the Holy Tongue: the walls were emblazoned with Hebrew verses— the Ten Commandments, the Lord's Prayer, and the Apostles' Creed, the latter two in translations made by a converted Jew. The church held a Hebrew prayer service (and still does so today) and even celebrated Jewish holidays. This was Shapira's church, a place where Jews who had converted to Christianity—"Jewish Christians," in church parlance—would not feel entirely out to sea. Although his attendance ebbed and flowed, Shapira felt very much at home there.

"Father remarked that, when [Shapira] began to pray, 'one might just as well try and make oneself comfortable,'" recalled Bertha Spafford Vester, whose family founded Jerusalem's American Colony and attended the church. "For he would go on and on ever so long."

When he was not putting on a display of piety, Shapira spent his church time reading—ignoring the bishop's sermon and losing himself in his Bible.

Shortly after his arrival in Palestine, Shapira applied for admission to the House of Industry, an Anglican-run vocational school that trained Jewish boys in trades like shoemaking and woodworking. In July 1856 he was accepted for a three-month trial period studying carpentry and turnery. He took to his apprenticeship there with aplomb, quickly gaining a reputation as both highly intelligent and hardworking. He was so successful that his initial appointment ended up lasting three years. In the minutes of the London Jews Society's Committee of Management meeting from July 28, 1857, Shapira's superior—a Mr. Rominju—applauded his charge's "diligence and regularity." The Reverend D. H. Hefter gave him good marks in weightier subjects, speaking favorably of his development "both in the knowledge and practical application of evangelical truth." The following year, the society produced a list of "unmarried proselytes," on which Shapira appeared as bachelor No. 22. The entry notes that the young émigré had been "twice baptized," indicating that he had undergone a second baptism once he arrived in Palestine. Shapira, the document goes on to say, is a "learned clever Jew, with a deep and original mode of thinking."

Shapira regularly proselytized among Jerusalem's Jews, although he and his compatriots had little luck minting new converts. Unbowed, he tried his hand elsewhere, making a missionary tour of the Galilee with stops in Tiberias and Safed, two of Judaism's holiest cities (along with Jerusalem, Hebron, and, according to more recent mystical traditions, Teaneck, New Jersey).

That summer, another member of the Anglican community departed Jerusalem for the mission in Cairo, leaving open his position as Christ Church's chief librarian. On July 12 the committee voted to offer the job to Shapira. The appointment came with a raise—Shapira would now earn a respectable forty-five pounds a year. The committee set very specific hours for his work at the library, allowing time for dinner and ordering that the depot be closed Wednesday afternoons "in order that Mr. Shapira may pay missionary visits to the Jews." In August 1860 the committee allotted eighty piasters a month for daily English lessons, which would foster improved communication with brother Anglicans and visiting pilgrims.

But even as his career prospects improved, Shapira's health threatened to derail him. Throughout his first years in Palestine he was often ill, suffering the fever, chills, and sweating associated with a condition known as "ague." Repeated bouts began to interfere with his work—both as a missionary and in the library. Eventually things got so bad that Shapira was sent to a Jerusalem hospital run by a team of German Lutheran deaconesses. There he met a nurse by the name of Rosette Joeckel, who had immigrated to Jerusalem from a small town near Düsseldorf. The prim daughter of a rural pastor, Rosette was among a group of women who had landed in Jerusalem in 1855 to tend to patients in this infirmary, to collect clothes for the city's poor, and, eventually, to look after a growing number of children at the Talitha Kumi orphanage, located on what is today King George Street. First, though, she would tend to Shapira, who would soon after be removed from the list of Jerusalem's unmarried proselytes.

FOUR YEARS AFTER his arrival in Jerusalem, Shapira launched a new business venture that would become the center of his life. Sensing an opportunity among the growing number of foreign pilgrims then beginning to descend on Jerusalem, the thirty-year-old entrepreneur opened his shop on Christian Street. Catering to these religious visitors, Shapira sold Bibles with made-to-order inscriptions on olive-wood covers, photos of holy sites, books about Jerusalem, breviaries, coins, and pressed flowers.

Shapira's Jerusalem was tiny—just one square kilometer, all told—and the romantic aura of its past was bathed in the gut-churning stench of the present. Blood and entrails spilled straight from slaughterhouses into the gutter. Sopping sloughs of trash decayed on ramshackle corners. The water was polluted and dangerous. Muslims, Jews, Christians, and Armenians lived in the city's cramped quarters, congregating around the monuments and shrines that brought meaning to their lives. Public squares oozed like sanitariums: sun-sleepy vagrants bathed open wounds in the blistering afternoon air; cripples—arms and legs ending abruptly in broad and poorly bandaged stumps—hawked measly beads imported from Hebron; blind men rattled beggars' cups as if to remind themselves they were still alive.

Mark Twain visited Jerusalem on a whirlwind tour through Palestine and would recount it in his classic memoir *The Innocents Abroad*. His account is a riotous catalog of disenchantment: the city he'd imagined was far superior to the one he found, where modernity and tradition ground awkwardly against each other, where the Bible was as much industry as inspiration, where locals seemed all too willing to exploit the past to scare up a piaster in the present.

Some years later, another American, Selah Merrill, described his own walk through Jerusalem's "dark, narrow and filthy" passages to call on a leading Jerusalem rabbi.

"He led me through the blindest and dirtiest of the passages until the way was plain, and then said he hoped I would not consider the Jews to blame for the filth which I saw," recalled Merrill, who served as America's consul in Jerusalem. "'We have often,' said he, 'tried to do something or get something done about this matter, but the government gives us no encouragement, but rather the opposite, and under such circumstances we can do nothing.'"

By the time Shapira opened his store, however, Jerusalem's sad situation had begun, slowly, to change. The previous decade, two European shipping concerns, France's Messageries Maritimes and Austrian Lloyd (Österreichischer Lloyd), had begun servicing Palestine with their modern steamships, opening the way to foreign tourism. Increasingly, European powers were establishing consulates in Jerusalem, and, through agreements known as capitulations, the region's Ottoman rulers granted them significant rights of operation—eventually loosening restrictions that had earlier prevented foreigners from buying land in the city. As an influx of Westerners made Jerusalem home, they brought with them improved standards of hygiene. A sanitation committee was founded to collect trash. Lights were installed along the city's streets. When Austrian emperor Franz Josef visited in 1869, the Ottomans upgraded the Jaffa–Jerusalem road so he could arrive by cart.

Along with developments in infrastructure came flocks of pilgrims and scholars nurturing visions of the lost Ark of the Covenant, the Ten Commandments, or any other artifact that, hiding just beneath the surface, might be dug up and brought home to at last "prove the Bible right."

Jerusalem's archaeology mania began in earnest when the Frenchman Louis Félicien de Saulcy explored the Tomb of the Kings. De Saulcy launched a survey of the site in 1850 and returned thirteen years later for what is widely considered the first archaeological dig in Palestine. Like almost all of the early explorers, surveyors, and archaeologists of the Holy Land, De Saulcy was a foreigner. Initially, local Arabs showed little passion for the work of these peculiar roving Christians. Eventually, however, natives got wise to the fact that there was money to be made off what lay beneath their feet, and involved themselves in a number of deals that led to fantastic discoveries—and unfortunate calamities.

For all his enthusiasm, De Saulcy proved a rank amateur, although it seems unfair to condemn him—professionals did not yet exist. In once instance, De Saulcy mistakenly believed he had identified the tombs of the House of David, though in fact he was excavating the crypt of a queen, Helena of Adiabene. But the site's name—the "Tomb of the Kings"—has stuck. Despite himself, the Frenchman helped launch an intellectual, religious, historical, and commercial industry that thrives to this day.

IN THE LATE nineteenth century, archaeology was still a fledgling science, and the idea that its practitioners could find hard evidence for the biblical version of history fired the public's imagination. The discoveries—and peccadilloes—of the new archaeologists populated flashy headlines. Newspapers from the *New York Times* to the *Times* of London gave extensive coverage to this contemporary breed of explorers, arousing sometimes frenzied public attention. The *Athenaeum*, a London-based magazine, would cover Shapira under its "Literary Gossip" banner. The Moabite Stone created such a stir that "politicians, lawyers, statists, men of business, nay, ladies—ladies, moreover, never previously suspected of having in their mental colouring the faintest tint of *blue*—talked of it, discussed it, argued about it, expressed opinions as to its age and its contents, and smiled if they met with any one who confessed to complete ignorance on the subject."

Relics from the Holy Land were particularly sought after, and in 1865 Queen Victoria herself helped launch the Palestine Exploration Fund, an organization that would go on to play a central role in nurturing not only the field of biblical archaeology but Jerusalem itself. Not to be outdone, enthusiasts in the United States founded the American Palestine Exploration Society, which their more successful English counterparts cheekily referred to by its acronym, APES. Many of those who arrived in the mid-nineteenth century to explore Jerusalem and, more broadly, Palestine—first to create maps of the region and later to locate and survey its ruins—were chapter-and-verse Bible aficionados. They knew the Holy Book's dramatis personae as though they'd grown up together on the playgrounds of Canaan; they could cite its cities and towns as though they themselves had shuttled between them collecting the half-shekel census payment mandated in the Book of Exodus; they could list its native flowers long before the opportunity arose to pluck one from the *terra sancta* and press it between the pages of their olive-wood breviaries. *A spade in one hand and a Bible in the other* was a popular sobriquet for these new searchers, who made a series of stunning discoveries suggesting that the Bible's stories were true. These finds, and the emerging archaeology of the Bible, engendered deep-seated desires among the faithful, chief among them what the Israeli writer Haim Be'er has called the "fetishist passion" to hold in their hands a piece of this disappeared world that was suddenly reemerging beneath their very feet.

For these travelers, the Bible was both living document and historical guidebook; to explore its sanctified geography was a divine pursuit and a rip-roaring adventure. A good number of these "sacred geographers" were Protestant missionaries and clergymen. Many of them passed through Christ Church and, later, Shapira's shop. As a young man new to the city, scraping by as an apprentice carpenter in the House of Industry while trying to figure out what to do with his life, Shapira was keenly aware of the explosion of archaeological activity taking place, sometimes literally, in his backyard. Through his affiliation with the Anglican Church, he came to know many of the players central to biblical archaeology's birth. Archaeology, like Shapira himself, was a growth industry.

THE NEW TOURISTS were very good for business. As Shapira well knew, if the Holy Land held a special place in the hearts of Christians, Jews, and Muslims, then Jerusalem was the holy land of the Holy Land. But the city, while slathered in history, was only beginning to excavate its hidden remains. Archaeology, of course, emerged from the yearning to connect with the past. But in Jerusalem, Westerners seeking to live where the Messiah had risen, and would rise again, helped turn the city toward modernity. Their desire to unearth relics that would shore up the Bible's narrative and, in so doing, tender proof for a belief system that had previously demanded faith alone was, ironically, a force propelling the ancient city into the future.

Shapira's shop became a gathering place for those seeking to do just that, or to profit from the seekers—curious scholars scavenging for new material, tourists on the hunt for keepsakes to bring back home, and Bedouin with relics to sell—nomads whose wanderings afforded them a deep knowledge of the region's geography that none of these others could match. The store was best known for its mementos of Jerusalem, many of which were in fact produced in Europe. Metal mice, of all things, proved strong sellers, several landing in Jaffa, where they joined a host of other antiquities in the collection of the Russian aristocrat Baron Platon Grigorievich von Ustinov. Along with his wife (rumored to be an Ethiopian princess) and a collection of monkeys and cockatoos, Ustinov made his home in Jaffa's Templars Colony. In addition to his mice, he owned a collection of ancient Jewish tombstones discovered near Jaffa by the noted French archaeologist Charles Clermont-Ganneau, who would shortly take on a central—and painful—role in Shapira's life.

JERUSALEM'S HISTORY DATES back to the city's founding in the fourth millennium BCE. According to the archaeologist Eric H. Cline, the much-contested city of peace has been destroyed twice, besieged twenty-three times, attacked fifty-two times, and captured and recaptured forty-four times. The city has a well-documented history of violence, born of its significance to the three great monotheistic faiths. It is a symbol, yes, but also a strategic asset. A beacon on the hill, and also a bunker.

Yet between the invasions and intifadas, the sieging and the pillaging, Jerusalem has also been a living, functioning city—an icon, but also home to kings and beggars; prophets and madmen; mothers and daughters; rabbis, reverends and imams. Abutting holy sites and shrines: shops and shepherds, shoemakers, fishmongers, and moneychangers. National and political conflicts abounded, and so did discord of a more humdrum variety: feelings hurt, sensibilities trampled, vows broken, marriages wavering, children rebelling.

Between the fighting and the living, Jerusalem has left behind an enduring physical record of its tumultuous history—a record that researchers have been digging up, dusting off, picking through, and putting on display for more than a century and a half.

The new shop allowed Shapira a measure of independence from the Church, which since his arrival had treated him as its child—at once looking after and enforcing his physical and spiritual welfare. This newfound freedom did not please the mission, whose leaders found his church attendance lacking. At one meeting, the Committee of Management passed a resolution requesting that Shapira "adhere strictly to the rule of the Mission in regular attendance at the Heb M.g. (Hebrew morning) service, and (resolving) to intimate to him that any future inattendance on this point will be reported to the Parent Committee."

Karl Baedeker's *Guide to Palestine and Syria* regarded Shapira's as the "best shop" in Jerusalem for books and photographs of the Holy Land. Centrally located on a bustling road just a short walk from the Jaffa Gate, one of six functioning entrances to the city (a seventh, Mercy Gate, had been closed for centuries, awaiting miraculous reopening with the Messiah's arrival), the store was appropriately sited for a man taken with Jerusalem's storied biblical pedigree. A left turn out the front door led directly to the Via Dolorosa, where Christ himself had collapsed under the weight of his cross. Through the rear window, Shapira could gaze down on Bathsheba's Pool, where, legend had it, King David fell for his comely neighbor after catching sight of her as she emerged from the water. Today the site is also known as Hezekiah's Pool, and, as in Shapira's day, one would bathe in it only if he wished to contract a staph infection. Such palpable religious and historical connections imbued Jerusalem with profound emotional appeal, eventually drawing pilgrims by the shipload. In the absence of these visitors, and their desire to find and bring home relics linked somehow to the Bible, Shapira might never have opened his shop, let alone turned to brokering manuscript deals with Europe's leading libraries and museums.

The pilgrims' romantic reveries about Jerusalem, of course, far outstripped its actual circumstances. The city was situated near the geographical center of the Ottoman Empire, which once had stretched from Hungary to the Persian Gulf and from Egypt up to the Caucasus. But by the time Shapira arrived, that mighty power was in the end stages of a long decline, and the Holy City, said the French playwright Jules Lemaître, was "the most pathetic spot in the whole universe."

"The city to which Christianity owed its earliest beginning is now so overrun with every description of rival creeds and heresies," he said, "that the religious differences within its sacred walls are far more present to the mind than the almost vanished traces of the Redeemer's presence are to the heart."

If the growing popularity of biblical archaeology paved the way for Shapira's career in antiquities, it was in large measure the emergence of the Palestine Exploration Fund that cleared a path for biblical archaeology to grow and thrive. On September 12, 1864, a party of men from the British Royal Engineers set sail for Palestine to begin work on the Ordnance Survey of Jerusalem, part of an effort to purify the city's polluted water supply. Under the stewardship of Captain Charles Wilson, later chairman of the PEF, these surveyors spent twenty-one grueling months mapping Jerusalem and its environs. Their work, almost inevitably, strayed into the realm of archaeology. The engineers set off on some early investigations of the city's ancient sites, and the remains of a stone arch that supported a road to the Temple Mount in the time of Jesus is still known as Wilson's Arch. When Wilson's work in the city was done, London launched the PEF. Over the coming years, the organization, whose goals were at once political, military, religious, and scientific, worked on two primary fronts: surveying the Holy Land, and excavating it.

The group attracted the best of English society. Aristocrats and military officers joined, as did more artistic types like Besant. PEF founders included Arthur Stanley, dean of Westminster Abbey, and the music critic Sir George Grove.

Shapira's life, meanwhile, had begun to grow into realms beyond his new business. After their chance meeting during his convalescence in the deaconesses' hospital, his relationship with Rosette deepened. In January 1861, Shapira asked the mission's leaders for permission to marry his onetime nurse. The committee supported his request.

As his personal affairs shaped up, Shapira moved to plug another gap. Stateless upon his arrival in Palestine, he applied now for protection from the German government.

"Owing to the political situation [in the Russian Empire], which restricted the migration of Jews of my status, we were forced to give up our passports and, by crossing the border, we relinquished our rights as Russian citizens," Shapira explained in his 1860 appeal for German papers. "Since I am without citizenship, I hereby request the protection of the Prussian consulate and ask that I be awarded a passport as testimony of that protection."

The Prussians granted his request; the Polish Jew was now a German Christian.

By the time he married Rosette, on April 23, 1861, Shapira

had abandoned one faith, adopted another, taken on a new national identity, and added the regal—and German—"Wilhelm" to his name. He had also begun to cultivate relationships with people in higher places, an objective he would pursue throughout his life. The Christ Church wedding was conducted by Shapira's instructor at the House of Industry, the Reverend D. A. Hefter. Among others attending was the well-known banker Johannes Frutiger, who would go on to become one of the richest men in Palestine, financing the country's first railway. For a young man on the make, these relationships would have embodied not only a means for advancement but an end in and of themselves: those cozy with the important and powerful were powerful and important in their own right. The union further established Shapira's place in Jerusalem's Protestant community. It also proved the rabbis right: hospitals were very dangerous places indeed.

THE SHAPIRAS MOVED into an old Saracen house behind Christ Church, its arched door—hung with heavy knockers and decorative brass nails—leading to a sun-bright courtyard where a well and a pomegranate tree offered relief from the heat.

Shapira had done well for himself: after arriving alone, he had beaten illness, found a wife, fathered a child—Augusta Louisa Wilhelmina Shapira—and established himself as a member of the Anglican community in Jerusalem. From the moment of his arrival in Palestine, he had shown himself to be a deeply intelligent and original thinker, and a relentless worker—impressing his instructors at the House of Industry and his elders among the London Jews' Society. Battling poverty, mistrust, and recurring infection, Shapira strove to better himself in his new homeland and to climb the ladder of Jerusalem's Protestant community—first mastering a trade, and next studying English, both of which, coupled with his background in the Hebrew language and Jewish texts, had allowed him to establish himself as an independent businessman. By the time his second daughter, Maria Rosette, was baptized on May 2, 1869, he was listed on the baptism certificate as "Bookseller." Although this was a step up from his prior work, it didn't begin to describe the international reputation he would come to earn as an antiquarian of the first order. Soon he would expand his business, moving seamlessly from Bibles and breviaries to the new beating heart of his work, and his life: a remarkable collection of ancient pottery and manuscripts, inscribed in Hebrew and Arabic, which he kept stashed away in the back room of his shop, his sanctum sanctorum, and pulled out only for special visitors. While average pilgrims were seen to by a number of hired hands, Shapira himself attended to the rich, attractive foreigners himself, usually in English. Roused from what his daughter would later call his "habitual abstraction," Shapira became garrulous—entertaining these guests with stories and learned discourse on his growing manuscript collection. He would invite pretty women to his work space for coffee and, while he regaled them with the story of David and Bathsheba—pointing out the very spot where it had unfolded—he would romanticize the mood, anointing his eager listener with a mist of rose water. Years later, his daughter Maria, who would achieve literary fame under the nom de plume Myriam Harry, would publish an autobiographical novel about life with her father. *The Little Daughter of Jerusalem* describes one of Shapira's customers, an American woman who became smitten with the merchant and his merchandise.

> *[He] devoted himself so exclusively to her that all his other customers ceased to exist for him. All his most precious rolls of the Thora were spread out for her benefit. He showed her his rarest*

parchments, his priceless MSS., his monoliths, his pottery and the little wild garden behind his back premises.

"Ah!" sighed the pretty young tourist, leaning over the mouldering balustrade, "if only, if only I could stay here for the rest of my life."

This kind of validation proved too much for Shapira to resist. In due course, Harry reported, the woman invited him to call at her hotel. He didn't make it home that evening.

When he *was* home, Shapira proved a loving, if distracted, father—alternately showering his daughters with affection and ignoring them entirely. He was similarly impulsive with Rosette—one minute resting his head on her lap while she stroked his hair and whispered her devotion, the next arguing bitterly over his business affairs and their daughters' schooling.

From the moment Rosette went into labor with Augusta, and a city-wide cholera epidemic left him rushing through Jerusalem searching for an available doctor, Shapira had taken an active role in his children's lives. He planned long horseback rides through Judea, during which he and Myriam nestled against each other atop his white steed. He found joy entertaining his daughters with stories of his own adventures in the Orient. He allowed Myriam to work beside him, drying plants and flowers to sell at the shop, and occasionally took advantage of her small hands, which were good for cleaning the narrow necks of his pottery. Shapira's shop was like a second home for Myriam, who felt the ground there was enchanted. In the evenings she enjoyed watching him empty his pockets of the dollars, rubles, and napoleons he had earned during the day. On Sundays she joined her father at church—when he went—and often fell asleep on his knee during prayer. He encouraged her to write poetry and instructed her in geology and botany. When he returned home from long trips away, he would wrap her in his arms and kiss her as she inhaled the scent of the desert in his beard. After one such trip, Shapira returned with a cohort of Bedouin associates, including a sheikh to whom a very young Myriam took a liking. Over the next several days her father and his guests played along, suggesting impishly that Myriam and the sheikh were to be married. When the girl recognized that it was a joke, she was forlorn. Shapira, sincerely distressed by his daughter's grief, reacted tenderly. He assured her that she would wed her sheikh one day—only not for a while, by which time she may have found someone else she liked even more.

Other times, however, Shapira was so involved in his work that he seemed to have forgotten he had children altogether—and remembered his wife only when they bickered. Winter was high season, with pilgrims descending on Palestine to celebrate Christmas where Christ himself was born. At this time of year, Shapira often worked late at the shop while Rosette and the children spent evenings at home without him. He suffered long bouts of loneliness and depression, periods during which he retreated into his office, and into himself. When she was young, Myriam wondered whether her father actually existed "or was only one of those imaginary heroes who figured in [her maidservant's] wonderful stories."

Often Shapira was occupied in the field procuring relics, or in his workroom deciphering them and writing detailed reports for buyers about their provenance and notable characteristics. He traveled abroad to hawk his merchandise to institutions such as the Royal Library in Berlin and the British Museum. It was an exhilarating time for him. But as his business grew, so did tension with Rosette. A conservative woman who saw holiness in a simple life (she once reprimanded Shapira for taking Augusta to the opera), she worried that her husband was a dreamer and that his efforts to elevate his station tempted fate. Shapira's forays into old manuscripts and pottery provoked angry exchanges between them, leaving Rosette frightened and Shapira gloomy. "Oh, dear Lord," she once prayed. "I thank you for having endowed my child with such a tender heart. God grant it may prevent her from developing her father's pride and love of display."

Rosette's concerns, however, paled beside Shapira's growing enterprise. In short order, he found himself catering not only to the foreign visitors who descended, scavenger-like, on his shop, but to the leaders of the very nations from which they had come.

3

LONDON

For nearly half a century, a single theory has dominated efforts to explain what happened to Shapira's scrolls after they were displayed in 1887 at the Anglo-Jewish Historical Exhibition in London. At the theory's center sits Sir Charles Nicholson, an English-Australian nobleman and gynecologist who arrived down under in 1834.

Over the next seventy years, Nicholson would amass a substantial fortune, allowing him to pursue passions outside his work as a physician. He served as a founding father of the University of Sydney, Australia's first university, and was an influential politician, an intrepid explorer, a generous philanthropist, the founder of at least six museums, a well-respected spiritualist, and a stalwart of the Anglican Church.

Among Nicholson's many enthusiasms was the burgeoning field of Near Eastern archaeology. Along with so many others, he had been captivated by the discovery of relics left behind by that region's ancient inhabitants. He was particularly infatuated with the Moabite Stone, swept away by "how wonderfully it proved the truth of ancient scripture history." Not satisfied simply reading about the ancient worlds then being rediscovered, Nicholson—with his friendly face and his ample lamb-chop sideburns, to say nothing of his well-padded wallet—strapped on a compass and a canteen and suited up to explore the region himself. In 1856, he departed for Egypt, where, sailing down the Nile, he acquired more than four hundred ancient artifacts, among them the mummified legs of a child. In 1860, Nicholson donated a collection of more than a thousand antiquities from Egypt, Greece, and Italy to the University of Sydney, thus inaugurating the Nicholson Museum, which displays his acquisitions even today.

From mummies and Moabites, Nicholson's interest turned naturally to ancient manuscripts. Wielding some of his considerable wealth, he acquired a trove of them. By then an old man, he began learning Hebrew so as to read the works in his growing collection.

Though well aware of Shapira's checkered reputation, Nicholson considered him "by far the most learned Hebraist of his day." It's no surprise, then, that when Shapira died and his remaining stock of manuscripts became available, Nicholson eagerly scooped them up. "I have generally had refusal of such [biblical] documents as have been on the market," Nicholson wrote to the Reverend Robert Story, principal of the University of Glasgow, "and suddenly overtures were made to me to buy (I believe) nearly the whole of the Sapire [*sic*] collection." With this purchase, Nicholson added to his holdings six more or less complete Torah scrolls that had belonged to Shapira, along with fragments from several copies of the Book of Esther, which Jews read aloud each year on Purim.

Then, on February 22, 1899, Nicholson's elegant estate north of London caught fire. While no one in the old man's household was injured, his home, known as the Grange, was devastated. Rebuilding was an enormous job—work went on for some fifteen months and cost more than the insurance would cover. "Documents and papers extending through many years" were consumed, Nicholson told a friend, as was a "considerable portion of the library contained in the upper floor."

Nicholson's passion for ancient Near Eastern manuscripts was undimmed by the incineration of his library. The following year, upon learning that the University of Glasgow did not possess any early copies of the Torah, he wrote Story to inquire whether he would be interested in receiving one as a gift. He had already donated similar scrolls from Shapira's collection to his alma mater, the University of Edinburgh, and to the University of St. Andrews. Now, as Nicholson made his offer to Glasgow, he acknowledged that the scroll on offer to the university had been obtained from the Shapira collection. "I am resolved to ask the acceptance of the University of Glasgow of one of the copies which I still retain," he wrote.

Such was Shapira's reputation sixteen years after his death that Nicholson seemed almost to be apologizing for daring to offer the university a valuable Bible scroll. Later, Nicholson would complain that a printed catalog of the University of Sydney's library holdings excluded any mention "of what is certainly the most remarkable object in its contents." That item, he explained, was a manuscript of the Torah—once owned by Shapira and donated to the university by Nicholson himself.

By the time he died in 1903, Nicholson had been knighted by the English crown, named a baronet, and publicly venerated at Oxford, Cambridge, and the University of Edinburgh, all three of which acknowledged him with honorary degrees. His influence in Australia is even more keenly felt. By one scholar's count, "a mountain, at least one river, a town, possibly two, several streets in towns and cities the length of Australia, and a museum all carry his name." That museum houses the largest collection of classical antiquities in the Southern Hemisphere. The University of Sydney, where Nicholson served as chancellor, today educates more than fifty thousand students and has been ranked among the thirty most reputable universities in the world.

It is only fair that Sir Charles remains better known for these honors and accomplishments than for any role he might have played in the Shapira saga. Nevertheless, sixty-seven years after Nicholson's death, another Englishman living in Sydney resurrected the Shapira story, and in doing so boldly placed the baronet at the very heart of the scrolls' unsolved disappearance.

That man was Alan David Crown, a professor of Semitic studies at the University of Sydney who researched the Dead Sea Scrolls. In 1970, Crown wrote what quickly became the seminal work on the fate of the Shapira manuscript, laying out a compelling theory in which Nicholson—who he said had demonstrated an interest in Hebrew, Deuteronomy, and the Moabite Stone—had come to possess the famous scrolls.

"It may well be that Sir Charles was the purchaser of the SHA-PIRA Scroll from QUARITCH, in view of his claim that most of the SHAPIRA collection fell into his hands and in view of his self expressed admiration for him as a scholar," Crown wrote. "If, indeed, this was the case, then we can readily understand the disappearance of the document."

"In 1899," he continued, "the Nicholson home, Totteridge, near London, was partially destroyed by fire and his study was gutted and the contents lost. Not all his library was housed in his study, however. Faded photographs of the study in the university archives indicate that it housed only the most valuable of his archaeological collection as well as a number of items of no interest here."

If Nicholson had purchased the Shapira manuscript, Crown concluded, it was "most probable that it was destroyed in this fire."

Crown's paper, though just two and a half pages long, quickly became gospel and has remained so ever since.

BERNARD QUARITCH'S GENERAL sales catalog for 1887 includes an entry that has been called "one of the most bizarre ever to appear in an antiquarian catalogue." Beside the heading for item No. 32270, the pamphlet—issued four years after Shapira brought his scrolls to London and two years after Quaritch purchased them at Sotheby's—registers the following description:

BIBLE. THE MOST ORIGINAL MS. of Deuteronomy, from the hand of Moses (? Ben Amram) as discovered by the late Mr. Shapira, and valued at £1,000,000; 15 separate fragments (7 numbered and 8 unnumbered), written in the primeval Hebrew character on strips of blackened leather, £25.
Ante Christum 1500–A.D. 1880

These are the famous fragments which Dr. Ginsburg so painfully deciphered and published in The Times, *and which led the religious world of England to sing hallelujahs. The scoffing atheists of Germany and France had refused to acknowledge them genuine.*

As soon as I read it, I realized that this odd entry was my own first clue, offering a concrete indication of what had happened to Shapira's manuscript after his death. Quaritch had acquired it at Sotheby's auction rooms, displayed it at the Anglo-Jewish Historical Exhibition, and put it up for sale in 1887. From there, if Crown was to be believed, Nicholson had purchased it. Now I had to figure out if that was true.

Late one evening in 2012, I entered "Bernard Quaritch" into my Internet browser. All these years later, it turned out, his company survived, dealing books out of offices on South Audley Street in London. It was just possible they retained a record of the sale to Nicholson. That night I booked a flight across the Atlantic.

Yoram Sabo had a thirty-year lead—but now he was only five clues ahead.

My interest in Quaritch had first been piqued in Israel, where, after meeting Sabo, I purchased a copy of *The Shapira Affair*, a slim volume written fifty years ago by the British scholar J. M. Allegro. Allegro was an odd figure: his work on the Dead Sea Scrolls had rankled colleagues, and his book *The Sacred Mushroom and the Cross* has been called "one of the strangest books ever published on the subject of religion and pharmacology." Even so, he was a serviceable narrator—though his Shapira book lacked drama, Allegro had done an admirable job of weaving together disparate sources, among them the "scoffing atheists" entry in the Quaritch catalog.

It was not long after my final meeting with Sabo that I flew to London. When I arrived I shot off an email to Shane Lapsys, a young bookseller at Bernard Quaritch Ltd. On the occasion of Quaritch's 150th anniversary, the *Book Collector*, a journal whose title well explains its content, had published an issue devoted entirely to Quaritch's storied history in the book trade. Among the sixteen essays that appeared in this "special number" was a curious tale about Shapira, Ginsburg, and an iconoclastic scholar named Ephraim Deinard. I wanted a copy of the article—but really I was hoping Lapsys would let me root around Quaritch's storerooms for evidence suggesting whether Sir Charles Nicholson had, in fact, purchased the scrolls.

Lapsys responded promptly, and we arranged a Friday afternoon meeting at Quaritch's elegant headquarters. London always feels to me like Manhattan's West Village just after the cleaning lady has come—its old brick buildings and quaint parks and wrought-iron gates swept and scrubbed as though the pope were in town. Located in the exclusive Mayfair district, the Quaritch facilities looked exactly as a venerable London bookseller's offices should: narrow, carpeted stairways leading to high-ceilinged rooms where bookshelves were neatly fit with leather-bound volumes of Voltaire; commission ledgers, recording auction bids from the 1880s through the 1970s; and a complete run of annotated Sotheby's sales catalogs from 1880 to 1960.

Lapsys, a genteel American then living in England, asked me to wait in one such room, where a portrait of the bald and bearded Quaritch hung above an ornate fireplace.

By now I was certain that the Shapira scrolls had at one point resided inside this very building. This was the closest I had yet come to them. I roamed the room, imagining the fragments laid out on the round, book-covered table near the door, or accidentally wedged between hefty editions of Voltaire's *Mahomet* and *Mérope*.

Lapsys returned with a copy of the *Book Collector* along with a color photocopy of the catalog listing. We chatted briefly about my search, and that was when he mentioned that Quaritch had only moved to this facility in 2009. This was disappointing. But then he mentioned something else: the company's stock cards—small notes listing the author, title, publication details, and physical descriptions for each book the company had in stock. Oftentimes these cards recorded where Quaritch had purchased a particular book and whom he'd sold it to. If I could find the relevant stock card, it might very well tell me who bought the Shapira manuscript. When I left that day, Lapsys promised to investigate how I might do just that.

FOR JEWS, THE number 613 looms large—it represents the sum total of biblical commandments issued by God to the Israelites. For Christians, 666 represents a fearsome trifecta: the dreaded unholy trinity. For Shapiramaniacs, the number 41294 is key—though for reasons far more prosaic. "Add. 41294" was the shelf mark assigned to a leather-bound file now located in the British Library that contains some eighty pages of material relating to Shapira and his Deuteronomy manuscript. For nearly sixty years, 41294—presented to the British Museum by C. D. Ginsburg's wife, presumably after his death in 1914—has been ground zero for Shapira research, the seminal font of primary documents relating to his attempted sale: handwritten letters to and from the story's protagonists, old news-paper clippings, scholars' notes on the manuscripts, and sketches of portions of the scrolls themselves commissioned by Ginsburg, who oversaw their examination.

Christian David Ginsburg was born in Warsaw on Christmas Day in 1831, though his name at birth was simply David Gins-burg. Like Shapira, he had added a suitable new handle when, as a teenager, he converted to Christianity. Protestant missionaries were active in Poland at the time—more so than in neighboring Russia. Travelogues of the era paint a lively picture of evangelicals hounding passersby, proffering books containing both the Old and New Tes-taments. Most Jews scorned these approaches. Many who did accept books never intended to convert, nor even to read them through. Rather, they tore their copies in two—saving the Hebrew Bible for themselves and chucking the Gospels into the trash bin. Ginsburg, it appears, kept on reading.

Beyond his labors as a biblical savant, which earned him a reputation as the "greatest of Oriental scholars in our own time," Ginsburg floated among the elite of English society. He counted England's prime minister, William Ewart Gladstone, as a close friend, and married twice into leading families, allowing him to pur-sue his scholarship without the distractions of an academic posting. An ardent liberal, Ginsburg was an original member of London's National Liberal Club, a gentlemen's association where his portrait still hangs.

Although I had been aware of 41294 before arriving in England—Sabo had mentioned it, as had Allegro—and had a sense of what it contained, I had not yet made a full accounting of the file's contents. Prior to publication of the Nicholson theory in 1970, researchers had conceived several hypotheses to explain what ultimately had become of Shapira's scrolls. Some were convinced they remained in the British Museum—hidden away by shame-faced staffers hoping they might soon be forgotten. Others assumed they had been misfiled among the museum's massive manuscript collection, or accidentally (or not) rerouted to another collection altogether.

I was certain that the scrolls themselves were not in the file—too many people had scoured it before me. But perhaps it held one or two more clues, hidden in plain sight. The morning after I met with Lapsys, I caught the Victoria line to Kings Cross/St. Pancras station, where, across from a Pret A Manger, an elderly man was playing Shostakovich on an upright piano while his cardiganed wife swayed lovingly beside him. Exiting a side door, I crossed the street and entered the British Library, by some measures the largest library in the world.

European libraries sometimes behave as if their aim is to deny public access to their collections. Before I landed in England, I'd had to complete a preregistration process to gain entry to the reading rooms. When I arrived, I took the marble steps to the Reader Registration Office on the enormous building's upper ground floor, where I was required to present a signature and proof of address (passport, national identity card, firearms license), full details of the items I planned to examine, and documentation supporting my request to utilize the library's materials.

After a short wait, I was called to a desk in the back of the room, where an attendant took my photo. She had a look at the result and swiftly offered to retake the picture. I blamed the lighting and, too proud to acknowledge I cared about such vanities, said the first shot would do. She raised her eyebrows and printed my reader's pass.

The Manuscripts Department's reading room was lined by wooden desks occupied by researchers squinting intently at a huge variety of documents—tiny calligraphed volumes, large vellum sheets illuminated in bright reds and regal blues, inscribed notebooks, and folios holding fans of yellowed letters and sketches. The security guard at the entrance glanced up from her paperback as I entered and nodded me through without comment.

At the help desk, I received instructions on calling up 41294 and, learning now that I could request several manuscripts at once, ordered 41293 and 41295 as well. If the scrolls had been mislaid, it seemed to me, the two adjoining files seemed likely landing spots. While I waited, I grabbed coffee and an astounding scone in the museum's café, where over the next several weeks I would pack on five pounds. Then I opened 41295. I was dying to see 41294, but because I didn't expect to find the scrolls themselves there, I thought I'd make a quick check of the other books first, in case my theory led to an immediate home run. It did not. Instead, Additional Manuscript 41295 contained several documents—an old passport, some poems—entirely unrelated to Shapira.

Putting that file aside, I turned to 41293 and was swiftly rewarded. The file contained a catalog of Hebrew documents on offer from Shapira to the British Museum in 1877. Labeled as a "List of Hebrew Manuscripts. Mostly from Saana in Arabia," and written in Shapira's own hand, the catalog offered detailed descriptions of some forty rare manuscripts that Shapira had acquired during a treacherous journey through Yemen. The sale, which had been concluded fully six years before Shapira brought his famous Deuteronomy scrolls to English shores, helped position his story in its larger context. Shapira hadn't arrived at the British Museum as a stranger—he was well known to its Manuscripts Department and others in the field as a purveyor of authentic and valuable Hebraica acquired in areas of the Near East that few Europeans had ever braved. He may have been a showman, but he also had a steady supply of excellent merchandise that museums and libraries were willing to pay for.

Take, for example, the item Shapira listed as No. 33—nearly four hundred pages excised from a book known as *Midrash HaGadol* in which the great rabbis expounded on the Torah's complexities. The section Shapira sold to the museum included their riffs on Deuteronomy. Written in 1496, Shapira's copy was probably the first ever to reach Europe.

Sitting there at my desk, I read the entire catalog. Shapira's handwriting was rushed and sometimes hard to decipher. As I slogged through the learned descriptions of his wares, a fascinating glimpse into the development of his thinking on biblical manuscripts began to emerge. Here was a Christian who was deeply engaged with Jewish texts—curious and knowledgeable about their language and vagaries of style. He was also, I discovered, a man very much concerned with establishing the relative antiquity of his manuscripts, and keenly aware of what it takes to make a text appear old. Comparing one Torah scroll with another document, he wrote—in his charmingly mangled English—that "we met with some what harder leather: yellow and even greenish, of also great age. Where we met the most of the above peculiarities we may be certain (it seems to me) of their oldness. We met often some red or brown skins, where, the ink are already gone taking with it the upper glossy part of the skin, the letters look thin, as, if having been nicely engraved into the skin or leather & it becomes such an oldish look."

Elsewhere, the catalog copy pointed to a man whose thinking, like his faith before it, was at that very moment undergoing a conversion.

"That piece of the M.S. [manuscript] is to me remarkable in consequence of the many many variations from our common codex," he wrote of a particular biblical scroll (not his Deuteronomy). The "common codex" is the traditional text of the Bible. The manuscript Shapira described is beset by abundant differences from that traditional version—a fact that called into question either the authenticity of Shapira's manuscript or, far more divisive, the accuracy of the common codex itself. Shapira cited 150 minor spelling oddities in this manuscript, along with near-wholesale divergences from prescribed rules on dividing paragraphs. These disparities, he wrote, are "systematical" and thus cannot be the result of occasional scribal error.

The discrepancies Shapira described here are small when compared with the variant readings, abridgements, and imports from other books that would later characterize his Deuteronomy. Still, that he noted their presence at all points to the fact that as early as 1877, he was beginning to notice inconsistencies. The idea that the traditional text of the Bible hadn't remained constant from revelation through to his own day would have been controversial, and Shapira was careful not to make such a claim too boldly. The catalog shows him to be circumspect, cautious—a man reluctant to oversell either the ancientness or the import of his own discoveries. "In the mean time I could not believe this our M.S. of a very remote age," he explained, downplaying the manuscript's unusual departures. "I could only account for this so strange variations by saying that the scribe copied some old M.S."

Cautious though he was, Shapira seemed to be quietly drawing a radical conclusion from the manuscript before him. If the curious textual variations he mentioned were, as he suggested, the result of a relatively recent scholar copying from an older text, it stood to reason that this more ancient, and therefore more original, version was unlike the standard edition. In other words, the common codex that believers quoted chapter and verse may have been a very different document from the original version of the Torah.

I was feeling good. In college two hours in the library usually meant the first half of my nap was nearing its end. Here I'd already gained insights into the development of Shapira's thinking on the textual history of the Bible and the physical characteristics of ancient manuscripts. It was a strong start. Turning now to the principal reason for my visit, I picked up 41294 and moved deliberately through its pages—which in every way, from their content to the formality of their address to the handwriting itself, transported me back to the late nineteenth century.

The file included two letters: one to the German scholar Hermann Strack and another to Ginsburg—in which Shapira himself recounted how he had acquired the Deuteronomy scrolls. "You will excuse me dear prof. if I shall trouble you now with a very long letter," Shapira began his note to Strack, an apologetic lead overshadowed by the studied fawning to come. "I hope you will read it with interest in spite of your having so little time to spare, over bourdened as you are, with such abundance of work of high scholarship."

Then there was Besant's invitation to Ginsburg, calligraphed on Palestine Exploration Fund stationery, asking him to attend the unveiling of Shapira's scrolls. "Dear Sir," Besant wrote.

Mr. Shapira of Jerusalem has brought to England an old Hebrew MS apparently of great antiquity containing the text of Deuteronomy with many important variations. He will bring the MS to this office on Thursday next the 26th just at 12 AM and will be very glad if you can meet him in order to see it.

Ginsburg, somehow interpreting the final sentence as an invitation to the royal "you," invited a number of his friends to join.

Farther along in the file, I found sketches of a few of the fragments themselves, complete with Ginsburg's initials in red ink. And there were photographs of the strips that were so dark and faded as to offer no real insight at all.

I was mesmerized by all this—the sudden freedom to peruse the private communications of players at the center of Shapira's drama, to hear their voices, to touch sheets of paper they themselves had touched. I felt as if I was shaking their hands across the many intervening years.

That's when I spotted it. Wedged between a letter from Besant and a memo by Shapira were a few lines on card stock small as a cocktail napkin, scratched in the loose hand of Edward Bond, the British Museum's chief librarian. Dated four months after Shapira's death, the note informed Ginsburg that Shapira's widow had been searching for two letters regarding her late husband. The notes, she believed, were in Ginsburg's possession. Next, almost as an aside, this:

> *She enquires after the Deuteronomy fragments & says she found two small pieces among her late husband's papers & sent them to Prof. Schlottmann.*

Shortly after Shapira died, probably while sifting through his things in advance of bankruptcy proceedings the following month, Rosette had discovered two pieces of the Deuteronomy scrolls that Shapira had left behind in Jerusalem. Seeking a second opinion, she had sent them off to the German theologian Professor Konstantin Schlottmann, the first person to have seen—and dismissed—the bulk of the scrolls themselves. If I could find Rosette's "two small pieces," they could, like the Dead Sea Scrolls, be subjected to modern testing that would establish their age. With the fragments in hand, modern paleographers, far more expert in interpreting ancient scripts than their nineteenth-century counterparts, could examine the writing without the filter of interpretation clouding reproductions like the ones Ginsburg commissioned. A really good paleographer could date the script to a narrow period of years, and the fragments could be carbon-14-tested to determine their date with even greater accuracy. Other tests might even indicate where the manuscript's leather had originated.

If the fragments, and so the scrolls, were real, they would reveal so much about how the Bible developed—how it was written, rewritten, and revised over the course of centuries. And if they were a forgery, whoever created this manuscript was some kind of genius—clever, creative, and profoundly learned. In conjuring a wild version of Deuteronomy, they had somehow managed to predict the Dead Sea Scrolls decades before their discovery. Who had the chops to pull off a fraud this brilliant?

A number of erudite scholars had already sought the scrolls. And Yoram Sabo was out there somewhere at that very instant—hunting, digging, progressing, even as I sat in central London, nervous that this would be the day he found them. If I was going to locate the scrolls, I'd have to think differently, conceive of new angles. This very brief reference in Bond's note to Ginsburg was just such an angle, and offered my second clue: Shapira's widow had sent two scroll fragments to Schlottmann. Maybe I didn't need to find Shapira's entire manuscript. If I could track down Schlottmann's papers in Germany, these fragments might still be among them.

First, though, I heard back from Shane Lapsys at Quaritch. I was not the only person who had come asking after the Shapira stock cards. Quaritch had been receiving similar inquiries since the 1950s, and staff had repeatedly rummaged through their files to no avail.

But there was another option. Quaritch had also kept "day-books," large lined notebooks in which his clerks recorded details of every sale. If Quaritch had sold the "most original" manuscript of Deuteronomy after listing it in 1887, the sale would be logged in one of these ledgers. Another young Quaritch staffer had for some time been seeking access to the firm's historical archive, but the institution currently holding it had not extended entrée beyond what was afforded the general public. All the Quaritch folks could do was tell me where to find the daybooks myself: in the Manuscripts Department at the British Library.

The Quaritch daybooks are large things—about eighteen by ten inches—and they were not designed for 130 years of use. Many are falling apart, their thick cardboard covers detached or hanging by gnarled threads, spines shrinking to dust at the touch. They reek of decay; after inhaling these volumes for six to eight hours a day over the next couple of weeks, I grew accustomed to the sharp taste of dust lodged in my throat.

Each book included an alphabetized index listing those who had made purchases from Quaritch in a given year. Starting with 1887—when Quaritch first offered the manuscript for sale—I scanned these lists for names of the scholars and noblemen who had been associated with the manuscripts: Nicholson, Ginsburg, Schlottmann, Besant. None of these names appeared, which left me no alternative but to read through each of the more than one thousand sales Quaritch made that year, in hopes the indexer had simply missed the transaction I was looking for—or that someone else, previously unsuspected, had swooped in to buy the scrolls.

Page by page, I immersed myself in what amounted to a retrospective overview of England's obsessions in the late nineteenth century. Quaritch dealt in a remarkable variety of books: poetry and novels; museum catalogs and encyclopedias; tomes on art, science, archaeology, the Bible, electricity. Some buyers specialized, limiting their purchases to books on a single topic—the numismatists sought insights to enhance their coin collections, the birders coveted diagrams of falcons and eagles. Others were Renaissance men who purchased volumes on multiple subjects. Still others were a drop less literary: Quaritch also dealt in booze, and certain customers—thirsty ones, like G. J. Mann of Lower Hawes Street in London—visited the respected bookman to procure Scotch and gin by the gallon.

After two days of searching, I was deeply educated on the nature of Bernard Quaritch's impressive business—and had become expert in deciphering the handwriting of his underlings, who, judging from their penmanship, moonlighted as physicians and/or serial killers. But I'd learned absolutely nothing about what had happened to the Shapira manuscript.

As far as I was aware, no one who had published on Shapira had taken the time to slog through these moldering notebooks. It was tedious, dirty work. But the daybooks, like Rosette's two small fragments, were just the sort of fresh approach I was after; searching them felt like a real step forward—and, I believed, held out the genuine promise of a breakthrough. Quaritch sold an enormous number of books and recorded, it seemed to me, every such transaction. If he had sold the Shapira manuscript, it would be listed in the daybooks. If it was listed, I would find it.

But I didn't find it, and as I neared the end of 1887's listings, my disappointment grew. Then I received another note from the folks at Quaritch—this time from a colleague of Lapsys named Katherine Thorn. Quaritch, she informed me, had in fact listed the Shapira scrolls a second time—in the general catalog published in September 1888. I hadn't found the Shapira manuscript listed in the 1887 daybook because it had not been sold that year. Although she had no information indicating a specific sale date, Thorn speculated that it likely would have occurred within a few months of the 1888 listing.

I ordered up the daybook that included September 1888 and the months following. While I waited, I had a scone and a coffee and proceeded to the Rare Books Room to see Sotheby, Wilkinson & Hodge's annotated auction catalog for July 16, 1885. This volume included the sale where Quaritch bought the Shapira manuscript. It listed the names of everyone who made purchases that day and the prices they paid.

Among the 375 books and manuscripts on offer that first day of a five-day sale, were an "Historical Essay Concerning Witchcraft," by F. Hutchinson, and "Five Hundred Points of Good Husbandry," by T. Tusser. The auction catalog also lists another group of items up for bid: "THE SCHAPIRA [*sic*] MANUSCRIPTS," seven lots that included a copy of the Kabbalah, the enigmatic book of Jewish mysticism; two Hebrew prayer books; a number of leather Bible rolls; and a Koran in Arabic.

Then there was Lot 302:

Deuteronomy in Hebrew, 7 numbered and 8 unnumbered Fragments, written on leather

Alongside this listing, in pencil, was the name of the buyer and the price he had paid for Shapira's scrolls: "Quaritch, £10.5." This brief notation seemed an apt summation of Shapira's fall from grace. Two years earlier he had bet his future on a manuscript destined for display in one of the world's great museums at the price of £1 million. Now it was headed to a nearby bookshop for about the price of a year's worth of coal.

I scanned the remaining "Schapira Manuscripts" up for sale:

Lot 303*: Exodus, Leviticus, Numbers and Deuteronomy— Genesis, Exodus and Leviticus; Leviticus written on leather 3 rolls*

Lot 304*: Genesis and Great portion of Exodus—Genesis, wanting last chapter—Numbers and Deuteronomy 3 vol.*

Quaritch had purchased both of these, too, each for just over one pound. Then I saw lot 305:

Lot 305*: Fragments of Hebrew manuscripts, a bundle.*

This one went for a mere twelve pence, but it wasn't the bargain-basement price that surprised me—it was the name of the buyer: Ginsburg. Bond's letter of July 7, 1884, reported that Rosette "enquires after the Deuteronomy fragments." This note indicated that he believed Ginsburg had held on to Shapira's scrolls, or at least knew where they were. Did Ginsburg consign them to Sotheby's in an effort to scrounge a few pounds for himself at auction? This struck me as unlikely. Not only would it have been remarkably bad behavior from the good reverend, but if he was looking to unload the famous scrolls, why would he have purchased a bundle of less valuable fragments at the very same auction? That said, the fact that I could place Ginsburg at the scene of the "Schapira Manuscripts" auction heightened my sense that he was key to finding the missing scrolls.

IN THE MANUSCRIPTS room again, I collected the Quaritch day-book for the latter part of 1888, when he had listed the scrolls for a second time. But before delving in, I called up the library's online catalog and searched for "Ginsburg, Christian David." A number of items popped up having to do with the Old and New Testaments, the Moabite Stone, and the Essenes—ascetic Jews believed by many to have produced the Dead Sea Scrolls. Three entries in particular seemed notable. The first was a letter from Ginsburg to his daughter, Ethel, written about a month after Shapira had brought his manuscript to London—and composed inside the British Museum. The other two were Ginsburg's diaries of a journey through Palestine and Moab in 1872. I added all three to my reading-room requests and cracked open, literally, the newest daybook.

While examining the Sotheby's catalog downstairs, I had made a list of everyone who purchased anything relating to the Bible during the five-day sale at which Shapira's manuscripts were auctioned. With Quaritch and Ginsburg, the list numbered ten people. Sir Charles Nicholson's name did not appear among the buyers, although it was possible he had engaged an agent to do his bidding. The most likely candidate was a man named Ridler, who purchased three Bible manuscripts at the sale—though none of them was a "Schapira Manuscript." I checked his name, and the others, against the index in the daybook but scored no hits. None of these men had purchased anything from Quaritch looking like the Deuteronomy scrolls. And so, again, I set out to read every sale Quaritch made from August 1888 (just in case he'd sold the things too late to remove them from the September catalog) through to the last sale recorded in that book—July 5, 1889. When that proved fruitless, I ordered up the next book, and then the next.

I was getting a little desperate. Over the previous fifteen years as a journalist I had been spoiled: when I wanted to know the answer to a question, I was accustomed to simply picking up the phone, setting a meeting, and asking. Now here I was, working on the largest investigation of my life, and everyone involved was long dead. I had endless questions—and no one to ask.

I turned to the three Ginsburg documents. The travel notebooks had been a gift from his wife, who inscribed the first page with quotes from 2 Samuel and Psalms:

Christian D. Ginsburg
From his loving wife
8 January 1872
"And the Lord preserved David whithersoever he went."
"He shall give his angels charge over thee
to keep thee in all thy ways."

Ginsburg, it turned out, needed a little help from these celestial entities. Toward the end of the expedition, he and his party were taken hostage by a tribe of Bedouin demanding a ransom for their foreign prisoners. Ultimately, Ginsburg and his compatriots were freed. I am not certain I would have been so kind had he described my wife the way he scorned Bedouin ladies. "The women," he wrote, "in addition to their natural plainness tattoo the lower part of their face including sometimes the lips and their arms which renders them double ugly. I was therefore pleased with the custom they have of covering the lower part of their faces."

The letter to his daughter was even more interesting. Dated September 3, 1883, the note added to my growing sense that Ginsburg was central to finding the scrolls. "My darling Ethel," it began:

I was so glad to have your loving letter this morning. It is indeed
a matter of [illegible] that dear grannie is so sick and I have no
doubt that your presence will do her a great deal of good.

The excitement about the MS has by no means ceased. You will probably have heard that last Saturday *The Spectator*, [illegible], *The Saturday Review* and other periodicals had still articles on the subject.

I do not think that the month which I spent on the MS is time thrown away though it is a forgery and though the deciphering of it has nearly blinded me. Though I am sure the first [illegible] of my examination that it was a forgery yet the extraordinary cleverness and skill displayed in the production of it as well as the fact that a company were engaged on it made it absolutely necessary thoroughly to make it out, to translate it and to publish it before I gave the verdict and before publishing the report. By doing so I made it impossible for this clever band of rogues to practice any more impositions.

Mr. Shapira has disappeared and the MS is still here. I do wish you could come up to town to see it for it is so wonderfully clever. If I could afford it I would give £200 for it. There is such a demand for my report that the British Museum have decided to reprint it with the original and my translation. Give my dear love to grannie. Accept much for yourself.

Your affectionate father

Ginsburg's letter raised serious doubts about the common wisdom on the Shapira scrolls' vanishing. The Nicholson theory posited that Sir Charles had bought the scrolls from Quaritch and that they had disappeared in a fire in 1899. That supposition was based on three pieces of evidence. First was the fact that Nicholson believed he had purchased most of the manuscripts Shapira left behind. Second, Nicholson had expressed admiration for Shapira. Third, as an old man Nicholson had demonstrated an interest in Deuteronomy, Hebrew, and the Moabite Stone.

But Ginsburg, too, had purchased merchandise from Shapira's estate—a "bundle" of Hebrew manuscript fragments, according to the auction catalog. In his letter to Ethel he had trumpeted his admiration for the "wonderfully clever" work involved in producing the Deuteronomy manuscript—so much so that he wished to buy it for himself. And while Nicholson had come late to Hebrew, the Bible, and the Moabite Stone, Ginsburg was renowned for studying and explicating all three.

Ginsburg, then, not only possessed all the qualities that led A. D. Crown to finger Nicholson, but had uniquely articulated the desire to own the scrolls. Significantly, he was present at Sotheby's when they were auctioned. That day, he had bid on and won eight books and manuscripts: three Bibles and two prayer books, along with copies of Dickens's *Nicholas Nickleby*, Schiller's *The Maid of Orleans*, and Coleridge's *The Friend*. He knew who bought the scrolls, and how much that person had paid. I could picture Ginsburg and Quaritch, elegant gentlemen in top hats, dark suits, and neckties, seated at the long wooden tables in Sotheby's book-lined auction room, bidding against each other for the Shapira strips. Quaritch, his firm's funding fueling his efforts, was able to outduel Ginsburg, constantly one-upping the brilliant scholar who had only his private accounts from which to draw. But then later, in flusher times, perhaps, Ginsburg—still in their thrall—may have mustered the cash to buy them back.

Examined side by side with the Nicholson theory, Ginsburg now seemed to me the more likely of the two men to have bought Shapira's Deuteronomy manuscript. The common wisdom was probably wrong.

This discovery offered me another new angle—and a third clue. I made a note in my journal: "Ginsburg?" Some months earlier, a Dutch historian who studied Ginsburg told me that, during a conference at Princeton, he had stumbled on a set of books that once belonged to the English scholar. The excellently named Complutensian Polyglot Bible was the first complete, multilanguage edition of the Bible (both testaments) ever printed, and included text in Hebrew, Latin, Greek, and Aramaic. Published in the sixteenth century, six hundred of these six-volume sets were produced. Only a hundred or so have survived.

When I first learned of Ginsburg's copy, it had seemed a curiosity. Now, suddenly, it felt important. If I knew where Princeton had secured this rare book, perhaps I could establish what had happened to the rest of Ginsburg's library. And if, as I now suspected, Ginsburg had purchased the Shapira Deuteronomy, this information would allow me to determine who had eventually bought the manuscript from him or his estate.

I wrote to Princeton's library, inquiring about the Polyglot, and soon heard back that in fact it belonged to William H. Scheide, class of 1936. Mr. Scheide's father, John (class of 1896), had bought the book in 1915 from none other than Bernard Quaritch. And Quaritch had acquired it two months earlier at the Sotheby's sale of Ginsburg's library. (Ginsburg had died the previous year.)

I ordered up the annotated auction catalog for July 14, 1915, and began searching excitedly for Shapira's Deuteronomy manuscript among the 928 lots for sale from the "Extensive & Important Library of the late Dr. C.D. Ginsburg, LL.D." A wide variety of books and manuscripts were up for auction that day—dozens of Bibles in a host of languages; comedies, histories, and tragedies from the pen of William Shakespeare; reproductions of famous paintings. The names of several buyers were familiar to me: they had been there thirty years earlier when Sotheby's auctioned off Shapira's scrolls. Quaritch himself purchased thirty-six lots at the Ginsburg sale, but nowhere in the catalog's ninety-six pages did anything appear that remotely resembled the Shapira scrolls. If Ginsburg had owned them, they hadn't been sold off with this portion of his library.

But there was another possibility. In Ginsburg's letter to his daughter, he had expressed the desire for her to visit London to see the scrolls for herself. Maybe he had left the scrolls to her—or another of his five children. Although Ginsburg was well known for his scholarship, when he died obituaries featured his role in the Shapira scandal. The *Daily Sketch* included a severe photo of the man beneath the boldfaced headline "Exposed a Great Fraud." The *Times* claimed outright that he had owned the manuscript. The affair had proved a highlight of Ginsburg's career—maybe he wanted the document itself to stay in the family.

A quick Google search turned up Ginsburg's will, in which he appointed as executors his wife, Emilie; his son, Benedict; and G. F. Barwick, assistant keeper of printed books at the British Museum. The trio were instructed to sell off his property and to divide the proceeds into five equal parts—one for each of his children. Upon their deaths, the will instructed, each portion should pass to the British and Foreign Bible Society. The document specified that "all the printed books of my works" were to go to Ginsburg's widow but made no mention of any books or manuscripts beyond those Ginsburg himself had written.

From there I turned to the wills of the three executors, but again Shapira's scroll was not to be found. It was still possible that Ginsburg had simply given or sold the manuscript to someone else. I began to comb through historical records, hoping to locate some living relative who might still, by some miracle, have old Uncle Christian's papers stowed away in an attic box—or know who did. Consulting birth, death, and census records, I was able to identify a number of descendants. Among them was a great-grandson of Ginsburg's named Roger Spottiswoode. He was, it turns out, a successful Hollywood movie director, having helmed, among many other movies, the James Bond film *Tomorrow Never Dies* and *The 6th Day*, starring future governor Arnold Schwarzenegger. I emailed Spottiswoode's agent and explained what I was up to. Later that same day, I received a friendly reply from the director himself.

"I would be perfectly happy to talk to you but I confess to knowing very little about our great grandfather, beyond a few common details," he wrote. "His painting of course hangs in the Liberal Club near Downing St. and is worth a visit."

Spottiswoode copied his brother and sister on the note and suggested that they might know more than he did about their progenitor. I wrote to both. The sister declined to speak; the brother never wrote back. And before I could arrange a meeting with Mr. Spottiswoode, I would learn that I, and every Shapiramaniac before me, had been digging in the wrong field all along.

4

AN EPIC BATTLE

In the summer of 1868, Frederick Augustus Klein made a spectacular find in the sands east of the Dead Sea. Klein was a hard-charging evangelical from Shapira's community in Jerusalem, and his chance discovery of what became known as the Moabite Stone would prove part of the Bible true. It would also trigger an international horse race to secure the ancient relic, foster a new trend in archaeology, and promote a thirst for Moabite artifacts that would drastically alter the course of Shapira's life.

Fluent in Arabic, Klein traveled widely in the region. Missionary work took him from Nazareth to Jerusalem to Cairo. But the journey from Jerusalem to Moab was an arduous go, even for such a practiced traveler. "The greedy, wild character of the inhabitants renders a tour in those parts one attended with considerable danger," the Reverend James King would later write in his book-length account of the Moabite Stone's discovery. To see them safely through to their destinations, Europeans often hired a *ghafir*—an Arab guide whose traditions not only proffered a hard-earned intimacy with the area's demanding politics and topography but allowed access to unexplored precincts that guarded artifacts left behind by ancient civilizations. Klein engaged the services of a man named Zattam, son of the Beni Sachr clan's chief, to negotiate his way through the tangle of tribal territories that lay along his route.

With Zattam at his side, Klein toured the stomping grounds of the Israelite tribes Reuben, Gad, and Manasseh before arriving at a site near Dhiban where the Beni Hamide had set up camp, much as the Children of Israel, fleeing Egypt, had done millennia earlier. Situated just a few miles from Wadi Mujib, Dhiban was an ancient capital of Moab's battle-hardened king Mesha. The Beni Hamide had a reputation as the "most savage and intractable tribe" in the Belka region, but greeted Klein genially, breaking out carpets and cushions inside Sheikh Ahmed ibn Tarif's tent as coffee was prepared. Klein and Zattam sank comfortably into their pillows for a much-deserved respite after a long day navigating in the heat of a Moabite summer.

Suitably pampered, sipping his coffee, and enjoying relaxed hits off his narghile pipe, Zattam began to tell a story. Not ten minutes from the spot where they now reclined, he said, and lying exposed among the ruins of Dhiban, was a large stone monument covered with an ancient inscription that no one had yet been able to decipher. It was early evening, and Klein—who, as a Jerusalemite, was keenly aware of archaeology's possibilities—was eager to see this unidentified pillar before the last light of the day. But Zattam had grown too comfortable on his cushions and could not be roused for a trek back into the sand. Their host, meanwhile, piqued Klein's interest further. The stone, the Beni Hamide sheikh announced, was surely one of the wonders of the region—and no European had ever seen it. Now, as a gesture of respect to his visitor, the sheikh offered to make him the first.

Klein was relieved—and skeptical.

"I, of course, took this for what it was in general meant to be," he later said. "A Bedouin compliment calculated to bring out a nice bakshish [gratuity]."

With daylight waning, the party straggled into Dhiban. There, lying "perfectly free and exposed to view," Klein was thrilled to find the black basalt pillar, its thirty-four-line inscription face up to the sky. The arch-shaped stone was large—about three feet tall, two feet wide, and a foot thick—and it was exceedingly heavy: four men had to lift it so that Klein could inspect the back, which was smooth and devoid of any further engravings. Age had dulled a portion of the inscription, but on the whole the stone was pristine.

Klein hurried to measure and sketch his find, collecting its alphabet as best he could. He didn't yet know it, but the script he copied that day was ancient Hebrew. The language was Moabite. The inscription was the longest ever discovered on a monument in the region. And the story those lines told would be familiar to anyone conversant in the Bible: the tale of Moab's rebellion against Israel, from chapter 3 of 2 Kings. This was the first confirmation of a biblical story from outside the Holy Book itself—only this version, unlike the Bible, took King Mesha's side.

While the Beni Hamide headman may have been hoping to exact a generous gratuity from Klein, he was also correct: no European had ever reported seeing the stone before the Anglican missionary. When Klein departed the sheikh's encampment, measurements and sketches in hand, he was in possession of a monumental secret—a secret that would prove to be one of the greatest archaeological discoveries of the nineteenth century.

WE DO NOT know a great deal about the Moabites prior to the story told in the Mesha inscription. Most of our information comes from the Bible, which offers a fairly one-sided take. What can be said with confidence is that much of the time, the Moabites and Israelites just didn't get along. Their relationship was characterized by a series of bloody territorial disputes that left corpses scattered over battlefields, survivors—when there were any—enslaved, and cities beat to hell. Considering the nature of intrafamilial quarrels, perhaps it is not surprising that, according to the Bible, these two warring nations had sprouted from the same Semitic stock: the Moabites' progenitor was the nephew of Abraham, father of the Jewish people. During the biblical period, Moabites and Israelites lived near one another and spoke similar languages. (A scholar I spoke to likened the linguistic differences to variants between English as spoken in the United States and England.) The geographical boundaries that separated them were fluid, and differences between members of certain Israelite tribes and the Moabites might have been indistinguishable to outsiders—something, say, like Czechs and Slovaks.

Literarily speaking, the Bible treats Moab as a punch line, a foil to powerful Israel. Their origin story, as told in Genesis, reads like an ethnic joke: Lot and his daughters took up residence in a mountainside cave after fleeing Sodom, which God had destroyed as punishment for its citizens' lifestyle choices. But while you can take the girls out of Sodom, you can't, apparently, take Sodom out of the girls. With no men around, and fearing they would end up childless spinsters, Lot's daughters conspired to get their father drunk. Over the course of two debauched nights, they plied the old man with wine, each one taking her turn with him in bed. Lot was so drunk, we're told, that he remained completely unaware of his progeny's betrayal. One can only imagine his surprise upon realizing a short time later that his daughters, who lived alone with him in a cave, were both pregnant. But they were—and each had a son. One called hers Ben-Ami, which means "son of my father's people," and the other named hers Moab, which translates roughly to "from my father."

"He," the Bible says of this child of sinful coupling, "is the father of the Moabites of today."

The Torah's early references to Moab paint a picture of a nation born to suffer and fail at Israel's hand. Eventually, though, Moab became an intransigent foe. Over the course of several centuries, the cousin nations engaged in a series of violent engagements distinguished by regicide, human sacrifice, and enslavement. In the Book of Judges, Moab's obese king, Eglon, mustered his own forces, along with those of the Ammonites (descendants of Ben-Ami) and the Amalekites, and led them to victory against Israel.

Later, an Israelite named Ehud would spark a rebellion against Moab when he opened Eglon's stomach with a homemade knife. "The fat closed over the blade and the hilt went in after the blade— for he did not pull the dagger out of his belly," the Bible tells us of Ehud's attack. Knife lodged firmly in Eglon's belly, "the filth came out." As the king's guts slithered from his stab wound, Ehud rushed back to Israelite country and ordered the ram's horn to be sounded—the ancient call to war. Emerging from the hills, armed Israelites descended on the River Jordan, where they captured the crossing points and slew ten thousand souls.

Then there's the war in 2 Kings 3, pitting Moab against Israel, Judah, and Edom. After Mesha bisected Israel's defenses and assumed command of Moab's primary thoroughfare, the three allied armies marched into Moab, where they tore up trees, destroyed fields, and stopped up wells. When the Moabites sheltered in Kir Hareseth, modern-day Kerak, the Israelite-led armies surrounded the city. King Mesha mustered a contingent of seven hundred swordsmen to cut through Israel's lines. Their effort was rebuffed. Trapped, the desperate Moabite king called for his firstborn son and slaughtered him, offering him up "on the wall as a burnt offering."

Mesha's extreme act paid dividends. Immediately afterward, a "great wrath" came upon Israel and the attacking armies withdrew. Mesha had won, and the prideful king engaged an artisan to commemorate his triumph. Laborers quarried a large blue-black basalt stone that a mason carved and shaped and polished into a three-foot-tall monument on which he engraved Mesha's version of the great battle. The inscription presents Mesha as a master builder and warrior who ruthlessly butchered entire Israelite towns and under whose military onslaught Israel "has perished forever." Conveniently, this rendition leaves out the child sacrifice, and the fact that Moab had nearly lost.

RETURNING TO JERUSALEM with his sketches of Mesha's stone, Klein went to see Dr. J. Heinrich Petermann, the Prussian consul. Like many envoys of the day, Petermann was a Renaissance man— both a diplomat and a scholar of Oriental languages. When Klein laid out his drawings, Petermann recognized the Hebrew script and quickly ascertained the potential importance of the discovery for science and for Prussia. He posted a letter to Berlin on August 29, 1868, asking whether the directors of the Royal Museum were willing to pay one hundred napoleons (about four hundred dollars today) to acquire the stone from the Beni Hamide. The museum responded by telegram, authorizing the expenditure. Petermann insisted on secrecy—he asked Klein, as well as three of Klein's friends who were present at their meeting, to keep the discovery under wraps. Anyone else who learned of the stone was sure to want it for themselves. But the secret didn't remain secret very long.

With funding secured from Berlin, Klein wrote to Fendi el Faiz, sheikh of the Beni Sachr Bedouin and the father of Zattam, Klein's guide in Moab. The sheikh was a respected leader in the Dhiban region, and Klein hoped he would smooth the way toward acquiring the stone. He dispatched his assistant, a "clever young Arab," to deliver the missive to Moab. Confident the young man would return with the totem in tow, he sent along a supply of felt in which to pack it. That decision was premature.

Fendi el Faiz did not reply until December 1868, and when he did, his response was equivocal: he could not offer assistance without permission from the Beni Hamide, who had first shown Klein the stone. Among Bedouin, who have historically earned livelihoods as agriculturalists and shepherds, land is everything. To stray into another tribe's realm was to threaten its very existence. This could, and often did, instigate violence. Perhaps Fendi el Faiz was standing on tradition, sagely seeking to avoid conflict. Maybe he was just delaying, as he never did consult the Beni Hamide. After responding to Klein's letter, he left for Damascus.

For the next six months, Mesha's monument lay unseen by Western eyes. Then, in March 1869, Petermann sent another messenger to Moab. Saba Cawar, a Jerusalem teacher, left for Dhiban with fifty-three napoleons in hand—fifty to buy the stone and three for expenses along the way. But yet again, the Prussians had been overly optimistic. The Beni Hamide upped their asking price to a thousand napoleons and Cawar, like Klein's "clever young Arab," returned empty-handed.

WITH GERMANY FLAILING, a new European contender made his move. Charles Clermont-Ganneau was a twenty-two-year-old dragoman, or translator, at the French consulate in Jerusalem. A brilliant and ornery linguist, Ganneau quickly became a vital figure in Near Eastern archaeology, though his cutthroat methods and bulldog enthusiasms would eventually lead to his ouster from the Holy Land. His rise in archaeology would coincide, unhappily, with Shapira's ascendance in antiquities.

Ganneau was born in Paris on February 19, 1846. His father

died before he reached the age of six, and Ganneau was raised by his mother. At age eleven he enrolled in Collège Sainte-Barbe and he later entered the Lycée Louis le Grand. At sixteen he earned his baccalaureate degree, and thereafter matriculated at the School of Oriental Languages, where he learned Arabic, Hebrew, Persian, and Turkish, alongside courses on the Bible and Semitic epigraphy—the study of inscriptions. In 1867, France's minister of foreign affairs appointed Ganneau to the French Consulate in Jerusalem, paving the way for his entrance into the field of biblical archaeology with a bold play for the Moabite Stone.

A Jerusalem banker named Bergheim first alerted Ganneau to the stone's existence, approaching him with a sketch and a few lines of its inscription. The drawings, he told the Frenchman, had been made by an icon painter named Salim al Kari. Rough and incomplete though they were, Salim's etchings immediately thrilled Ganneau, suggesting, as they did, the monument's historical import.

"There was no more possible doubt," Ganneau would recall. "I determined at once to procure at any price an impression of a monument so precious."

To this end, the Frenchman hired Yaqoub Caravacca, "an Arab of great intelligence," and dispatched him to Dhiban along with two horsemen from yet another Bedouin tribe. The trio arrived and, after some initial back-and-forth, persuaded their hosts to grant them access. They did not intend to take the monument away, the men assured their interlocutors, only to prepare a "squeeze" copy of the inscription. Caravacca would lay a wet piece of paper over the artifact and gently tap along its length, urging bits of the paper into the inscription's grooves. Once the sheet dried, he would slowly peel it back, revealing a three-dimensional trace.

As the outsiders began their work, some of the onlooking Bedouin became agitated. Words were exchanged, threats were issued, and the situation, tenuous to begin with, quickly escalated. Ganneau later reported that this was nothing more than "one of those quarrels so frequent among the Bedouins." But in his zeal to secure a squeeze "at any price," Ganneau also seems to have misread the delicate political balance that obtained among rival Bedouin clans, carelessly sending members of one tribe into the territory of another with designs on a valuable relic from which all hoped to derive benefit.

What happened next reads like a scene from *Lawrence of Arabia*.

While Caravacca was down in the pit, applying damp paper to the stone, "the jabbering Arabs stood round, one party from the mountains, the other from the plains, each asserting its own interest in the monument and eager to turn that interest to the best possible account. The excitement and gesticulation became so frantic that it became plain that neither the stone nor the squeeze would easily pass into the hands of the Europeans."

Angry words turned threatening. Tempers soared. Members of the horde began jostling one another before finally turning their attention to the cause of their distemper: Ganneau's emissaries. Caravacca, the party's leader, quickly became the focus of their ire, and several Bedouin closed in around him. Realizing that his life was in danger, he dropped what he was doing and made a break for it. But as he scrambled out of the pit, one particularly aggressive local stabbed him with a spear. Caravacca staggered to his horse and labored on, racing away alongside one of the horsemen he had come with.

The third rider, a fellow named Jemil, proved braver than the others. Alone now, his mission's leader wounded, Jemil leaped into the hole where the Bedouin had hidden their stone and ripped the still-damp squeeze paper from the monument. The operation was fast and rough, and the impression came off in seven tattered pieces.

Jemil, fearing he too would be speared, or worse, shoved the fragments into his robe, jumped up onto his horse, and, "narrowly escaping a graver fate," galloped off at full speed.

For Ganneau, safe at home in Jerusalem, the excursion was a success.

"The aim of the expedition was then attained," he recalled. "I had an impression, but in what a state, alas! The fragments, quite damp, were torn and crumbled in drying, and traces of the characters were almost imperceptible. One could not distinguish them but by their transparency, whilst interposing the sheet between the eye and a candle or a ray of the sun. I read enough of it, however, to convince me of the great importance of this discovery."

Around this time, yet another bidder moved on the stone. Aware of the foreign interest, Fendi el Faiz of the Beni Sachr Bedouin entered into negotiations with the Beni Hamide. Changing their asking price yet again, they quoted the sheikh a fee of 375 medjidies, about four times what the Prussians had agreed to pay. He headed to Jerusalem to inform Ganneau of this latest offer. "Burning with a desire to get possession of the precious relic," Ganneau advanced the sheikh two hundred medjidies toward the purchase.

Ganneau's drive to win the relic at almost any cost would become a recurring theme. A gifted scholar who made many important contributions to the field of biblical archaeology, Ganneau was, according to a colleague, "the master" of archaeology in Palestine. He, "more than any other person, opened up the way, set the methods and enriched the modest treasures of it."

But his evident joy in defeating the competition would also lead to accusations of bad behavior. Blasting Ganneau's "hasty and precipitate action," Ginsburg insisted that the Frenchman's "endeavours to secure the stone for himself were indisputably made at the very time when it was perfectly well known that the German Consulate's negotiations were being carried on, thus bringing into collision two opposite bidders and thereby imperiling the monument itself."

In his account of the stele's discovery, the Reverend James King, an "authorized lecturer" with the PEF, wrote that "when it is remembered that the sanguine temperament of M. Ganneau led him to offer for the stone four times as much as the Prussians did, we would doubt the expediency of entrusting to that gentleman the means to be employed in securing the stone."

AS GANNEAU WAS outbidding the competition, three Ottoman functionaries inserted themselves into the chaos, and what was already a confused situation turned tragic. The wali of Damascus ordered the pasha of Nablus to compel the stone's Bedouin keepers to hand it over to the Prussians. Under instructions from his boss, the pasha immediately engaged a third Ottoman bureaucrat, the modir of Salt, to exert pressure on the natives.

This proved to be an enormous miscalculation. When the modir arrived, the Beni Hamide went into "paroxysms of terror" that the stone could serve as the pretext for an Ottoman invasion. In a misguided effort to preclude such a ploy, the Beni Hamide lashed out. Building a bonfire around the monument, they heated it until it reached a skin-melting sizzle, then doused it with cold water, repeating the process a number of times until the pristine relic—its text still undeciphered—burst into multiple pieces. The remnants, some large, some terribly small, were handed out to tribesmen, who stashed them in their granaries to bring blessings on their crops.

It was Fendi el Faiz who brought word to Ganneau that the monument he had vowed to acquire was decimated. The very real danger now loomed that the inscription would never be read, deciphered, or translated. On receiving the sheikh's bad tidings, Ganneau all but gave up on acquiring the pillar itself, electing instead to focus on recovering its message through the badly torn impression he had already received.

News of the stone's destruction also reached Lieutenant Charles Warren of the PEF, who was en route from Lebanon. Fearful, like Ganneau, that the stone could be lost forever, he sent a Bedouin named Goblan back to Dhiban with a supply of squeeze paper and instructions to copy any and all of the stone's fragments he could track down. On January 13, 1870, Goblan returned to Jerusalem with squeezes from two more fragments. The copies highlighted a welcome bit of good news: at least two of the stone's surviving pieces were relatively large, together making up about half of the original. Warren offered use of his new impressions to Ganneau.

Even as the men cooperated, their Bedouin agents were working at cross-purposes. Warren had sent Goblan back to Dhiban to purchase what remaining stone fragments he could; Ganneau had sent Jemil to do the same. By the time they arrived, the Beni Hamide understood that even these fragments were valuable, and so they put the remaining pieces up for auction, compelling the two men to bid against each other, Goblan on behalf of Warren, and hence England, and Jemil on behalf of Ganneau and France.

Jemil secured the smaller of the two fragments then and there. Later, Ganneau managed to buy the larger one as well. Warren apparently purchased several much smaller fragments. The rest of the monument, dozens of shards reduced to rubble, seemed to be lost.

Even before he received the large stone fragments, Ganneau set to work on the stele's text. Over the course of just four days, making do with the damaged resources available to him, Ganneau transcribed and translated the inscription into Hebrew and French. His work was remarkable; that he completed it in less than a week was almost incredible. "Not wishing to keep back the knowledge of a monument so precious to science," he sent his translation quickly to Paris. What Ganneau did not mention, even once, in his report to l'Académie was the name Frederick Augustus Klein. Nor did he cite the Prussian Consulate. His version of events gives the distinct impression that Ganneau himself discovered the Moabite Stone—an impression he had no doubt hoped to convey.

Ganneau sold his pieces of the stone to the Louvre and by January 1875 had returned to France to begin restoring the badly damaged monument. Nine months later the repairs were completed, and by November it was on display in the Louvre's hall of Jewish antiquities. What visitors saw, and still can see today, was about two-thirds of the original monument, meshed with new black stone that was inscribed based on the squeeze materials available at the time. Ganneau was never able to match the color of the ancient material to the modern stone, and the overall effect is the archaeological equivalent of Frankenstein's head. Every now and again, the Louvre considers renovating the stone, but ultimately this suggestion is always rejected. The story behind its discovery and destruction has an important historical value of its own. For many years, hanging beside the stone at the Louvre was a vivid reminder of this rollicking tale: the framed and reassembled squeeze that Jemil had snatched from oblivion at grave risk to his own well-being.

HAD KLEIN NOT discovered the Moabite Stone, Shapira likely would have remained a relatively anonymous merchant, hawking touristy knickknacks in Jerusalem's bustling souk. But once it became clear that the stone was valuable, a flood of relics from Moab surged onto Jerusalem's antiquities market, feeding a growing frenzy for the stuff. First it was more engraved stones. Next came pottery. Both found their way to Shapira's shop.

Ginsburg was among those hoping to get in on the action. In January 1872, while strolling along Christian Street, the English scholar spotted something interesting. "I saw in the window of Mr. Shapira a bookseller and [unintelligible] in antiquities a fragment of an old stone with an inscription which at a cursory glance looked almost exactly like a piece of the Moabite Stone and I at first sight took it to be so," he recalled.

Ginsburg had just arrived in Jerusalem and was well aware that much of the damaged monolith remained unaccounted for. The previous year he had published the most extensive account yet of the stele in a book he called *The Moabite Stone: A Facsimile of the Original Inscription, with an English Translation, and a Historical and Critical Commentary*. Stumbling on this fragment so soon after the volume's publication seemed to him a stroke of tremendous luck.

Ginsburg approached Shapira and inquired about the stone in the window. It was, Shapira said theatrically, only the first of many such pieces in his possession. In fact, he told Ginsburg, he had received a shipment only the previous night. Ginsburg was elated. That evening he paused to record his good fortune. "[I] rejoiced with the thought that I at last would obtain the missing fragments of this celebrated memorial."

GINSBURG HAD ARRIVED at the port of Jaffa four days earlier aboard the Russian steamer *Wladimir*, departing immediately for Jerusalem with a party of ten mules, six horses, three servants, and a donkey. Having been forewarned by a number of PEF comrades to keep the expedition small, he was dismayed at the circus-like caravan his handlers had assembled. He worried that locals would mistake them for European kings and charge exorbitantly should he discover anything of interest along the way.

Like many travelogues written by nineteenth-century tourists, Ginsburg's record of his journey tenders a view of the Holy Land imbued alternately with reverence and disgust—sometimes on the same day. Along the way from Jaffa to Jerusalem, the party stopped at the biblical village known as Upper Beit Horon—mentioned in the Book of Joshua—to eat and rest. As they filled their bellies, the interlopers noticed that a group of locals had gathered to gape at them. Ginsburg could not help but gape right back, utterly incredulous. Among the onlookers, he reported, were several boys walking on all fours.

"As this was the first time in my life that I saw human beings on four I examined them most minutely and found that they could not walk otherwise," he wrote. "When resting they sat down crassly like monkeys. Indeed it was difficult to distinguish them from monkeys."

Eleven hours after leaving Jaffa, the traveling menagerie finally approached its destination as the sun set. On spotting Jerusalem in the distance, Ginsburg found himself deeply moved. "The impression which the lights of the city made upon me I can scarcely describe," he wrote.

Ginsburg was so stirred by the sight of the long-dreamed-about city that, approaching the Jaffa Gate, he handed his gun to his translator, unwilling to breach its walls bearing arms. Then he headed straight to Jerusalem's best hotel. Formerly the home of the Anglican bishop, the Mediterranean was located around the corner from Shapira's shop and was popular among the well-funded foreigners on whom he doted. Mark Twain had stayed there a few years earlier. Charles Warren, who had shared his Moabite Stone squeezes with Ganneau, slept there, too, as did Claude Conder. A third PEF explorer, Charles Tyrwhitt-Drake, died there in 1874. As for Ginsburg, all that first night he found it hard to shake the initial excitement of first laying eyes on the city.

"The weariness of the journey having been eleven hours on horseback and the solemn feeling that I was actually lodging in Jerusalem on the slope of Mount Zion with the pool of Hezekiah at my feet kept me awake the greatest part of the night," he wrote. "The bedroom which I occupied faced Christ Church on Mount Zion, the Bishop's residence, David's tower, the market and the gate of Jaffa."

Ginsburg had intended to stay only briefly, but when negotiations dragged on between his representatives and some Bedouin guides over the logistics of protecting him during the upcoming Moab portion of his trip, he decided to "make the best of unpleasant things." Over the next several days he toured the city and its environs, taking in its history and lively archaeological scene. Almost immediately he encountered an inscribed stone that Ganneau had recently discovered. It bore an engraving that warned gentiles away from the Jewish Temple at the peril of their lives, confirming a report of such inscriptions by the first-century historian Josephus Flavius.

"Ganneau in his usual way [had] offered £50 for it when it might have been obtained for £5," Ginsburg wrote.

The effect of Ganneau's high bid was much the same as it had been with the Moabite stele: it alerted the Ottoman pasha to the relic's value. Taking the inscription for himself, the Turk decreed that, going forward, antiquities discovered in his realm were not to be removed.

Ginsburg also visited the village of Siloam, on the site of the biblical City of David, where his companion, a certain Mr. Baily, informed him that Ganneau had discovered yet another ancient inscription located above the house of a village Muslim (this is the famous epitaph of a royal steward, probably Shebna, who is mentioned in the Book of Isaiah). They headed off to view the engraving, only to find, to their "surprise and disgust," that it had been roughly chiseled from its stone and taken away. When the men inquired into what had happened, they were told simply, "Ganneau did it."

Baily went off to investigate and returned later with word that Ganneau had, in fact, removed the inscription, but only in the interest of its safekeeping. The Frenchman, Baily said, had placed it in the custody of the British consul. At first blush the story seems peculiar—Ganneau, who had only recently pursued the Moabite Stone for France with such partisan gusto, had acquired a valuable relic and simply handed it over to the Brits? But his career had flourished since the discovery of the stone, and he had recently switched allegiances, accepting a position with the PEF.

A few days later, Ginsburg visited the Temple Mount. Noting that the plaza was in Muslim hands—in Arabic it is known as Haram al-Sharif—he was filled with "awe and indignation."

"The children of the Kingdom are cast out and strangers desecrate their sanctuary was the thought which haunted me at every step which I took through the gigantic and curious structure," he wrote. "I left the place with the most painful feelings and with the thought that I should not like to see it again as a mosque."

IT WAS ON his fourth day in Jerusalem that he discovered the stone fragment in Shapira's window. Impatiently entering the shop to see the rest of the collection, Ginsburg believed that, so soon after arriving, he had already managed to discover the missing fragments that would allow for a fuller understanding of the famous monument.

Under Shapira's expectant gaze, Ginsburg examined the trove carefully, holding each piece, feeling its weight, rotating it in his hands, running his fingers along its extrusions and crevices. There was writing on the stones, and it was similar to the Mesha stele. But years working with ancient scripts told him that his initial assessment had been overly optimistic. While on the whole the inscribed letters were "identical" in form to those on the Moabite

Stone, some bore slightly different shapes. The fragments them-selves were so small that no sense could be made of the inscrip-tions without bringing into play "an extraordinary amount of imagination."

Concluding that Shapira's fragments "were pieces of quite a different stone," Ginsburg began to wonder about their origin, mustering a hypothesis that ascribed to Moab's Bedouin equal measures of ignorance and cunning. Having grasped the value of ancient stone fragments, these Arabs, Ginsburg speculated, had dis-covered another such pillar and broken it into pieces to sell. By this "clever trick," he wrote, the Arabs had duped Shapira and ruined yet another ancient stone inscription.

Disappointed by Shapira's wares, but appetite whetted for the real thing, Ginsburg set a meeting with Ganneau to examine the large, confirmed Moabite Stone fragments for himself. The city's Jewish shops where he might have done more exploring were closed on the Sabbath, so Ginsburg had left Saturday open for this purpose. When he arrived, however, the light was bad, precluding a proper inspection. Ganneau agreed to welcome his guest back when con-ditions had improved, but when Ginsburg returned the Frenchman refused to grant him access to the monument.

Twice disappointed, Ginsburg listened as Ganneau explained. He was at this point still seeking a buyer for the stele, he said. If Ginsburg compared Ganneau's transcription of the monument with the stone itself and came up with a different interpretation, it could devalue the piece. Ginsburg promised not to publicize his findings until Ganneau had secured a sale, but to no avail. Ganneau was steadfast, and Ginsburg headed off into the Jerusalem afternoon empty-handed. If he had arrived that day with doubts about Gan-neau's methods, the Frenchman's refusal to grant this courtesy can only have raised further questions.

ALTHOUGH HIS MOABITE stones were not *the* Moabite Stone, the celebrated stele proved a terrific boon for Shapira. Early in 1872, local Arabs began arriving at his shop, stooped beneath bags full of clay relics they said had been dug up near the site in Dhiban where Klein had first seen Mesha's inscription. Chief among Shapira's suppliers of such "Moabitica," as the area's relics quickly came to be known, was none other than Salim al Kari, the icon painter whose sketch had alerted Ganneau to the existence of the Moabite Stone. Sheikh Ali Diab of the Adwan Bedouin was another purveyor. Suddenly, relics from Moab, this long-forgotten kingdom, became, in the words of one writer of the period, "the rage."

"The talk of Jerusalem, and of the travelers then crowding in and around it was the great Shapira collection," wrote Lieutenant Claude Conder, then leading the PEF's survey of western Palestine. The collection sported a rogue's gallery of bizarre pieces possessed of a "grotesque uncouthness all their own." There were coneheads with lips turned up in spooky smiles. A disembodied cranium, its long tongue dangling like an exhausted dog's. Grotesque, distended faces with tiny eyes and giant noses. Clay men sporting impressive erections beside sculpted women with crudely formed genitalia. Human faces carved in stone.

Pots and jars and urns arrived each day, and many of them—like some of the statues—were pierced with a curious constellation: seven holes dotting their exteriors, seemingly to convey some unknown symbolism. Many of the pieces were covered in saltpeter, imbuing them with the appearance of great antiquity.

As puzzling as their odd forms was the curious writing that adorned some of the relics—they were emblazoned in a script nearly identical to the Mesha stele's ancient Hebrew. Might these words tell a similar story? Confirm another biblical narrative? Explain aspects of Mesha's religion? The stele had shined a light on the region's history, and Shapira's collection promised to do the same for Moabite culture, which had until then remained obscured by time.

SHAPIRA'S POTTERY COLLECTION grew fast. Tourists and scholars chatted about the stuff over drinks at a local coffeehouse and debated its meaning in the lobby of the Mediterranean Hotel. Some curious Jerusalemites made the pilgrimage to Shapira's shop to see the pieces with their own eyes. To feel their cool weight. To finger the ancient handiwork of some long-dead artisan.

Among Shapira's visitors was a German cleric named Hermann Weser. Some years back, Weser had studied with Konstantin Schlottmann, the professor to whom Rosette Shapira would later send those two small fragments of her husband's Deuteronomy scrolls. Now, caught up in the Moabitica hubbub, Weser made sketches of Shapira's new acquisitions and dispatched them to Germany. Schlottmann, a meticulous scholar who had already written extensively about the Moabite Stone, had from the beginning hoped that the pillar's discovery would herald more such finds in Moab. He proved a most welcoming audience.

Working from Weser's drawings, Schlottmann began to publish details of Shapira's finds. He theorized that the statuettes—many of which were undeniably crude and ugly—were none other than *shikutzim*, a nasty term for idols used frequently in the Bible, notably in Kings and Ezekiel.

More daunting than identifying the pottery was interpreting its inscriptions. The writing was maddening. While the letters on many of the pieces were nearly identical to those on the Moabite Stone, some came from other alphabets. A few appeared to be Nabatean. Others were South Arabian—an alphabet that had not emerged until years after the pottery's supposed manufacture.

The most confounding difference between the Moabite Stone and the writing on Shapira's pieces had to do with meaning—or the lack thereof. The Mesha stele, even in its damaged state, told a story. The writing on the pieces in Shapira's collection made no sense at all. While the letters were recognizable, they did not form any known words, to say nothing of sentences or stories. Rather, they seemed to have been randomly dropped onto the pottery.

For Schlottmann, this was evidence of a hitherto unknown Moabite script—and he went energetically to work deciphering it. He managed to decode a word here and there but, by all accounts, even these efforts were strained. On one figurine, for example, Schlottmann read the personal name Atchakh. According to one scholar, for that reading to have been correct, the scribe would have had to be writing simultaneously in two different scripts, one of which did not exist during the period when the Moabite pottery was thought to have been created. And those were the easy pieces. Many of the inscriptions simply proved indecipherable.

In November 1871, an Englishman named Henry Lumley stopped into Shapira's shop. Always eager to engage a foreign guest, Shapira hauled out a stone pillar, about three feet tall and a foot and a half wide.

"No more valuable a record of biblically stated facts, made at nearly a contemporary moment with the events which it records, has yet been discovered," Lumley recalled Shapira saying as he displayed this latest find. The pillar, Shapira told him, "may be, indeed, of more powerful interest than the Moabite stone, for it contains the name of Moses, who may have directed, seen and approved the inscription himself as a memento of the conquest of Moab by Israel under their great leader, and in addition the stone, so far as the inscription is concerned, is in a perfect state."

To have located an inscription made in the time of Moses, and bearing the name of the prophet himself, was nothing short of magnificent. If one compared the lines etched into this stone with verses in Deuteronomy, Numbers, and Joshua, Lumley said, "a remarkable coincidence of narrative will be seen." In other words, the monument in Shapira's shop may have been some kind of precursor to, or original version of, the Bible—written, no less, on a stone tablet and dictated by Moses himself in the desert of Moab.

Except that it wasn't. After his meeting with Shapira, Lumley wrote to the *Times* of London to describe the remarkable encounter. The note was printed under the headline NEW MOABITE STONE. Immediately after publishing his account, Lumley, by then back in England, met with Emanuel Deutsch, a Semitics scholar at the British Museum. In the course of their conversation, Deutsch informed Lumley that a nearly identical inscription had already been discovered. Charles Warren wrote about it in the PEF's *Quarterly Statement* and it was analyzed in the newsletter of the Deutsche Morgenländische Gesellschaft (DMG), the German Oriental Society, of which Schlottmann was a leading member.

Further, Deutsch said, Lumley's stone said nothing like what he'd claimed it did. In fact, it was a poor copy of the original, possibly fashioned using the PEF and DMG publications as a guide. Red-faced, the Englishman sent a second letter to the *Times* the very next day, recanting his original report.

On learning of the affair, the poison-penned Swiss scholar Albert Socin dispatched a blistering letter to the *Academy*, a London-based magazine covering literature, science, and the arts, leveling a ferocious personal attack against Shapira, branding him a forger and even questioning his Christian bona fides.

"There is no misunderstanding here, as some might be inclined to think," Socin railed, "for this is not the only suspicious inscription which has passed through the hands of Shapira."

To buttress his point, he noted two additional "suspicious inscriptions" linked to Shapira: a slightly altered copy of one Ganneau had discovered banning Gentiles from the Jewish Temple and a stone engraving of Psalm 117 made in letters like those found on the Moabite Stone.

"The facts seem to establish the existence of a flourishing manufactory of inscriptions in Jerusalem," Socin wrote. "Whether Shapira is the only partner in the concern or not is uncertain; but we feel bound to address a warning to scholars, and particularly to travellers in Palestine. Mr. Lumley is not the only person who has been deluded by Shapira."

Then Socin got really nasty. "Being personally acquainted with Shapira, we can state that he embraced Christianity from purely sordid motives," he wrote. "His character is just suited for a forger of inscriptions."

The attack must have hit Shapira hard. Not only could such a letter, coming as his new collection of Moabite pottery took shape, damage his reputation and his livelihood, but—considering the disdain with which Jerusalem's Jewish community viewed converted Jews—to have his Christianity impugned by a fellow Christian can only have left him feeling unmoored.

A few weeks later, however, Socin repudiated his own attack, acknowledging that he had slurred Shapira on the basis of scanty evidence. What's more, his mea culpa cites Jerusalem's Protestant bishop as among those who had since come vocally to Shapira's defense.

"I have now the pleasure of informing you that these doubts are unjust to M. Shapira," Socin explained in a second letter to the *Times*. "According to the testimony of reputable persons in Jerusalem, such as the bishop, who is staying at Basel, he was even honourable enough to refuse to sell a stone of (to him) doubtful genuineness except on the understanding that he should be free from blame should the inscription turn out to be spurious."

The bishop's tale indicated that Shapira not only understood the hazards inherent in his line of work, but acknowledged that he was not immune to them. As the popularity of biblical archaeology grew, Jerusalem naturally became the center of the antiquities trade. Just as naturally, it became a hotbed for fakes. Even today antiquities dealers must contend with a glut of forgeries creeping into the market. Part of their job is sifting the real from the fraudulent, but sometimes they miss. Unscrupulous dealers, of course, may knowingly sell fakes. But selling a fake does not necessarily make one an unscrupulous dealer.

Socin conceded as much in his apology. Take the inscription of Psalm 117 that he had earlier condemned. In fact, he now said, upon learning that it was inauthentic, Shapira himself had made a laudable effort to expose it as a fraud. Notably, Socin did not disavow his claim that the monuments in question were fakes. Rather, he said, Shapira was "not the deceiver, but the deceived." The stones were forgeries—but Shapira was not the forger. He was a dupe.

"I regret not to have been better informed in the matter," he added. The letter closes with a righteous entreaty to the people of Jerusalem, urging that they "bestir themselves to find out the real forgers."

Socin's call for a manhunt was a lonely one. Shapira's collection of Moabite statuettes continued to grow and Schlottmann, in his position as secretary pro tem of the DMG, recommended that Prussia purchase the available pieces for its Royal Museum. Fresh off the embarrassment of losing the Moabite Stone to the French, the Prussian government jumped at the suggestion, naming Shapira as its official agent. In the autumn of 1873 Prussia purchased the first collection of 911 pieces, followed in short order by a second set of more than 700, paying Shapira the astonishing sum of 20,000 thaler (about $235,000 today). So taken were the Germans that Kaiser Wilhelm I himself donated a portion of the money to ensure that Shapira's collection reach the fatherland posthaste.

Shapira was moving up in the world. His collection was the talk of Jerusalem, his name bandied about by Europe's intelligentsia and political power brokers. He had weathered a painful attack with the backing of powerful people. He had money in the bank. And he was no longer a stateless apostate, a sickly bachelor, an apprentice carpenter, a bookseller. He was now M. W. Shapira, agent of the Prussian government; a successful antiquities dealer in a place where antiquities were prized like prophecies. No sooner had he sold the first two collections to Prussia than he began to assemble a third. As before, new pieces arrived in a torrent.

BY THIS TIME, Shapira had moved his family out of what would come to be known as the Old City of Jerusalem and into a home near the Russian Compound, a neighborhood located in the New City then emerging outside Jerusalem's walls. Shapira was among a growing number of Jerusalemites who had begun to escape the crowded and disease-ridden Old City for the roomier wilds outside. The sale of the Moabite pottery afforded him a comfortable nest egg, and his new home befitted a man of his growing stature. Known as the Villa Rashid, the elegant stone house was built in 1864 by the prominent Jerusalem Arab Aga Rashid Nashishibi and was among the very first constructed outside the city walls. As described by Shapira's daughter, Myriam Harry, the ground floor was "completely Turkish in style," with a large arched front door, domed ceilings, and square windows masked to filter out the noonday sun. Upstairs, low ceilings were adorned with murals in which swallows drifted dreamily among "delicately tinted clouds."

Outside, two balconies overlooked Jaffa Road and a roomy back-yard with a "complete labyrinth of alcoves and niches, and irregular little buildings with miniature hanging gardens." A wooden terrace encircled the yard, where rosemary bushes grew in barrel planters and a lemon tree climbed over a latticed window. Shapira's young daughters relaxed on a stone divan, beneath which was a paddock hedged by a stand of pomegranate trees.

Shapira made another small show of his wealth by acquiring an exotic pet—an eight-foot-tall ostrich with a singularly bad attitude. One can't blame the bird for its disposition: hatched in Arabia and carted up to Jerusalem by some of Shapira's associates, it now found itself inhabiting a ninety-foot pen tracing the merchant's backyard. The Shapiras were terrified of the grouchy creature.

One afternoon, Selah Merrill, the American consul, called on Shapira. The men were visiting with three or four other people on the patio when the ostrich broke free and unleashed a lightning kick toward their heads. Its aim, thankfully, was poor. The bird's foot smashed into the door fully six feet above the ground, flinging it open. Shapira's servant heard the commotion and came barreling around the corner brandishing her broom like a Moabite warrior. As the guests gathered themselves, the poor animal suffered a swift and violent rebuke.

"It has now almost no feathers, and its bare skin is red," Merrill wrote of the attack's sad aftermath. "It doubtless finds the winters of Jerusalem severe, compared with those of the region whence it was brought, but in Mr. Shapira's hands it is well cared for, and is in every way a curiosity worth seeing and studying."

For the moment, at least, the same could be said of Shapira's growing collection of Moabite pottery.

5

ROTTERDAM

I left England with three clues in hand: a year after Shapira's death, Bernard Quaritch, the venerable London bookseller, had purchased the controversial Deuteronomy scrolls at Sotheby's; Shapira's widow sent two small pieces of the scrolls to Konstantin Schlottmann, a theologian at the University of Halle in Germany; and C. D. Ginsburg—an expert in Hebrew, the Bible, and the Moabite Stone who had purchased manuscript fragments from Shapira's collection— had announced his willingness to pay two hundred pounds for the Deuteronomy scrolls. This last clue called into question half a century of Shapira scholarship, indicating that Ginsburg was more likely to have bought the scrolls from Quaritch than was the prevailing suspect, Sir Charles Nicholson.

Almost as soon as I returned home to San Francisco, Caroline Dijckmeester-Bins, a Dutch journalist friend, sent me an email that, unbeknownst to her, contained my fourth clue.

Shapira had died in Rotterdam, and I was planning a trip to the Netherlands to see what clues remained there. I'd asked Caroline if she would call the city's archive to get a sense of what relevant materials were on file. Archival research is hit or miss— sometimes you find what you're looking for quickly, filed under the names or subject headings you expect. More often, the really useful information is cataloged elsewhere—under a more general heading, or the name of a more famous person with whom your subject is associated. The Rotterdam archives probably didn't have a folder labeled MOSES WILHELM SHAPIRA, but it was possible they did hold records on foreigners who died there, or paupers' graves, or coroners' inquests.

I didn't speak a word of Dutch and hoped Caroline would be able to push buttons I could not. She came back with new information before she'd even picked up the phone. Trolling an online archive of Dutch newspapers, Caroline had hit upon a number of nineteenth-century articles reporting Shapira's death. The details were upsetting—he had died altogether alone, in a city far from home, and his final exit was ugly.

But there was more. According to *Het Nieuws van den Dag* (*The News of the Day*) for Wednesday, March 12, 1884, investigators had spotted Shapira's valise lying beside his stiff body. And they described it as being full of documents: some letters, some brochures—and some manuscripts. In Hebrew.

"It sounds like an amazing detective novel," Caroline wrote when she sent over the clipping.

She was right. I was still holding out hope that Ginsburg's relatives might yet yield some lead, but as I waited, this article reanimated the search, offering up the next clue: at the moment of his death, Shapira's suitcase was bloated with documents, some of which were in Hebrew. Who was to say that one of them was not the famous Deuteronomy?

It's true that in Ginsburg's letter to his daughter, he noted that the manuscript had remained in the British Museum even after Shapira "disappeared." But was he right? Reading old letters and manuscripts over the course of some years, one thing had become evident: people err in their recollections—constantly. But Ginsburg's claim was different. He wrote that letter just days after Shapira had left London for the final time, and did so from inside the very institution about which he was reporting. It is even possible that the Shapira manuscript lay open beside his inkwell as Ginsburg exclaimed to his daughter, Ethel, about the cleverness of the "forgery."

What, then, was in Shapira's luggage? It was possible, of course, that in the six months between his departure and his death, he had sent for the manuscripts. That was the neatest explanation and, if true, meant that the strips might still remain among evidence collected at the scene of his passing. Alternately, if Rosette had found two small slips from the Deuteronomy manuscript among Shapira's things in Jerusalem, perhaps he had more such pieces in his possession at the end. Maybe the documents described by police investigating his death were, in fact, portions of the very scrolls that had precipitated his demise.

But why had Shapira escaped to the Netherlands to begin with? Was he running from the shame of having been exposed as a forger—a guilty man too weak to face his accusers, his friends, his family? Or was he an innocent man fleeing a scholarly world that seemed hell-bent on vilifying him? Was he a scoundrel hiding out until the embers of scandal were extinguished? A Christian exhausted by the mistrust of his fellow Christians? A Jew tired of abuse from other Jews? Or was he just the unluckiest man on earth, cornered and driven mad after finding an authentic gem that he simply could not prove was real?

Whatever Shapira's motives—and no matter his guilt or innocence—the idea that he had died with some portion of the manuscript that had devastated him right by his side was too sad and cinematic to dismiss. That these manuscripts could still be sitting in some Dutch police storeroom, unexamined for the past 140 years, was too enticing. The only way to know for certain was to find the suitcase.

WHERE TO BEGIN? I started with an email to the Rotterdam police department in hopes that someone there—perhaps a distant successor to Adjunct Inspector G. Putman Cramer, who had discovered Shapira's body in 1884—could point me in the right direction. I still hadn't heard back by the time I landed in Holland and so, after checking into a dark and disorientingly narrow hotel along one of Amsterdam's 165 canals, I caught the train to Rotterdam.

It was Sunday and still too early to try the police station, so I went to St. Mary's, the only Anglican church in town. I was hoping someone among its parishioners might be knowledgeable about nineteenth-century Anglicans.

By the time I sneaked into a pew near the back of the neo-Gothic sanctuary, the service had begun. Worship here was in English and was being led by a woman. There was very little in the way of overtly Christian iconography. Save for the wooden cross on the front wall, the room—with its stained-glass windows and HOLY, HOLY, HOLY emblazoned in gold across the front of the lectern—could as easily have been a synagogue.

When the lightly attended service let out that Sunday morning, congregants adjourned to the all-purpose room for coffee and cake. I hadn't eaten yet and was happy for the opportunity to nosh (can one nosh in a church?) and mingle. The lady doling out coffee had a kind face, so I broached the reason for my visit with her. She said the person I should really talk to was Anneke Barends, a phlebotomist and local history buff.

"I'm writing a book about the oldest Bible in the world and how its outing as a possible fraud in 1883 led to the death of a man here in Rotterdam who may have worshipped at this church," I told Barends after the coffee lady introduced us. She was an attractive woman in her forties with short hair and a floral skirt, and as I delivered my Sunday morning homily—delving into the particulars of Shapira's tale—her eyebrows climbed above her glasses. "He was a Jew, later an Anglican—and I'm trying to learn anything I can about him. So far I can't find the scrolls, or the suitcase, or the hotel where he died."

Barends was immediately taken with the story. It felt as if she'd been waiting for someone like me to shuffle through the door and ask for help. She had, it turned out, spent much of her free time studying and reenacting the region's history. She'd met her husband at a celebration marking the 750th anniversary of Spijkenisse, the small village in South Holland where their ancestors had lived. They were married in historical costume, an oddity that generated a series of newspaper articles and a television appearance.

"But he wouldn't have worshipped here," Barends said. "This church wasn't built until 1913, after the old one fell apart."

She dashed off for a moment as I examined the hinges on a door, trying desperately to seem occupied, worrying that, beyond the coffee, my visit was already proving fruitless. She returned with a short history she'd written of St. Mary's—from its founding in 1708 to its use as a prison during the French occupation, through to a 2008 visit by the Netherlands' Queen Beatrix. At no point, Barends told me, did the church have its own burial ground, so he would not have been buried here or at the church's previous location. But she might be able to help me find where he died, and that was a start.

MANY OF THOSE who have written about Shapira suggest that he died in a hotel called the Bloemendaal. In fact, in the months before his death, Shapira spent time in a district by that name, but died in a second-rate hotel called the Willemsbrug (Williams Bridge), on a busy thoroughfare known as the Boompjes. I had been trying to find some reference to the hotel that would tell me exactly where it had been located, but, beyond a photograph that offered very little context, I'd had no luck. The following day, Barends and I went out looking.

It was drizzling and cold when we pulled into the parking lot just behind the last remaining column of the bridge from which the hotel had taken its name. Barends parked her car and we ventured out into the chilling rain, past the Witte Huis, one of Europe's first high-rises, and the Mariners Museum, with its neon sign barely visible in the mist. The whole time, Barends was on the phone with her husband, Hans, who was acting as her GPS. Finally, on a street corner across from the Health City gym and a red suspension bridge, Barends shut her phone.

"It was right about here," she said.

"Where?"

She gestured to the slick street on whose edge we were standing. "Here."

I tried to picture a hotel on this spot, but there was absolutely nothing left. On May 14, 1940, two Luftwaffe bomber formations had pummeled the city center. Hundreds were killed, thousands were left homeless, and the medieval city center was leveled. Winds kicked up over the following days, igniting a ferocious firestorm that inflicted a subsequent layer of destruction on the terrible wreckage.

The Hotel Willemsbrug was among the buildings that were pulverized. Barends and I paused on the spot where it had stood. Where once there had been a front door, there was now a zebra-striped traffic pole. To stand in what had been its lobby would entail the very real possibility of being run down by a motorist. A little roller skate of a car puttered past, followed by a truck. Even in the rain, a few hardy Dutch skimmed by on their bicycles. I was having trouble imagining the hotel, so instead I scanned the skyline for landmarks that appeared old—I wanted to look at something Shapira himself may have seen on that last, worst night of his life. But the Luftwaffe had done its job well. The remaining pillar of William's Bridge wasn't visible from where I stood. The banks and insurers that had once served this industrial city were now relegated to its collective memory. Then I spotted the river. Surely Shapira had seen the river.

I spent the next few minutes looking out at the choppy black water. The rain thickened and a cold wind hopped in. Standing there, it was easy to understand how a man who had been dismissed as a fraud, who hadn't seen his wife and daughters in months, whose career was finished and whose reputation was smashed, could idle on this spot, gaze out at the silent river, and conclude that there was nothing left for him in this world.

BARENDS HAD TO take her daughter to a piano lesson, but on the way she dropped me at Rotterdam's police headquarters, on Doelwater Street. With its green-tiled facade and mirrored windows, the building was the architectural equivalent of Hawaiian Shirt Fridays—a boring person acting out in a boring way. The interior was no more inviting. A man sat behind a long desk. Behind the desk was a wall of windows. Behind the windows, members of the police force opened and closed doors, entered and exited anonymous rooms. As I approached the desk, a young uniformed officer with a blond buzz cut stopped me and asked if he could help. His name was John Kagenaar, and a moment later he was rendered mute as I informed him that the case I was there to inquire about was closed in 1884. I cycled quickly through Shapira's story, and Kagenaar came back to life. Especially intriguing to him was the idea that portions of Shapira's missing scrolls could have been collected by officers called to his hotel room to investigate his death. Kagenaar dialed the police archives and spoke briefly to someone on the other end. When he hung up, he said, "They have no idea." Then he scribbled an address in my notebook and said, "Write to the Rotterdam Police Museum."

BACK IN AMSTERDAM the following morning, I stopped into the Bibliotheca Rosenthaliana—the large Hebraica and Judaica library housed at the University of Amsterdam. If Shapira had any portion of his scrolls with him when he died, they could have ended up on the manuscripts market in the Netherlands, and so I decided to spend a few days searching the library's collection of sales catalogs published by Dutch booksellers in the late nineteenth century. When I arrived that morning, I took it as a good omen that the library held a copy of my father's Deuteronomy commentary. Over the next two days, I searched more than a decade's worth of catalogs. They listed many interesting items—from old Bibles, prayer books, and Passover Haggadoth to silverwork and ritual rams' horns. But nothing that looked like Shapira's scrolls.

On a break from combing the catalogs, I received a reply from José Michels, an officer in Rotterdam's Police Control Room Unit and a volunteer at the Police Museum. Michels knew who Shapira was—there was a picture of him among the museum's holdings. But his belongings were long gone: items confiscated by the police at that time were stored in a facility that had burned in World War II. Like the Hotel Willemsbrug, the suitcase and whatever was in it had gone up in flames.

6

SCULPTING A CIVILIZATION

Even as the Prussians took delivery of their prized new museum pieces, Shapira began building a third collection of Moabite pottery. As it grew, so, too, did doubts about its provenance. Much of the early concern focused on the sheer volume of material that was landing in one man's lap. No one had ever before discovered inscribed pottery in Moab, and now, suddenly, there was no end to it? The proposition struck some as suspect.

While Schlottmann's warm embrace persisted, scholars in England and America began to ask questions. Charles Tyrwhitt-Drake, a PEF member who had taken part in expeditions to Sinai and the Negev and in 1870 had joined an unsuccessful hunt for a "new Moabite Stone," harbored doubts about the pottery. He made sketches of Shapira's jars, idols, and inscriptions and sent them to PEF headquarters for examination. Later, when Conder arrived in Jerusalem to helm the PEF's Western Survey, he painted his own watercolors of those objects in the collection he deemed most important. Between them, the two men sent London two hundred illustrations of the Shapira pottery.

Over the next several months, Tyrwhitt-Drake's doubts intensified. In a letter home to the PEF dated June 19, 1872, he wrote:

"[Shapira's] being a converted Jew goes much against him. But I believe him to be ignorant of any forgeries if such are carried on."

Then in August he wrote to Besant, wondering if the British Museum was still sticking to "their idea of Shapira's pottery being worth as much as 1£ each." Six months later he said he was "not competent to pronounce on [Shapira's] inscriptions but will maintain his pottery till it is *proved* a forgery."

He wasn't alone in his concerns. As Shapira's Moabitica collection grew, so, too, did tension with Rosette. A religious woman with a puritanical worldview, she saw her husband's efforts to expand his business as arrogance and folly.

"Remember," she warned him, "God blasts those trees which try to touch the sky."

Family dinners became dreary. Rosette was "silent and irritable." Shapira sat in "gloomy silence." Two deep furrows channeled his forehead like fault lines. Arguments would erupt suddenly—Rosette fretting that the Moabitica would be the family's ruin, Shapira countering that no one had the right to criticize his work. *I would rather die,* he would say, *than give up my excursions to Moab.* Then, pushing his dish away like a child, he would march upstairs to pace alone on the terrace.

With so much hanging in the balance—his career, reputation, finances—even marital discord couldn't halt his project. Shapira departed for Moab to inspect the sites where his collections were allegedly being unearthed, hoping to prove that authentic pottery could indeed be found east of the Jordan. Teaming up with Hermann Weser, the Protestant pastor who had sent sketches to Schlottmann, as well as Wilhelm Duisberg, the German consul in Khartoum, and Salim al Kari, Shapira set off on an eleven-day journey.

The expedition was beset by problems from the start. Running low on water and fearful the horses might die, the party was forced to send the beasts back four hours to drink. Spent, they arrived at the encampment of Shapira's friend, the Bedouin sheikh Ali Diab, which they used as a jumping-off point for a visit to nearby El'Ab, where Ali was said to have discovered a number of the jars that he had delivered to Shapira. There they observed a "rock-cut repository" large enough to fit two such jars, which pointed to the possibility that Moabite pottery could have been found there, even if none remained.

In Madeba, Weser and Duisberg turned up two pieces concealed beneath a pile of more recent pottery. One was inscribed with two lines of "crowded Phoenician characters"—a nineteenth-century term for Hebrew letters—and the other with the letter *mem* (*M*). Later, while Shapira plied locals with coffee, the two Germans dug twenty-three feet into the ground, discovering several more specimens at various points along the way. As they worked, a host of local Bedouin arrived bearing broken pottery pieces for the foreigners' perusal. Wary of giving them an idea of what it might be worth, which could lead to exorbitant demands later, Weser and Duisberg threw most of it aside like garbage.

From Madeba the group traveled to Dhiban, where they found a two-foot-long stone inscribed with Phoenician characters.

These were minor discoveries—nowhere near as significant as the Moabite Stone, certainly, nor even much of the Moabitica. In some corners, though, the outing quelled the doubts then dogging Shapira's collections. Conder, for one, concluded that "the late visit of Pastor Weser and of M. Dinsberg [*sic*] (a German resident at Jerusalem) has placed the authenticity of the pottery beyond dispute."

THIS WAS VERY good news for Shapira. So, too, was the fact that he took easily to the desert. His daughter describes observing his return from one such trip, using the name of her literary alter ego, Siona:

When she ran out into the paddock, she found it transformed into a regular caravansary. It was alive with strange men and their beasts, and piled up with bales of stuffs and calabashes filled with roses of Jericho and the balm of Gilead and bitter apples from the Dead Sea. One corner was filled with rows of coal-black sacks which terrified Siona. They were said to contain wheat from the banks of Jordan and barley from the land of Moab. A Bedouin with a long spear was in charge of this particular corner, and Siona thought he looked just like a demon in a fairy tale mounting guard over priceless treasure. Such sacks as these were never opened when her father was not present. He always stood by, whilst Selim, the factotum of the household, plunged his hands into the grain, extracting urns and idols and sundry articles in pottery. These [the girl's father] would carry away with the greatest care to that mysterious upper room at the top of the stone steps. But whenever he passed Ourda, bearing his precious spoils, she would promptly cross herself, whilst Siona's mother would sigh audibly:

"Oh, my God, my God, what more of these Moabitish idols!"

Then there came another morning when Siona woke up to find the paddock empty and silent. Men and beasts had vanished as if by magic. The "sidi" resumed his Roomi garments, but the subtle scent of the desert still hung about the house, and underneath his usually grave demeanour, there lurked a certain gladness.

Rosette was suspicious of the Moabitica from the start. Her response here—"What *more* of these Moabitish idols!"—pithily summarizes the initial arguments scholars proffered against the statuettes, namely that there were too many of them to be believed.

But Shapira was swept away. Though by then his temperament

was "usually grave," when he returned home from Moab, he gathered his daughter in his arms and proclaimed that he was "King of the Desert."

HIS REIGN DID not last long. In Germany, the majority of scholars had by now concluded that Shapira's pottery was fake, an opinion echoed by Ganneau, who insinuated himself into Shapira's life now with all the subtlety of a jaw tumor. In December 1873, he published a long letter in the *Athenaeum* in which he not only labeled the Moabitica a "colossal deception" but offered up a deceiver.

"My opinion is, and always has been, that the collections of M. Shapira, all derived from the same source, are false from beginning to end," he wrote.

And the forger?

Salim al Kari, Shapira's partner and supplier.

Since 1868, Ganneau explained, he had carefully preserved Salim's "rough but faithful" copy of the Moabite Stone, delivered to him by the banker Bergheim. This allowed him to detect "from the very first, in the fantastic inscriptions of the Shapira Collection, the characteristic and peculiar manner in which our artist sees, understands and designs the Moabite letters."

These letters were at once "much too similar" to those on the Mesha stele and formed words that were wholly unintelligible. This, Ganneau said, indicated that the pottery had been inscribed by a forger who had access to the stone's alphabet but no understanding of it—who was able to copy the letters but not to make meaning of them.

Ganneau dismissed efforts by men like Schlottmann at siphoning meaning from the dry font of the pottery's inscriptions. "For it is impossible to receive as serious translations certain unfortunate attempts made in Germany and England to make sense of these inscriptions—attempts often contradictory, which have served to show, not only the ingenuity and erudition of their authors, but the impossibility of translating texts, supposed, from the alleged circumstances of the 'finds,' and their paleographic appearance, to be contemporaneous with the Moabite Stone."

When he read Ganneau's attack, Shapira flew into a tantrum—he crushed the magazine in his hands and, "white with anger," hurled it onto a table. "Then," Myriam recalled, "snatching it up again, he read its contents to his wife in a voice that shook with rage."

Rosette was as concerned about the impact Ganneau's accusations could have on Jerusalem's Protestants as she was about her husband. Shapira's daughter, meanwhile, wanted simply to comfort her father. She reached out to hug him, but he shook her off.

Over the coming days, a steady stream of visitors marched through Shapira's home—clergy, ministers, and missionaries huddled in his office in a series of "solemn conferences." But whatever counsel and succor they offered could not mitigate the shock of Ganneau's very public shaming.

"Oh, my poor children," Rosette said. "[Ganneau] will certainly be the ruin of you both."

SINCE HE HADN'T seen the pottery himself, Ganneau's theory was pure speculation, or worse, and he decided to follow his attack with a visit to Shapira. When he arrived, Shapira refused to show his visitor what he'd come to see.

"[He] believed me, I do not know why, animated by some hostile sentiment," Ganneau wrote. Considering that Ganneau had freely admitted in his letter to the *Athenaeum* that he'd dismissed

Shapira's collections as badly done fakes before ever having seen them, it is not hard to understand why Shapira, grown accustomed to such men's scorn, would have been circumspect. Nonetheless, when an English acquaintance intervened, Shapira relented, and Ganneau inspected the pottery as its owner looked on.

"The figures," Ganneau reported, "are rudely formed, and yet betray the hand of a modern." On certain pieces, the mark of threads was visible, accidental impressions from the linen on which the soft clay had been laid before shaping—a modern practice, he said, evidence of which was clearly overlooked by Salim.

"In short," Ganneau wrote, "I did not see in the whole collection, *one single object which could be regarded as genuine,* so that I remarked . . . when we came out, 'There is only one thing authentic in all that we have seen, the live Ostrich the Arabs have brought here with the pottery.'"

GANNEAU BELIEVED THAT he recognized Salim's style, but wasn't it possible someone else had a similar approach? He viewed readings like Schlottmann's as forced, but were they necessarily wrong? Convinced the pottery was Salim's handiwork but lacking concrete evidence, Ganneau undertook a crafty intelligence operation meant to catch Shapira's factotum *"la main dans le sac"*—with his hand, as it were, in the Moabite cookie jar. The investigation began at a pottery shop between the Spanish consulate and the Damascus Gate. There, Ganneau happened upon a journeyman clay worker named Abd el Bagi. Careful not to disclose the nature of his investigation, Ganneau proceeded to question this man, who divulged that he had once worked "for a certain Salim al Kari, *who made statues and vases in earthenware (terre cuite) with writings.*"

"In order not to awaken suspicions, I did not press my questions any further," Ganneau told his readers, "but confined myself to asking him if he knew to what potter Salim now sent his vessels to be baked."

Abd el Bagi pointed Ganneau toward an apprentice named Hassan ibn el Bitar. Certain he was getting close, the Frenchman tracked down and interrogated the young potter. "What follows is the exact narrative which I took from the mouth of Hassan, always being very careful to let him speak, without suggesting anything by injudicious questioning," Ganneau wrote. "He was formerly apprenticed to [a potter named] Ahmed, with another boy named Khalil, son of Said the barber, and Abu Mansura (Abd el Bagi), journeyman . . . Salim al Kari got soft clay of Ahmed, made out of it, at his own house, statues of men, dogs, and women, with noses, hands, feet and breasts, the whole covered with writings . . . then he sent them to Ahmed's to be baked. Ahmed made vases for him in turn, and Salim wrote letters on them."

Hassan told Ganneau that he and another apprentice had been charged with carrying the clay items back and forth between Salim's house and the pottery shop, surreptitious outings the boys made only during the Maghrib and the Isha'a—Muslim prayer times that fall after dark. Per Salim's instructions, Hassan tried his best to keep the pottery hidden as he went about his deliveries. Whenever he returned with a shipment of newly baked pieces, Salim would carefully count each one. If any were dropped and broken, Salim saw to it that even the smallest slivers were carefully picked up. After taking a delivery from Hassan, Ganneau continued, Salim would dip the pieces into a cauldron of water "'to make them grow old.'" The boy had quit this job for fear he would be arrested.

Hassan's story "contains details which cannot have been invented, and the exactness and veracity of which I have been able to establish by other means," Ganneau wrote. "I believe it conclusive: it is notably instructive as to the process adopted by Salim in order to impregnate his things with that *couche* of saltpeter which was to be their brevet of authenticity. I think that we can henceforth, with these elements of information, consider the matter as settled."

Ganneau's letter landed like a grenade. For the PEF's Tyrwhitt-Drake, who had earlier sent sketches of the pottery back to the PEF, it confirmed a story he'd heard not long before. While he was camped at Mar Saba—the ancient Greek Orthodox monastery in Bethlehem that had been home to St. John of Damascus—a "very trustworthy and intelligent Arab" had approached him with a sensational report identifying Salim as the forger. Tyrwhitt-Drake could not independently confirm the story and so, sending details to the PEF, asked the committee to hold off on publishing them until further notice.

"There seems, as far as I can at present judge, to have been an original trouvaille [lucky find] of many specimens of which I sent some sketches, while late forgeries have been made in imitation of these," he wrote. "These I begin to look upon as forgeries, while still feeling inclined to believe in the genuineness of some of the original lot. Mr. Ganneau agrees with me in believing that if the things are forgeries, Mr. Shapira is in no way a party to the fraud."

The Ottoman Empire granted foreign governments the power to interrogate and imprison those they suspected had crossed them, and several weeks after Ganneau's letter, Tyrwhitt-Drake dragged Abd el Bagi, the first potter the Frenchman had interviewed, before British consul Noel Temple Moore to make a "voluntary" statement explaining what he knew of Salim's business. His account, published in the *Athenaeum,* closely echoes Hassan's declaration: Salim and his father, he said, paid him to make clay pots. They also bought clay from him, which they themselves would sculpt into hundreds of birds, hands, and heads, inscribe them with writing, and bring them back to Abd el Bagi for baking. They counted each item carefully, paid him, and told him to keep his mouth shut.

Prior to publication, Tyrwhitt-Drake alerted Besant. "Keep this quite to yourself, as a word spoken too soon would put the forger on his guard," he wrote. "I am in hopes of getting material proofs. Ganneau is also working with the same object."

Ganneau's letter in the *Athenaeum* only reinforced Shapira's sense that the Frenchman was out to get him. He grew visibly depressed and began to ignore both his family and his business, devoting himself entirely to refuting the accusations. True, Ganneau acknowledged that Shapira was probably ignorant of the fraud and, as in the case of Lumley's bogus "Moses" stone, was merely "the first dupe." But being first dupe does not inspire confidence or sell antiquities. And so Shapira struck back.

"Allow me to inform those of your readers who have perused M. Ganneau's letter . . . that the evidence adduced therein is just now being sifted on the spot by four gentlemen of the highest character, one of whom is an Englishman," Shapira wrote in the *Athenaeum*. "And, although the Minutes of the Proceedings are not yet in my hands, I am warranted in telling you that all the witnesses on whom M. Ganneau relies have been found utterly worthless."

Ganneau and Tyrwhitt-Drake, it turned out, were not the only Europeans then in Jerusalem out to ensnare Salim. Weser, who accompanied Shapira to Moab, had launched an inquiry of his own. Along with Prussia's consul-general in Jerusalem, he'd begun by thoroughly searching Salim's house for evidence of conspiracy. They found nothing. Undeterred, they had Salim arrested and held in the German Consulate. Meanwhile, a litany of Jerusalem potters was paraded before Weser, Duisberg, and Tyrwhitt-Drake and energetically interrogated. One by one, the men changed their testimony, each telling a very similar story: that Ganneau had threatened, thrashed, imprisoned, or bribed him to implicate Salim in a large-scale fraud.

Rather than question them, the men now swore, Ganneau had browbeaten them all, insisting they tell the story as he wanted it told. Ganneau claimed the allegations were preposterous, and that the puppeteer behind the potters' swift and unanimous change of heart was "the only man among them really compromised" by his allegations: Salim al Kari.

GANNEAU, OF COURSE, did not leave it there, taking again to the pages of the *Athenauem* to go after the pottery. This time Schlottmann responded in kind, claiming that the French scholar's ideas were not only wrong—they were stolen. In a private conversation shortly before Ganneau published his first letter, Schlottmann said, Tyrwhitt-Drake had expressed suspicions about Salim, on the condition that Ganneau keep this information to himself. Ganneau, however, did quite the opposite.

"Inspired by a desire to derive *éclat* by publishing a piquant revelation, [Ganneau] wrote on Dec. 29 the letter which subsequently appeared in the pages of *The Athenaeum*," Schlottmann said. That letter essentially repeated and extrapolated on the evidence Tyrwhitt-Drake had presented to Ganneau confidentially.

Perhaps Ganneau's exuberance can be attributed to his age. Though later in his life he would wear a white beard, an upturned white mustache, and oval glasses pinched to the top of his nose, Ganneau was now just twenty-seven. Then again, Tyrwhitt-Drake was the same age and, despite his own growing doubts about the statuary, he had insisted on discretion. Significantly, Schlottmann's letter would not be the last instance in which Ganneau was faulted for publicly pronouncing a forgery without having seen the object in question. Nor was it the last time he was charged with taking another scholar's theories, offered in confidence, and publishing them under his own name.

All this was not the only bad behavior of which Ganneau was accused. Some time earlier, Tyrwhitt-Drake had discovered an engraved stone at a site in the foothills of Judaea. Subsequently, Ganneau had learned of the Englishman's discovery. Tyrwhitt-Drake died in 1874, succumbing to fever after weeks of suffering. Now, even as the Moabitica scandal flamed, Ganneau decided he wanted Tyrwhitt-Drake's stone and, taking credit for its discovery, made plans to ferry it home to France (though he was then in the employ of the PEF).

"The acquisition and removal was contrary to Turkish law and Ganneau hid the slab at the house of Peter Bergheim, a banker's son," writes John James Moscrop in *Measuring Jerusalem,* his comprehensive history of the PEF. Although Conder thought Ganneau in the right, he wrote home to Besant complaining of the Frenchman's "imprudence" and his tendency to claim others' discoveries as his own. The Ottomans protested, and France was left with little choice but to recall Ganneau. In essence, he had been kicked out of the country.

Schlottmann, meanwhile, was among an ever-shrinking minority, and his ardent defense of the Moabitica did little to aid Shapira's prospects for selling his third—and largest—collection. Shapira sent specimens to the Oriental Museum in Vienna for consideration, but they were rejected. This was a serious setback. Whether out of economic concerns or a growing suspicion about his role in the affair—or, perhaps, coming to recognize that his agent's reputation was simply bad for business—Shapira fired Salim.

Salim did not go quietly into the Jerusalem night. Reduced

to poverty, he petitioned Germany's imperial consul in Jerusalem, Baron von Münchhausen, for wages he claimed Shapira still owed him. Incredulous, Shapira produced two bills demonstrating that Salim, in fact, owed *him* money. The evidence was convincing, but Salim pressed his case with the Germans. Münchhausen referred him to the city's Ottoman authorities, who dismissed his claims outright.

"On that occasion," Münchhausen reported, "[Salim] told several persons, so that I came to hear of it, that if Mr. Shapira did not satisfy his demands to the last farthing he would 'expose the whole of the Moabitic antiquities.'"

IN PRUSSIA, THE purchase of nearly two thousand pieces of Shapira's dubious Moabitica was such a blow to national pride that the controversy made it all the way to the Diet, where Professor Theodor Mommsen (who years later would be awarded the Nobel Prize in Literature) spoke passionately about the affair, acknowledging the error and forcefully questioning the process by which the pottery had been vetted. Following his speech, the majority of the Moabitica was declared fraudulent. Burned by their support for the supposed relics, Schlottmann and his German Oriental Society abandoned efforts to publish further data.

Although his government had just made it official, Baron von Münchhausen was still not convinced that the pottery was fake. On November 1, 1877, just a few weeks before Shapira left for London to conclude a large manuscript transaction with the British Museum, Münchhausen told him that he believed the Diet's hearing had been "comical." Despite all the Sturm und Drang, Münchhausen told Shapira, he remained confident that "nothing at all" had been proved, positive or negative, about the true nature of the Moabitica.

That all changed, he said, with the recent expedition of a man named Almkvist to Moab. Almkvist, a professor of Oriental languages in Uppsala, Sweden—who had traveled with Shapira to Moab's Wadi Mujib in 1875—had just then embarked on his own search for Moabitica. Setting out into the mountains of Moab, Almkvist selected a cave at random and began to dig. For two hours he hammered away at the cavern's wall until he'd managed to carve a hole two feet deep. There, lying behind the thick stone, Almkvist discovered a clay jar like those Shapira had been selling.

"All of a sudden," Münchhausen reported, "the state of things was altered."

But the professor, it turns out, had not been alone in the cave. Joining him on the expedition was none other than Salim. The "scoundrel's" presence seemed an obvious red flag, a clear indication that Salim had salted the site with fakes in advance of Almkvist's arrival. Münchhausen was not bothered. "Honest Dr. Almkvist" had selected the cave himself. To suspect Salim's complicity, then, would be to call Almkvist a fool or, worse, a liar.

Although the Prussian Diet had only the previous year dismissed the majority of Shapira's pottery as fake, elements in government now began to grumble. For them, Almkvist's discovery must have rekindled hope that they had not made such a colossal blunder after all. Shortly after the Swede's expedition, Prussia dispatched Münchhausen to Moab to definitively establish what was—or was not—going on.

Münchhausen was joined by three men. Conrad Schick, a Protestant architect who had worked at the House of Industry while Shapira was apprenticed there, would draw up a technical report; Ser Murrad, an Armenian antiquities dealer and Prussian dragoman, would employ his Arabic to negotiate with local Bedouin; and A. Niepagen, inspector of the ruins at the Convent of St. John, would excavate using the latest archaeological methods. The delegation, Münchhausen was sure to point out in his letter to Shapira, was "perfectly impartial and unconcerned in all matters relating to the disputed Moabitic question."

Like Almkvist, Münchhausen's party confined their digging to caves, and it was immediately clear, Münchhausen reported, that they were not the first people to have entered these hollows since Almkvist's outing. Many of the caves, he said, appeared to have been "materially changed" by individuals who had continued digging after the Swede's departure. Among the diggers, the German speculated, was a certain Mutlak, the Bedouin proprietor of the caves in question.

"Here I mentally hear the learned critics exclaim, 'Ah! Very well; those are Mutlak's own formations, behind which he has hidden his or Salim's manufactures,'" Münchhausen wrote.

He dismissed this imagined attack unconditionally. "I should like to see the great conjurer who is able to create artificially that stratum of flint protruding from the side wall of one of the caves more than one metre high above ground, and losing itself in the depths of the earth."

It was behind that stratum of flint, Münchhausen said, and under a fine layer of gray moss whose integrity indicated it had not been disturbed by human hands, that the party discovered large fragments of inscribed clay, several bones, and two idols.

Achieving what appeared to be real progress in the cascading narrative that had until then defined the Moabitica, Münchhausen's discovery seemed to prove Shapira right: authentic items of Moabite culture could be found in the wilderness of Moab. Had it continued, perhaps the expedition would have uncovered more such illuminating treasures—or evidence proving the pottery false. But as Münchhausen's team dug, geopolitical fault lines thousands of miles away shifted and he was recalled to Jerusalem to assist resident Russians, whose homeland had just declared war on the Ottomans.

Münchhausen's subsequent letter to Shapira was published in the *Athenaeum* on December 1, 1877. It was followed, in the paper's left-hand column, by a short addendum from Shapira himself, who theorized in some detail about the geologic process by which small "earth bubbles" form in cave walls—walls made of soft rock that, over time, dissolves into powder, which eventually rehardens.

"The same thing must, in my opinion, have happened in the hundreds of caves I have seen, all of which are hewn in the original rock," Shapira noted. "The upper parts resolved themselves into powder, and the idols, vases, &c, hidden in the natural holes there (and used as talismans? or monuments?), also fell down to the bottom of the caves, and are, consequently, often found under ground near the rocky walls of the caves."

Shapira signed off with an ominous postscript to his scientific exploration, meant to demonstrate that Mutlak—the caves' proprietor—and Salim could under no circumstances be working in cahoots.

"Mutlak . . . is Salim's greatest enemy," Shapira wrote, "and would have long ago killed Salim if not afraid of me."

IN THE WINTER of 1877, five new Moabite idols appeared on the market. This was not, in and of itself, noteworthy. What made these pieces interesting was the fact that their owner, a young Arab tradesman named Kattan, was explicitly selling them as forgeries. With so many in Jerusalem eager to prove the Moabitica fake, Kattan understood that demonstrably fraudulent pieces could, under the circumstances, be every bit as lucrative as the real thing.

That December, Kattan had secretly approached Lieutenant

Horatio Kitchener, then the PEF's top man in Jerusalem, and offered him, in strict confidence, a number of Moabite idols. The statues, Kattan told his English client, were fakes—and he was prepared to lead him to the house where they had been manufactured. Convinced that he was about to bring the whole affair to its end, Kitchener purchased two idols. Kattan guided him to the suspect building. It was the home of Salim al Kari.

Police quickly descended on Salim's home, undertaking a thorough investigation of the premises as Salim stood by, unperturbed. He watched calmly as officers rifled through his rooms, and he didn't seem to mind when they discovered a freshly molded clay idol, inscribed with ancient-looking letters but as yet unbaked. Lying beside it were four small chisels that had been used in the statuette's manufacture.

Münchhausen interpreted Salim's equanimity as proof of a diabolical plan to punish Shapira for his firing. "The conviction is almost forced on one," he suggested, "that [Salim] procured the unburnt idol and the four chisels, and cautiously directed public attention to them, in order to compromise Mr. Shapira, and thereby perhaps manage to extort something from him for himself, or simply by way of revenge."

Despite Münchhausen's refusal to implicate Shapira, scholars raced to their desks to pen letters trumpeting just how early they, and only they, had concluded that the Moabitica was a sham—and how shocked they had been when the Germans bought it up. William Hayes Ward, an American clergyman and orientalist, recalled how six years earlier he and a number of well-regarded East Coast academics had examined squeeze copies of the Moabitica on behalf of the American Palestine Exploration Society.

"Our judgment was decidedly averse to their genuineness, although they came endorsed by Mr. Shapira's signature," he wrote.

"The Palestine Exploration Society was advised not to purchase Mr. Shapira's collection, which was afterwards secured, much to our surprise, by the German Government."

A. D. Neubauer, an Oxford expert in Semitic manuscripts, directed his aim squarely at Schlottmann and his "strange method of decipherment."

"Allow me to express the hope that, in the further discussion concerning these Moabite antiquities, no one will imitate the example of Prof. Schlottmann, who declares, in the *Norddeutsche Zeitung*, M. Clermont-Ganneau's statements to be the result of *chauvinism*," Neubauer wrote. "Science is, and ought to be, cosmopolitan, and professors have to give the first example to the general public of confraternity and candour."

Aggrieved and aged by scandal, Shapira felt he'd been unfairly denied such humane treatment. Now, Harry would recall, "whenever his glances traveled in the direction of the blue hills of Moab, such nameless sadness crept into his eyes that [she] would burst out crying."

7

PARIS

Early in 2012, I applied for a professorship in the Creative Writing Department at San Francisco State University. I had been writing for a number of newspapers and magazines and, growing tired of the freelancer's life, was hoping that full-time employment would not only offer a stable source of income but serve as a solid base from which to pursue my quest for Shapira's scrolls.

As I prepared for my interview that March, I received an email from a man I'd never before met, Rabbi Adam Rosenthal. Rosenthal lived in Cincinnati and had found my name while doing Shapira-related research online.

What he said floored me.

"I imagine that you are fully aware of the fact that following Shapira's [death], many (all?) of his remaining literary antiquities were sold to Adolph Sutro, of San Francisco," he wrote. "Thankfully, they were part of the collection which survived the fire (that followed the great earthquake of 1906), and remain in San Francisco to this day."

I was not "fully aware" of anything Rosenthal was telling me. But I immediately recalled that, during one of our meetings in Jerusalem, Sabo had mentioned Sutro, the mining magnate and book collector who had gone on to serve as San Francisco's mayor near the turn of the twentieth century. Still, I could not remember the context. I went back to my notes and found the following unhelpful entry: "Sutro." That was all.

If Sutro had, in fact, scooped up most, or even all, of Shapira's texts, it was possible that among them were fragments of the missing Deuteronomy manuscripts, like the ones Rosette had sent to Schlottmann. (Quaritch bought the scrolls themselves a year after Sutro's purchase, so they could not have been among those acquired by the San Franciscan.) A wholly new avenue for investigation had just opened up and, by sheer happenstance, it was in my backyard. Add to this the insinuation that some of Sutro's collection had been destroyed in a fire—an increasingly common theme—and the connections were growing.

I contacted Rosenthal right away. He was hoping eventually to write a book about Sutro's collection of Jewish literature and over the previous few years had made several trips to examine it. He confirmed my suspicion right away—the scrolls were not there. Nor, it seemed, were any of its fragments. This wasn't particularly surprising. What was surprising was what Rosenthal told me next: this collection of Shapira's manuscripts, he said, was housed in the Sutro Library. I had never heard of this institution and asked him where it was located.

"San Francisco State University."

In 1917, the California State Library had established the Sutro from what remained of the mayor's private collection. The books had subsequently bounced around to a number of sites. When Rosenthal wrote, library staffers were busy transferring Sutro's collection, totaling some one hundred thousand volumes, to their newest home—the fifth floor of S. F. State's J. Paul Leonard Library. The coincidence was uncanny. The likelihood that a collection of Shapira's old religious texts from Yemen would find their way to a San Francisco university was extremely low. That I was up for a job at that very same school seemed preordained.

A few weeks later, I was hired. The Shapira collection, I then learned, contained 167 items purchased from his estate. The number was startling—far greater than I had imagined. Nicholson assumed that he'd bought the majority of the manuscripts Shapira left behind, and he had owned about six. It was based on this assessment that A. D. Crown had posited the nobleman's purchase of Shapira's famous scrolls and their subsequent destruction in a house fire. I was already convinced that this theory was erroneous, but here was more definitive proof: Sutro owned 167 Shapira manuscripts—thirty times the number Nicholson ever had. Crown's hypothesis rose and fell on Nicholson's assumption, and Nicholson's assumption was wrong.

I asked if I could come in to see the collection and was told that it would not be available until late August—the very month I was to begin teaching.

I had been waiting for a break—the kind of serendipitous opening that always seems to underlie great discoveries. Rosenthal's email about a cache of ancient scrolls straight from Shapira's storeroom presented the opportunity I had been hoping for. The Deuteronomy scrolls I sought weren't there—they'd been sold to someone else—but maybe the collection held some clue that would push my search from the quixotic to the realistic.

WHILE SHAPIRA HAD not himself been involved in the Moabite Stone saga, its discovery charted the course for the remainder of his life. Without the stone, the Moabitica craze would have been unlikely. And without the Moabitica, it's not clear the Deuteronomy scrolls would have landed in his lap. Put another way, in the absence of the Moabite Stone, it's unlikely anyone would still know Shapira's name. Having now read all the contemporary material about his Moabitica, it occurred to me that to truly understand the man, I would need to see the pillar that had been so central to his life—and his death.

I flew to Paris in the middle of July and caught a cab to the fifteenth arrondissement, where I'd rented an apartment on the top floor of a six-story walk-up. It was blazing hot and, like most Paris apartments, this one lacked air-conditioning. As soon as I arrived, it was clear that I'd need to procure a fan—and that I'd be spending a great deal of time in my underpants.

Tired after a long flight, I grabbed dinner at a nearby restaurant and turned in early—which is more than I can say for the revelers who flaunted their lung capacity at the bar below until the early hours of the morning. A few hours after they at last shut it down, I caught the Metro to the Louvre, where Mahmoud Alassi, the youthful manager of preservation and restoration for the museum's Department of Near Eastern Antiquities, led me into a storeroom lined with glass-doored cabinets full of all manner of pottery—jugs, vases, and amphorae that ranged in condition from perfect to piles. I was looking forward to seeing the stele itself, but before that, Alassi, one of ten children raised in Gaza City, took me on an unexpected detour. I followed him into a bright alcove overlooking the museum's iconic glass pyramid. Only about 6 percent of the department's holdings are actually on display on any given day. Most of its 130,000 or so inventoried pieces are stored in back rooms like this one. Alassi, who was in his early thirties, set two items on a table. The smaller of the two was a rudimentary drawing on yellowing paper. I leaned in to see it better and noticed an old label affixed to the bottom of the frame:

COPIE DE L'INSCRIPTION DE MÉSA EXÉCUTÉE
À DIBÔN EN 1869 PAR UN ARABE—COPY OF THE
MESHA INSCRIPTION MADE IN DHIBAN IN 1869 BY
AN ARAB.

This was Salim al Kari's sketch, the drawing that led Ganneau to join the race for the Moabite Stone. The label captures many early European archaeologists' attitudes toward the people who lived in the lands they explored. In their memoirs, Arabs don't talk, they jabber. When a particular Arab is intelligent, this fact is pointed out as if greatly surprising. And the sticker I was now looking at did not say, "Made by Salim al Kari." Instead it said simply, "Made by an Arab."

I turned now to the larger of the two items and saw immediately that it was the squeeze copy of the Moabite Stone that Yaqoub Caravacca had made before a Bedouin stabbed him with a spear. His assistant, Jemil, had torn the copy paper from the face of the monument in several ragged pieces that were now encased in a black frame and covered in glass. The heavy-stock paper was the color of rice pudding. Rumpled and torn in the field, it had been carefully pieced back together by Ganneau—but a long gash still dipped diagonally from top left to bottom right. Elsewhere it bubbled like pizza. It was nearly impossible to make out letters, let alone words.

Although the stone was discovered in 1868, Alassi told me as he leaned over Jemil's squeeze, scholars still scrutinize this ravaged document for long-obscured secrets. In the mid-1990s, André Lemaire, a Sorbonne professor of paleography and epigraphy, took a new look at it with the aid of infrared technology. In doing so, he noticed something remarkable. A badly broken section of the stone that had long proved impossible to read but was now visible on the squeeze seemed to say "Beit David," or House of David. This reference to David's kingdom was a revelation, cutting to the heart of a controversy between biblical scholars, some of whom—known as minimalists—accept as historical fact only that portion of Israelite history that occurred after the sixth century BCE. Prior to that, they say, the historical evidence for the biblical account is too scant to be trusted. Their approach would exclude King David from the record; the Israelite monarch, said to have lived prior to the sixth century BCE, is not mentioned in sources other than the Bible itself. But if Lemaire's reading was correct, here was the Moabite Stone, all these years later, offering up evidence that the lute-playing, poetry-writing warrior king himself was not simply a figment of the Bible's imagination—he was a real man, whose existence was recorded for posterity by none other than Israel's Moabite enemies.

Years ago, the Louvre displayed the *estampage*—the French word Alassi used for the squeeze—beside the stone itself, as evidence of the extreme efforts required to obtain it. Encountering it in the Louvre's storeroom, I was reminded of Near Eastern archaeology's wild infancy—and how it compares with the relatively orderly and scientific pursuit of today. Surely there was something romantic about the early shoot-from-the-hip (sometimes literally) approach wherein brave and occasionally greedy men traversed deserts on horseback, did battle with spear-wielding Bedouin, grabbed what they could, and dashed for home.

Alassi led me to the Moabite Stone through a warren of hallways and stairwells accessed only with an electronic key card. I had, of course, known the pillar was marred, but it wasn't until I stood two feet away that I grasped just how badly—and what a feat of intelligence it had taken for Ganneau to decipher its inscription.

With a little imagination, it was possible to visualize what the piece had looked like when Klein found it lying face up in Dhiban. Now it was an ugly mash-up of different-colored stone—the smooth, dark portions marking what remained of the original, the gray bits Ganneau's attempt to fill in the blanks. I wanted to feel sad or disappointed at the decrepit state of this marvelous relic, the way I feel during the Oscars when once-virile actors shuffle onto the stage to receive their lifetime achievement awards. But I didn't. I felt more the way I do about other actors, the ones whose scars imbue their faces with character. The stone was amazing, but so was its backstory. That's why the Louvre had never fully repaired it, and had once displayed it alongside the roughed-up squeeze.

Alassi took my picture beside the stele, and it occurred to me that to see the best of Near Eastern antiquity, one must visit Europe. Standing before artifacts at the British Museum, the Pergamon in Berlin, the Louvre, one can sense the battles won and lost to obtain them. But what about Egypt? Syria? Iraq? Jordan? Israel? Today, laws limit the removal of archaeological treasures from the nations in which they are discovered. But the Rosetta Stone still draws thousands of visitors to London, the Ishtar Gate brings throngs to Berlin, and the Moabite Stone attracts people like me to Paris. I told Alassi what I was thinking and assumed that, as a Middle Easterner himself, he would concur. He sympathized, but not entirely.

"It is better to get your fish from a lake than a grocery store," he said. He gazed intently at the stone. "But look what happened to the stele of Mesha when they left it at the lake."

We stood in silence now before the famous monument. I knew what Alassi meant. Left to the locals, the stele had ended up in tatters. But I realized something else then, and it came to me like a cramp: if Klein had never found this stele, or if Ganneau had never extracted it from Dhiban—in short, if all its suitors had simply left the Moabite Stone at the lake—Moses Wilhelm Shapira might have lived to enjoy old age.

THE FOLLOWING MORNING I returned to the Louvre to meet Elisabeth Fontan, then the chief curator for the Department of Near Eastern Antiquities. Her office was crowded—she sat behind a desk layered in books, and the rest of the small space was strewn with binders, sketches of ancient artifacts, more books. We spoke of frauds (the Louvre, Fontan told me, has so many known fakes in its storerooms that executives have considered mounting an exhibition), about Ganneau (he lived with his mom), and about Shapira's pottery (the Louvre definitely never bought any).

Fontan consulted a number of books in which Ganneau's contemporaries presented their renditions of the Moabite Stone story, and translated for me as she went along. Several lines into one such volume—a 1912 catalog of the Louvre's holdings from Palestine—she reached a paragraph about the donation of additional fragments in 1891. After the stone's destruction by the Beni Hamide, Ganneau managed to collect the largest pieces. Segments obtained by Charles Warren were also brought to the Louvre. But the French did not initially get everything. Several tiny pieces ended up in the collection of Konstantin Schlottmann, Shapira's early champion in the Moabitica affair. In addition to his roles as theologian, professor, and secretary of the DMG, Schlottmann was also, I was learning, quite the fragment magnet. When he died, this report noted, his daughter had donated these stone chunks to the Louvre.

Up to that point, everything I'd learned about Schlottmann hinted that he was a lifelong bachelor who never had children. Now it turned out he had a daughter. If he had left her his Mesha scraps, it was plausible that he also had passed down the widow Shapira's two small manuscript fragments. Fontan read on, and the book gave the donor a name, Mademoiselle Anna Schlottmann. Per Schlottmann's wishes, Anna had donated the stele fragments to the Louvre through the auspices of the DMG, the German Oriental Society, of which her father had been a leading member.

This was a solid lead, a contemporary report making mention of a child. That Schlottmann had a daughter who inherited archaeological relics from his collection and handed them to the Louvre was more than intriguing. It seemed entirely possible that she would have sought a similarly suitable home for another set of famous fragments.

That afternoon I contacted the Martin Luther University of Halle-Wittenberg, Germany, where Schlottmann had taught before his death, and asked if I might visit to have a look at any documents they held relating to Konstantin or Anna Schlottmann. I sent the same note to the DMG. Then I headed out to the sixteenth arrondissement to find the grave of Shapira's daughter.

MYRIAM HARRY WAS buried at the Cimetière de Passy, a small, crowded graveyard in a chichi Right Bank neighborhood not far from the Champs-Élysées and the Trocadéro. Since its opening in 1820, Passy Cemetery has served as the final resting place for the cream of Paris society. Among other notables interred there are Claude Debussy, Édouard Manet, Marcel Renault, and Princess Leila of Iran. In the waiting room, just off a cemetery entrance designed by René Berger, I told a kindly older lady at the desk that Harry had died on March 10, 1958. She pulled out a burial log and quickly located the site—Harry, she said, had been buried in the family tomb of her husband, the sculptor Émile Perrault.

A wide, paved road ran through the center of the cemetery, but the graves were located, often haphazardly, off extremely narrow lanes. Some lay east to west, others north to south, and all were pressed close, like tenements. Because it was a see-and-be-seen cemetery, a large number of people sought burial there, and the proprietors, it appeared, had tried to accommodate them all. Approaching the Perrault family tomb, I stopped for a moment by a smooth black headstone on which a talented mason had emblazoned the image of the Concorde in flight beside a photograph of an attractive young woman, neatly attired in her airline uniform.

Harry was buried several yards down this cramped artery in the cemetery's most tightly packed section. Someone had visited recently: fresh flowers added a dash of color inside the concrete tomb's metal gate. Peering out from a ledge at the back was the white bust of a mustachioed man—Léon Perrault, Harry's painter father-in-law. Beside that was a small, framed photograph of another man, Monsieur Faouaz Perrault, Harry's adopted son. Years after she had left Jerusalem, Harry traveled widely throughout the Orient—writing books and magazine articles about her experiences. She published articles in respected dailies such as *Le Journal* and *Le Temps* and in the prestigious magazine *L'Illustration,* including one about the last harems of the Middle East. She was photographed tooling around in a little vehicle, built by her husband, which looked like the love child of a motorized rickshaw and a wheelchair. Like her father, she appeared to change costumes frequently, often appearing in Levantine garb.

On one such journey abroad, Harry adopted an orphan whose parents had been killed in Lebanon. Young Faouaz was living with his grandfather at the time, and the old man asked his famous visitor to take the boy with her. Faouaz was ten when he arrived in France, and he lived there until his death, in 2009, at the age of one hundred.

Cécile Chombard Gaudin, Harry's biographer, met Faouaz a decade before he died. He received her cordially and announced that he held a large archive of his mother's private material—including an unpublished novel. This was welcome news for the writer, although she had just begun her research and didn't have enough information during that first meeting, she told me, "to ask the good questions."

"Afterwards it was too late," she said. "He didn't want to talk anymore."

Indeed, as the years passed, Faouaz became increasingly reluctant to discuss his mother. Perhaps he was frustrated with frequent inquiries into his family's affairs. One relative believes it was something deeper. Not long ago, Gaudin traveled to Geneva to interview Faouaz's cousin. Harry, he told her, had been the cornerstone of Faouaz's career as a painter. She had marshaled her extensive group of contacts to commission artworks from her son, among them a series of hard-to-find portraits of Syrian officials. When she passed, he understood that his career was nothing.

"As Faouaz was not an artist of great success," Gaudin said, "I think when his mother died that suddenly the world was very small around him."

And so Faouaz took drastic action.

"He burned everything," Gaudin told me. "All the private archives are lost completely."

When Gaudin was about to publish her biography, she sent a copy to Faouaz, who asked that she remove details of the Shapira affair taken from nineteenth-century newspaper accounts. "It had been the drama of his mother's life, and he didn't want it published again," she recalled. She trimmed this section of the book and sent it off to the publisher. Shortly before its release, Faouaz dispatched his lawyer to quash the project.

"I could not understand it," Gaudin told me. "I showed him the

[book] manuscript before giving it to the publisher. He told me I understood very well who his mother was."

Gaudin's book was published in 2005. Faouaz died four years later and was buried in a vault with his mother. Neither one of their names appears on the tomb.

WHEN I RETURNED to the apartment that evening, an email was waiting from an archivist at the Martin Luther University of Halle-Wittenberg. She had a file pertaining to Schlottmann's time at the university and would be happy to let me see it. The next morning, I received a similar invitation from the German Oriental Society. If Schlottmann had kept Rosette's two small fragments, in all likelihood they would now be in one of these institutions.

8
GERMANY

I flew from Paris to Berlin and from there caught a train into Halle. When I arrived, the Maritim Hotel on Riebeckplatz was full of rugged-looking men with no necks and noses shaped like potatoes. Sidestepping my way from reception to the elevator, I dodged these men, their trainers, their girlfriends and wives, all of whom were in town for a boxing tournament I quickly gleaned would begin that very night. My journey through the German hinterlands had already made me feel a little short and acutely hirsute, and rubbing shoulders with these hairless he-men wasn't helping my self-esteem. I waited next to one and imagined myself ducking into the ring with him. My only hope would be my body—the wings of hair flapping on my shoulders and the corpse-white shade of my slack midsection. Perhaps when I removed my shirt, my opponent would simply become so upset that he'd forfeit. Needless to say, I was relieved to be heading out to the archives at Martin Luther University of Halle-Wittenberg, where I expected to encounter more of my own people—bearded, bespectacled, atrophied.

Halle is better known as the birthplace of George Frideric Handel than as Konstantin and Anna Schlottmann's home—or the possible repository for the two small fragments Rosette Shapira had sent to Schlottmann in 1884. Still, Schlottmann's daughter, Anna, had given the Louvre several pieces of the Moabite Stone from her father's collection, and I suspected she might have done something similar with Rosette's segments.

The university's archives are located in a four-story stucco building with graffiti on the outer walls and bars covering the first-floor windows. It was a quick walk from the hotel full of boxers, but halfway through it had started to rain and, poorly equipped, I arrived dripping.

Dr. Michael Ruprecht, the archive's manager, saw me in. A welldressed man who looked like Ralph Fiennes, Ruprecht directed me to the restroom to dry off before we headed upstairs to the archive's book-lined reading room. Another archivist had already pulled Schlottmann's file from the 3,500 linear meters of documents stored at the institute, and after asking that I fill out a number of forms, Ruprecht retreated to his office.

The file was much smaller than I had anticipated. It did not, as I had hoped, contain any of Schlottmann's personal papers, but, rather, documents pertaining to his employment at the university. The briefest glance made clear that it held no portion of the scrolls. I had come a long way, and this swift failure was a disappointment. But the folder did contain a number of letters relating to Schlottmann's relationship with Anna—who was not his daughter, I learned, but his sister. In Schlottmann's day, Ruprecht explained when I went back downstairs, family members typically trashed dead relatives' papers. But later, searching through an old issue of *Zeitschrift der Deutschen Morgenländischen Gesellschaft*, the DMG's journal, I discovered that Anna Schlottmann had made gifts to the DMG beyond the Moabite Stone pieces. The article did not specify what those gifts were, but if she had inherited Rosette's fragments, she could have given them to her brother's organization.

I immediately checked with the DMG's library to see whether its records included any mention of gifts from Anna Schlottmann. They did not. I checked again with Ruprecht, who agreed to search his archive for all files relating to the DMG, but he found nothing.

"We have again researched intensively in the stock of DMG," he said, "unfortunately, without success."

Rosette's fragments were not in Halle. I made a mental note to do better preparatory work the next time I decided to travel to Bumblefuck, Germany, in a rainstorm.

SIX MONTHS LATER, while helping me translate some letters Rosette had written to the executors of her husband's estate, a former graduate student at San Francisco State named Allan Webb stumbled on a recent article in a small German newspaper about a woman who had curated a local exhibition on the life of Myriam Harry. When Webb told me what he'd found, it immediately struck me as odd. Though Harry was an integral player in her father's story and once was a writer of some note, she is (Gaudin's biography notwithstanding) a largely forgotten literary figure. The most recent edition of one of her novels was released by a publisher specializing in hard-to-find books. Who, exactly, was putting on a museum show chronicling her life? Webb sent over a copy of the article, but translated only the headline:

ANNETTE SCHWARZ-SCHEULS INTRODUCES MYRIAM HARRY—JEWISH AUTHOR WITH ROOTS IN STOCKHAUSEN AND LAUTERBACH

Schwarz-Scheuls, it turned out, was interested in Harry because the two were cousins. The reporter makes several errors in his story but, significantly, closes the piece with a short account of the Shapira story, indicating that, though Harry was its primary subject, Shapira had featured in the exhibit.

Schwarz-Scheuls, I realized immediately, was my own fifth clue.

From the beginning, it had seemed plausible that the scrolls, or some portion of them, had ended up with a relative of Shapira, but until now I had been unable to locate any. Now here was word that not only did family still exist, but they remained in rural Germany. As significant, one of them had taken an interest in Shapira. Could a relative have bought the scrolls from Quaritch to ensure they remained in the family? Or maybe—and this seemed even more likely—Schlottmann had returned the two fragments to Rosette, who held on to them until her death in Stockhausen in 1904. From there, it was easy to imagine that they had been passed down among kin, all the way to the family's resident Myriam Harry expert, Annette Schwarz-Scheuls. I needed to see her.

A quick search produced her phone number in Schlitz, a small town in eastern Hesse, and Webb offered to make the call in case Schwarz-Scheuls didn't speak English. He reached her that night. She was very friendly, he told me, and seemed happy to meet. She gave Webb her email address, and I wrote to her.

Then I waited a week to hear back. All the while I worried that Sabo had approached her to suggest that she not cooperate with me. But when Schwarz-Scheuls at last responded, she was apologetic. She worked arduous hours at a home for the disabled, and in the past few days a family member's health had deteriorated. She was extremely busy and under a lot of pressure, but she could make some time for me. She even recommended a small pension around the corner from her house.

SCHLITZ IS NAMED for its river but is better known for the romantic castles that ring the hill at its center, shoring up the quaint cottage vibe that gives it the feel of a giant B&B. The town looks exactly as someone might imagine Germany if their only impression of the place came from fairy tales. The cobblestone streets are narrow and coiled, lined on each side by immaculate half-timber homes, biblical tableaux carved in their ancient frames to confer luck on the families living within. The growling pipes of a church organ can be felt from blocks away, choir voices wafting ethereally up the building's stone turret, which leans like the tower of Pisa.

Outside the church, consecrated in 812 by Archbishop Richolf of Mainz, the severed head of a rebellious Schlitzman is said to be buried beside his corpse, secreted home in a trunk labeled DISHES after a financial scandal in Scandinavia lured the ax to his neck. At Christmas, the Hinterturm, an enormous fourteenth-century castle remnant, is draped in red fabric and topped by an electric "wick," creating, I'm told, the largest non-wax candle in the world. (The closest competitor, apparently, is in Easton, Pennsylvania.) At one of the castles, a large clock breaks into song each day at two and five. And in a building nearby, craftsmen at Germany's oldest distillery produce schnapps and whiskey—bottled courage for a winter's day as cold as the one on which I chose to visit.

There once were Jews in Schlitz—Aaron Stein, the innkeeper; Julius Wintmüller, the textile dealer; Bacharach, who sold horses and cows. But, until I showed up, that was no longer the case. Just outside town, though, on farmland where horses still graze, there is a Jewish cemetery, and Schwarz-Scheuls drove me there as part of a tour that quickly morphed into a lesson on Schlitz's Jewish history. There was a layer of frost on the ground when we arrived at the graveyard, and a number of sturdy horses stood nearby breathing steam. The small cemetery—it can't have held more than a hundred headstones—opened in 1899, and its final grave, Stein's, was dug in 1938. After that, no Jews remained to be buried.

That same year, Schwarz-Scheuls told me, Wintmüller sold the building that had served as Schlitz's synagogue and, before hurrying out of town, used the proceeds to build a fence around the graveyard. Schwarz-Scheuls is not herself Jewish, though she suspects there might be some Hebrew blood in her veins. She has spent years study-ing the town's Jewish history, learning a bit of Hebrew along the way, and hopes one day to install stone plaques in front of homes like Wintmüller's, where Jewish families made lives before the Nazis snuffed them out.

Her house was built in 1780, and later that day, after warming up with tea and pastries, we descended the steep staircase from the top-floor kitchen to a small room where she keeps the collection that formed the core of her Myriam Harry exhibit. Schwarz-Scheuls pointed to family photos lining the steps and began to map out her relationship to the Shapiras. Her great-grandmother was Rosette's sister. This, she told me, made her a fourth cousin to Harry.

"Ever since I was a little child, my grandma and her sister talked about the family, and they let me look at little pictures from Jerusa-lem and little albums of olive wood," she said in her thickly accented English. "And they told me the story of *The Little Daughter of Jeru-salem*."

Tales of her relatives' lives in faraway Palestine roused her imag-ination, and over the years she amassed a large collection of memo-rabilia to go along with a vibrant oral tradition, passed down among family members eager to tell of the misfortune that had befallen their ancestors.

She led me into the room now and began to show me around. We spent much of the next two days together, and the entire time Schwarz-Scheuls—always polite, always accommodating, always sweet—seemed a little nervous to have me there: concerned that my long haul to her doorstep would not prove worthwhile, apologetic for her English, and, I sensed, wary of my motives. This was her family, and I had parachuted in to get their story—a story she had spent years gathering and organizing and cherishing. Now, she told me, she was at work on a book of her own, and she worried that offering up items or information might later deprive her of proprietary rights.

She wasn't wrong to be cautious. I did want to know how the family viewed the Shapira scandal and to experience the town Rosette had retreated to once Shapira died. But really I had come to see whether Rosette ever got her two small fragments back and, if so, were they still here?

Schwarz-Scheuls was a bright woman and had a strong sense of ownership over her research on Myriam Harry. The room where she stored her collection was filled with carefully arranged mementos. Photographs of Harry. Magazines in which her articles had appeared. Postcards. Letters. Panels with descriptive material that Schwarz-Scheuls had written for her exhibition. And there were multiple copies of Harry's novels in a variety of languages—books, Schwarz-Scheuls told me, in which spot-on characterizations have allowed her to match family members with their fictional counterparts: *The Little Daughter of Jerusalem, La Petite Fille de Jérusalem, La Muchachita de Jerusalén*. All the while she was vigilant about what she would allow me to photograph.

For the next two hours we rummaged through the collection, accumulated over years from relatives, antiquarian book dealers, and the Internet. After hauling out a large number of these curios, Schwarz-Scheuls opened a cabinet by the wall and removed a small book with a cover made of polished olive wood.

"This," she said, handing it to me, "was made by Mr. Shapira. It's from the shop. Shapira wrote the lines for Rosette."

The "lines" were a hand-calligraphed verse from the Song of Songs, inscribed along the book's outer edges: *Ani havazelet haSharon, shoshanat ha'amakim.* "I am a rose of Sharon, a lily of the valleys." The floral reference to Rosette was clear. The biblical verse continues, "As a lily among thorns, so is my love among the daughters." Rosette, Schwarz-Scheuls told me, had kept little postcards inside, which she sent to her daughters in Berlin and Paris on their birthdays.

I had by then read a great deal of material written by Shapira, almost all of it to do with his business affairs. I had handled a large amount of his merchandise. But this booklet with its inscription, fashioned with skills learned as a new immigrant in Jerusalem's House of Industry—this was personal, a handmade gift to a woman from a guy in love. So often it is the little things that bring home the sadness of a death, the tragedy of a departure. The dead man's toothbrush, still damp from the final brushing. The deceased woman's slippers, still set neatly by her bedside. When Rosette sent those postcards to her daughters, it was as if they were, in some small way, also from their dead father. Suddenly the tragedy of Shapira's death came at me with force. Until now he had been "Shapira"— antiquities dealer, controversial figure, subject. As I held this sweet gesture in my hand he became, abruptly, jarringly, Moses.

"Can I take a photo of this?" I asked.

"But only for you," she said. "Not for the book."

This seemed fair. I liked the idea of taking a photo of something so meaningful for no reason other than its meaning. And if it was evocative for me, certainly it held great value for my host. Much of what Schwarz-Scheuls knew of Shapira and Rosette had come down from her great-aunt, Charlotte Weinberger, herself a nurse and deaconess who had played the role of family genealogist—drafting a family tree, curating stories, collecting keepsakes, visiting Israel on a de facto fact-finding mission. Lotte herself never met Shapira, his wife, or either of their daughters. But Rosette told Lotte's sister stories about life in Jerusalem—stories she later told to Lotte, who passed them on to Schwarz-Scheuls. Where newspapers of the day condemned Shapira as a villain or a dupe, these family stories emphasized the injustice that had been perpetrated on their innocent forebear—and its disastrous aftermath.

"My great-grandpa said [Shapira] was right," Schwarz-Scheuls told me now, returning the olive-wood booklet to its shelf and gently closing the cabinet door. "The journalists and the people around him killed him in a very simple way."

This, then, was how the story had come down to her: Shapira had been condemned by unscrupulous reporters and trigger-happy scholars whose premature accusations of fraud led to his death. As a result, Rosette and Myriam were forced to leave behind their lives in Jerusalem, so promising when Shapira had departed for Europe, and set sail for Germany, where Augusta was already in school. Once well-off, the family sank swiftly into poverty. Myriam had always found the Hesse region altogether boring—a sleepy backwoods nowhere near so lively (or, to be fair, filthy) as Jerusalem. On their return to Germany, she joined her sister in Berlin, where she was enrolled in a boarding school. Eventually she made her way to Paris and became a literary star. I would later learn that Augusta, too, ended up in Paris, where she worked as a teacher. But Rosette—widowed, miserable, and stuck on her husband's innocence—never remarried, living out her days at the large family home in Stockhausen, about twelve miles from where I was standing.

"They never forgot Shapira," Schwarz-Scheuls told me. "Lotte Weinberger said to me that they are proud about Shapira. He was a tragic figure—but they said he wasn't false with the scrolls. Excuse my English."

"And you?" I asked. "What do you think?"

"When you go in a museum and want to talk about Shapira, they say to you, 'What? You talk about false things,'" she said. She was referring here to an exhibition mounted by Jerusalem's Israel Museum, called "Truly Fake: Moses Wilhelm Shapira, Master Forger." "He's a part of my family, and I saw it a little bit differently and I can't be neutral. I'm on the side of the family. And so I think it's sometimes false to say he is 'master forger.' They didn't really know the whole story. They only see parts like—like blind people. . . . And so I think it's not right in my eyes. It's only a personal opinion, a very personal opinion, that he is 'master forger.' It is not true in my eyes. It is false. You understand this?"

I did understand. I'd spent the past three years searching for her relative's scrolls in hopes she was right. The reporter in me should have pressed Schwarz-Scheuls further—did she take Shapira's side strictly because they were related? What about all the red flags? Did she have evidence? Two small leather fragments, maybe?

But I couldn't. She seemed vulnerable just then—genuinely sad. More than a century on, Shapira's family still had not gotten over his death. Like her great-aunt Charlotte's stories about Shapira's life, sorrow at his death had been passed between generations.

That afternoon, Schwarz-Scheuls invited me out to her parents' place in Stockhausen. This was the opportunity I had been hoping for. Her parents now occupied the house where Rosette had lived following Shapira's death. If Schlottmann had returned the fragments to her, it seemed likely that this was where they would now be located.

We set a time to meet the following morning, and I returned to my room at the nearby Gasthof & Pension Lenk. I seemed to be the only overnight guest—but when I headed downstairs, the bar was packed. Local men with hacking coughs swilled beers between hearty drags on their cigarettes. Smoking seemed to be required here, and these men were good at it. I sat down next to a guy with Jeffrey Dahmer glasses and a fly open wide as the Hessian plains. The ash at the end of his cigarette was as long as his finger. I ordered a beer from the owner's ponytailed son, and another man at the bar stopped me.

"You must drink only beer from Schlitz!" he said.

He recommended one, and I nodded my assent to the bartender. The man introduced himself as Hans Peter Sauerwein—reporter on the local newspaper. When I told him why I was in town, he handed me his business card.

"Write to me when you are finished and I will make a story in the newspaper," he said.

We chatted a little while longer and then, in an effort to escape the thickening cloud, I repaired to my room. I woke early the following morning, had breakfast, and, just before nine, left to meet Schwarz-Scheuls. We scraped ice off the inside of her windshield before making the twenty-minute drive through beautiful, frozen pastureland. Schwarz-Scheuls had slept poorly the previous night. All the talk of Shapira, she told me, had worked her up.

"It's so personal for me," she said, her voice climbing half an octave. "I cannot be neutral about it."

By the time we arrived in Stockhausen, the sun was out and the air had warmed. Schwarz-Scheuls's childhood home—the house in which Rosette had died—was very large. A century earlier it had served as a pub and the town post office. Now her parents, Karin and Erich, lived there, and they welcomed me into their comfortable living room, where they poured mimosas in champagne flutes and toasted my arrival. Several painted landscapes hung above fringed beige sofas. An ornate wooden armoire sat in one corner, and dominating the opposite wall was an enormous family tree tracing their clan back to the 1630s. In the next room, a gleaming teakettle sat atop a 1930s-era wood-burning stove, neatly chopped logs stacked expertly beside it.

We chatted for quite a while about Rosette and Shapira and Harry, Schwarz-Scheuls serving as interpreter. They were lovely people—both of them smiling and urging me to drink more champagne. I was thrilled to be in this house, and I asked if they knew which room Rosette had occupied. They did—it was upstairs.

"May I see it?" I asked.

Schwarz-Scheuls murmured something in German, and her mother smiled shyly as she responded in kind.

"She did not have time to clean it properly before you have come, so it's not possible now," Schwarz-Scheuls said.

I didn't press the matter. I just figured that the longer I stuck around, the more comfortable they would become with me. Maybe, ultimately, they'd let me poke around. Erich invited me out into the yard to show me the original water pump. Visible across the street was another castle, occupied today by a home for the disabled. Down a brick path, Erich pulled aside some shrubs that were growing over a relative's headstone, which they'd removed from the cemetery when their lease on the grave was up. In Germany, Schwarz-Scheuls told me, as in Holland, burial plots are rented temporarily. When the allotted time is done a new body is buried on another level in the same plot. Sometimes the contents of the grave are emptied as well.

"Is Rosette buried in that cemetery?" I asked.

"Yes," Schwarz-Scheuls said. "She is."

I followed her up some stairs, past an old redbrick church and through a gate into the quiet town graveyard. The ground was dusted with ice, crunchy beneath our feet. Stepping carefully through terraced burial plots, we descended to the bottom, where Schwarz-Scheuls gestured to a stretch of grass and said, "Here is where Rosette is."

I looked around. There were no headstones here.

"Where, exactly?" I asked.

Schwarz-Scheuls traced a rectangle in the air. "Near this place."

She headed back toward the gate, but I lingered a moment. Standing by Rosette's grave, I thought about how unendingly sad her final years must have been. She believed the scrolls were real; her husband's death, therefore, had been not only unfair but avoidable. The more I learned about Shapira, the more convinced I was becoming that she was right. I wondered whether his scrolls could have been something like the Samaritan Pentateuch. An ancient sect, the Samaritans adhere to their own special version of the Torah in which various episodes and details from the traditional text are repeated in new locations, language is borrowed from elsewhere in the Torah to create a new Tenth Commandment, and select words are replaced with synonyms. Shapira's Deuteronomy did all of these things. Had his scrolls, far from being forgeries, been like the Samaritan Pentateuch—ancient, but not quite as ancient as the eighth century BCE?

This, along with a number of other bread crumbs I had picked up along the way, led me to believe that at the very least, Shapira's scrolls had been too hastily dismissed, debunked in a callow rush to judgment. Rosette must have considered this, felt it deeply, every lonely day of her life—from the moment she arrived, newly widowed, in Stockhausen to the day she died and was buried here, in the grave beneath my feet.

As Schwarz-Scheuls and I headed back to the house, I decided it was time to broach the topic I'd been avoiding until now. "You know, you were saying earlier that you think Shapira's scrolls were authentic," I began. "But the only way to know for sure would be to find them."

"Yes," she said. "The scrolls are lost. Mr. Quaritch bought them from the British Museum and . . . later the house of [Sir Charles Nicholson] burned down, and so they are lost."

"Maybe," I said. "But, you know, it's interesting. Because everyone thinks that this guy Nicholson bought the scrolls from Quaritch and that Nicholson's house burned down. But I don't think Nicholson actually bought them from Quaritch. Maybe they still exist somewhere."

"Maybe they exist," Schwarz-Scheuls said, laughing a little.

"One of the possibilities is, of course, that they stayed in the family. After Shapira died, apparently Rosette wrote a letter to a scholar in Germany named Konstantin Schlottmann. She said, 'I'm sending you two little pieces of the manuscript to examine.' So it's possible that these two little pieces still exist—wherever the material from Schlottmann is, or maybe, you know, one thought was that it's still in your family. That someone has a box in an attic somewhere."

"But the house where Rosette lived burned down," Schwarz-Scheuls said. "Half the village did, in rapid time."

I was under the impression that the house I'd just visited was the one Rosette had moved into after Shapira's death. That was, in large measure, why I had been so eager to visit.

"The village burned down?"

"A half part. And so it was—"

"Stockhausen?" I asked.

"Yes. So it was impossible to save many things from the house."

"How'd it burn down? Do you know?"

The fire had begun in a bakery around the corner. Billowed by a country wind, the blaze spread quickly—first to a neighbor's house, next to Rosette's. Eventually half the village was consumed. The house in which Karin and Erich had just served mimosas was not the original family home. It was the replacement house August

Weinberger had built after the fire. If Rosette ever had the scroll fragments, they were lost in the conflagration.

"When was the fire?" I asked.

"Eighteen ninety-nine."

"Eighteen ninety-nine?"

"Yes. Eighteen ninety-nine."

This was remarkable: 1899 was the very year in which fire had destroyed the home of Sir Charles Nicholson—the fire most people believed had consumed the scrolls themselves. That was not true. But now I was learning that another fire that very same year might, in fact, have consumed their last remnants.

"Okay," Schwarz-Scheuls said when, incredulous, I mentioned the coincidence. "Like a miracle. Like a miracle."

For me it was the opposite of a miracle. I had hoped to trump the challenge of finding the much-searched-for scrolls by tracking down those remaining bits. Now I knew they were gone—tossed by Schlottmann's descendants or consumed by fire—and still I had no better sense of what had happened to the rest of the manuscript after Quaritch bought it in 1885. I could feel myself ceding more ground to Sabo. Three years in and my search had fallen apart.

FOR SEVERAL WEEKS after I returned home from Germany, I licked my wounds. My search was at a standstill and, depressed, I did not know what to do next. I'd stomped around Israel, Jordan, England, France, Germany, the Netherlands—and hadn't found a trace of the scrolls. At that moment, lying on my couch eating Fruity Pebbles from a salad bowl on my chest, I felt envious of Sabo, whose confidence seemed only to have grown with each passing year. Why couldn't I be more like him?

But I was not yet ready to give up. Rosette's fragments were gone, but I still believed the scrolls were out there somewhere. I'd been able to show that they hadn't burned in England, and so it stood to reason that they still existed. But where?

Getting up from the couch and dusting off the cereal crumbs, I began combing through all the material I had amassed over the previous couple of years in hopes I might happen upon yet another new angle. Over the following months, I reread everything from 41294, the press clippings from 1883, a book by Ganneau on archaeological frauds. I read books on the Dead Sea Scrolls, Rosette's correspondence after Shapira died, *The Little Daughter of Jerusalem*. I read through all the notebooks I'd filled during my travels, trying to parse my scrawl, making notes on my notes. I contacted many of the people I had met along the way to press them again for details, insights, conjecture. But there was nothing new.

Then, on September 13, 2013, the eve of Yom Kippur, the holiest day on the Jewish calendar, I received an unexpected email that would break my search wide open.

It was late in the afternoon and I was on my way out the door for the Kol Nidre service when I heard my computer ping.

Would you know when your book . . . is due for release?

> Regards,
> Matthew Hamilton
> Sydney, Australia

My first thought on reading the email was to wonder how a man from Australia had gotten wind of my project. Then I remembered that someone had recently appended a few sentences about me to the Wikipedia entry on Shapira. I clicked out and headed to the synagogue.

But as I struggled up the palm-lined hill along Dolores Street, I couldn't push Hamilton's note from my mind. I suppose I was flattered that someone so far away was already interested in my book—of which I had at that point written exactly zero pages. But why did he care about the release date? Was he so eager to read it? Or—and this is the thought that spurred my heart rate and led me to pull my iPhone from my tallis bag—was he, too, looking for the scrolls?

I thumbed out a quick reply, letting Hamilton know that there was, as yet, no publication date and inquiring why he wanted to know. Then I shut off the phone and headed inside. Kol Nidre, to my mind, is the most beautiful piece of Jewish liturgical music. The haunting melody puts one in the mind of something ineffably sacred. The text, however, is decidedly prosaic—an Aramaic legal formula prophylactically annulling as-yet-unuttered personal vows. I have often wondered if Perry Como and Johnny Mathis knew this when they recorded their own versions. But that night, while music transported those around me to a plain on high, my mind was moored firmly down under.

I elbowed my way out of my row, apologizing as I drew each person I passed momentarily from reverie. On the sidewalk, I removed my yarmulke so passersby wouldn't judge me for fussing with my phone when I should have been inside praying. At the very top of my inbox was another note from Hamilton.

Hello Chanan,

Researching early biblical MSS over the past 25+ years and in particular early OT [Old Testament] MSS I've always been aware of the Shapira MS but like most people accepted the hypothesis of A. D. Crown that the MS was destroyed in the fire at Sir Charles Nicholson's home. In late 2011 I was fortunate to find a reference showing who actually purchased the MS—and it is definitely not Nicholson nor anybody else who has been considered over the years . . . which explains why nobody has yet found the MS. I'm not yet ready to broadcast the person's name as I'm expecting to finish a short paper on Crown's hypothesis in the next few months.

My interest in your book is to see if in it you had succeeded in finding out what became of the MS after the purchaser died.

Regards,

Matthew

Over the past three years, I had searched ceaselessly for these scroll fragments. I had logged endless miles on treks through Europe, the Middle East, and North America. I had conducted hours of interviews; read and reread dozens more books, essays, and articles; examined hundreds of manuscripts in a long litany of libraries and archives. I had engaged translators and transcribers. Sought out archaeologists and epigraphers. Hunted down rabbis, conservators, and antiquities dealers. I had thought and talked and pried and dug. And yet, to that point, I had succeeded only in ruling out a series of theories as to the scrolls' whereabouts. I had not been able to significantly advance the ball down the field. But here now, on the holiest night of the year, this: Matthew Hamilton knew what happened to the scrolls after they were last seen in the late 1880s—and, as I suspected, they hadn't burned at Nicholson's estate.

I sent him another email.

Hello Matthew. Thanks for your very interesting note. It sounds like you'd have much to talk about with my father, Jeffrey Tigay, an Old Testament scholar who recently retired from the University of Pennsylvania.

I'd love to talk with you. My book will be coming out long after your article (earliest possible publication is 2015), so certainly anything we discussed would not be broadcast before you publish! I have already concluded that Crown's hypothesis was incorrect, for a variety of reasons—and your note reinforces my suspicions.

Would you be willing to talk with me on condition that I don't publish anything at all that you tell me until your article has already been published? This would allow you to be the first to publish your new information and hypothesis, and would let me forge ahead, quietly, in my research.

Happy to be in touch.

All best,

Chanan

I didn't immediately return to services. Instead I paced. I refreshed my email. Then I refreshed it again. And again. Eventually I switched the phone to vibrate and went back inside, but I didn't hear from Hamilton that night, or the following day. Or the day after that. I went about my business, tried to put it all out of mind. I taught my classes, walked my dog, shared meals with my wife. But not a moment passed during which some portion of my consciousness wasn't circling around one of two questions: Is Matthew Hamilton going to write back? And that query's corollary: If not, why not? I could think of about a hundred reasons, ranging from the mundane to the insane.

That weekend I flew to Los Angeles to watch my nieces perform in *Mulan*. I'd brought some student work to read during the flight but couldn't get past the first line of the first paper. I read it over and over, comprehending nothing—my mind flitting constantly to Australia. There were many reasons for Hamilton not to respond, but increasingly my thoughts turned conspiratorial. On the ride from the airport to Veterans Memorial Auditorium in Culver City, I decided to stop waiting and shot off a brief and polite follow-up. Then, again, I waited.

At the intermission, I checked my email. Nothing.

I had trouble sleeping that night. When at last I did nod off, it was only half an hour before I woke up in a panic and checked my phone. Hamilton had written back.

> Hello Chanan,
>
> I will get back to you shortly and I assume I will be sharing the name of the buyer of the Shapira MS with you. Just need to check with one person first.
>
> Regards,
> Matthew

I could have focused on the part where he said he'd probably give me the information I was seeking. Instead I began obsessing over the second sentence, the one where, I suspected, he was cryptically acknowledging having promised the information to someone else. My thoughts immediately went to Yoram Sabo. If he now had Hamilton's information, he would be that much further ahead of me—that much closer to the scrolls.

I waited an excruciating ten days to hear back and when at last I did, the news wasn't good.

> Hello Chanan,
>
> There is much information I can share with you, but the only person [with whom] I have shared the name of the buyer of the MS from Quaritch—they have asked that I keep that under wraps until 2014.

I responded immediately, gently pressing Hamilton to reconsider, but he didn't reply. I wrote again a week later, then two weeks after that, but this note was the last I heard from Matthew Hamilton. Once he'd refused to tell me the buyer's name, he summarily cut off all contact. I had no idea why. I wrote again as the days and weeks dragged on, but he held firm in his silence. The whole thing was extremely odd and upsetting. To begin with, *he* had contacted *me*. Then, having dropped this tantalizing bombshell, he had broken off communication.

Some days I told myself that he was probably just a wing nut who never had any real information to begin with, the kind of guy who got off on issuing grandiose statements and being pursued by whoever had the misfortune of believing him. Other days I imagined he had simply decided to keep the find for himself—for his own book, maybe, or an exhibition. But all the while I suspected that something darker was afoot: I was sure it was Sabo who had gotten to Hamilton. For some time I had considered Sabo to be my Ganneau. When we had first met, he was friendly and genuinely enthused to meet a fellow traveler. The problem, it soon became clear, was that he and I were racing to find the same thing. And so, after a brief flirtation with cooperation, he, like Hamilton after him, had cut me off. I didn't like it, but I understood Sabo's reluctance to share—we were rivals. I was an upstart horning in on the prize he'd been after for thirty years.

While catastrophizing, I recalled that in one of Hamilton's early emails he mentioned having discovered the reference to the scrolls' purchaser late in 2011. It occurred to me that if I could determine what subject he had been researching at the time, I could work backward to identify the materials he would have been looking at. Once I had those, it would simply be a matter of reading them myself until I spotted the Name. Like searching for Rosette's two small fragments, pursuing this angle would allow me to bypass Hamilton himself and get right to the heart of the issue.

I scoured the online chat rooms in which he occasionally posted but found nothing. Next I looked into securing library records, hoping to identify books he'd been reading. This, it turned out, would have been illegal. So I searched for contact information—a home address or phone number. When that, too, proved futile, I began combing Australian obituaries. Maybe he wasn't writing back for the most dire reason of all: he was dead. But his name didn't appear in the papers. Aside from his email account, the man seemed to live off the grid.

My options were being steadily whittled down. Finally, only one remained: a Hail Mary, a shot in the dark, a wing and a prayer—a flight to Australia to find Matthew Hamilton.

If I managed to locate him there and convince him to share his information, I could return to auction catalogs, bills of lading, genealogical records, museum accession logs, receipts, correspondence, newspapers, email, and even the telephone to trace them to their present-day owners.

But if he refused, my search was emphatically over. Hamilton, I suspected, had already divulged the Name to Sabo. If Sabo had it and I didn't, I would never catch him. Here was the problem: even if I managed to find Hamilton's house, the idea of showing up unannounced—"doorstepping" him, in journalism argot—disturbed me. I had once heard doorstepping described as something "nasty journalists do when they want to speak to someone who doesn't want to speak to them." I didn't think of myself as a nasty journalist—and I had no idea how Hamilton would react to my sudden appearance. Certainly he'd be surprised. He'd probably be upset; I would be if our roles were reversed. There was a good chance he'd yell, or at least tell me to leave. And what if he was some kind of nervous homesteader? Or a gun enthusiast who'd greet me with some ghastly high-capacity rifle tipped by a shiny bayonet?

One evening, after another day of failed Internet searches, I took my dog out for a walk. We passed the private medical center that had once been a hardware store and the upscale kids' clothing shop that was once a dry cleaner. As the dog sniffed at the door of the cosmetic dentistry center that had displaced a video store, I had a thought: *The Insider.* A couple of years earlier, the journalist Lowell Bergman had awarded me a fellowship at the IRP, the investigative reporting outfit he runs out of the University of California, Berkeley. *The Insider* tells the story of Bergman—immortalized in the film by Al Pacino—and his efforts to unmask the Machiavellian evils of Big Tobacco. In it, I now recalled, he doorstepped a recalcitrant source. I remembered the scene, which took place outside in the pouring rain, as particularly compelling. I tugged the dog from her sniffing and jogged to the only remaining video store in the neighborhood, perhaps the world. I grabbed a bag of the free popcorn and a copy of the movie, and though later that evening I was captivated by the film, I didn't pick up any doorstepping pointers. So I decided to check in with the man himself.

Bergman had always been smart, levelheaded, and generous. When we met at his office in Berkeley later that week, I explained the situation and told him I was thinking of heading off to Australia.

"What's your plan?" he asked.

It was a good question, and a deceptively tough one. The kind of straightforward query Bergman wielded on camera as he backed overmatched interlocutors into tight corners. Now I was sitting in the corner. Because going to Australia *was* my plan. I just figured it'd be easier to find Hamilton if I was already there. Bergman was unimpressed. He'd seen too many young (and not so young) reporters head down that road—blowing large sums of cash and time on ill-planned excursions that led nowhere. Kicking back in his modest second-floor office above the *Daily Californian,* he crossed his legs and made several recommendations. Among them, he offered the name of a private detective in Australia with whom he'd worked in the past. Maybe he could help. As I left, Bergman issued one final admonition: once I did find an address, he said, I needed to approach Hamilton before he got inside.

"That way," he said, "there's no door for him to slam in your face."

As soon as I left Bergman's office, I contacted the Australian detective. A few weeks later, his colleague sent over a sixty-seven-page report. What I'd wanted was a phone number—in hopes a call would suffice, precluding the need for a two-thousand-dollar flight to Sydney and an uncomfortable face-to-face encounter. Instead the report included an old email address, a list of more than three hundred Australians named Matthew Hamilton, a paper in which a Dead Sea Scrolls scholar had thanked Hamilton in a footnote, and a couple of old blog posts in which someone named Matthew Hamilton had commented on something to do with the New Testament.

But beyond that? Nothing.

Well, not quite nothing. There was also a home address that the investigator said looked promising. The house was located in a marginal neighborhood thirty miles outside Sydney and was owned by a couple, Gary Matthew Hamilton and Toni Maree Hamilton. It seemed a long shot, but the PI thought she'd linked Hamilton's email address to someone living in that house.

If news reports were to be believed, privacy was dying or dead. Why, then, couldn't we raise a phone number for this guy? His age? And, of course, the most important question of all: did Hamilton, in fact, have the information he claimed to have?

On May 23, 2014, I boarded Delta flight 417 for the grueling nonstop from Los Angeles to Sydney. I had checked my luggage an hour earlier and was now carrying nothing but the detective's report, pressed tight between my elbow and side. At that moment the file felt like the most important object I had ever held. I was edgy, to say the least—and, considering the fifteen-hour flight staring me in the face, the garlic breath curling in from the guy in 30E was alarming.

More alarming still was the fact that I was about to embark on a 7,500-mile trip and didn't know if Hamilton was alive. And if he hadn't died in the past eight months, one more thing was abundantly clear: he did not want to talk to me.

I was on my way to Australia to change his mind. My hastily sketched plan involved renting a car, parking it near the address the investigator had given me, and waiting for Hamilton to emerge. Not quite SEAL Team Six. But beyond my dislike for confrontation, there were difficulties: For one, I did not know if Hamilton actually lived at this address. If he did, I had no idea if he would be in town when I was. I didn't know what he looked like, and I had no phone number to call in case no one entered or exited the house. And if I never managed to meet him, he could easily continue ignoring my emails. There was a very good chance that my plan, such as it was, would end in failure. And not spectacular failure—Bay of Pigs failure, O.J.-trying-on-the-glove failure, Geraldo-opening-Capone's-vault failure. In short, not the kind of failure that makes for great reading. More likely was the fizz-pop kind of failure where I fly all the way to Australia and simply don't find the guy I'm looking for. This would, once again, put an end to my search for Shapira's scrolls.

I slipped the report into the seat pocket, then immediately took it back into my lap. I buckled my seat belt. The woman behind me was coughing incessantly. I was suddenly grateful to be seated next to the guy with the garlic breath.

I intended to spend the flight combing the dossier's pages for clues the way scholars like Ginsburg close-read the scriptures— some tiny connection I'd missed, some name that had escaped my notice, some footnote that, on the tenth reading, illuminated some new idea.

As flight attendants rushed up and down the aisles instructing passengers to straighten their seats and turn off their cell phones, and as the woman behind me struggled to keep her lungs in her chest, I opened the file. A squat tractor backed the plane away from the gate. We began the short taxi toward the runway, and I reread a brief reference that previously had seemed insignificant and out of date. I'd seen it a dozen times already, but now its meaning became clear. Some years earlier, the report noted, Hamilton had been employed by the Moore Theological College, a small Anglican school near Sydney.

Just like that, I had a plan.

"We're first in line for departure," the captain announced over the intercom. I closed the report and peeked out the window. "Cabin crew, take your seats."

And then, engines growling, we were off.

9

THE ANTIQUARIAN AND THE MURDERER

As his Moabitica crumbled under withering attack, Shapira fell into a depression that put his business and his family under strain. His reputation had been marred. He spent a growing amount of time fighting to regain it—holding meetings, dashing off letters to the editor, trekking into Moab to prove his point. But receipts at the shop suffered. He argued with Rosette and ignored the children. Myriam cried just looking at him.

Shapira was not yet fifty years old and his career was at the edge of a cliff. The pottery that had once seemed the key to his prospects was now the source of financial strain and embarrassment. The scholars he had so hoped to impress dismissed him. Schlottmann was livid. But it was Ganneau's attacks that did the most damage. If Shapira was teetering at the cliff's edge, that "horrid man" Ganneau was right behind him, sticking him in the flank with a hot poker.

But now—as he had done following his grandfather's death, a series of illnesses, and a lowly start in his adoptive country—Shapira rebounded. Over the next several years he would boldly carve a niche for himself in a new line of work, one that was far enough afield from pottery to make a clean start but played sufficiently on his talents that he would not need to begin from scratch. Pivoting once again, Shapira established himself as a dealer in antique Hebrew manuscripts.

As early as 1870, he had consigned two Torah scrolls to the Frankfurt book dealer Johannes Alt, and seven years later he expanded that side of his business dramatically. In the fall of 1877, Shapira negotiated a sale of forty manuscripts to the British Museum, among them a number of Bibles he had obtained in Yemen. That an institution of this stature would see fit to engage him even in the aftermath of the Moabite pottery scandal was a victory for Shapira. Perhaps the museum's executives were convinced that he was not responsible for the Moabitica. Perhaps, in their zeal to amass the finest collection of old Hebrew documents in the world, they were willing to hold their noses. The texts Shapira sold them were not only unquestionably authentic—they were extremely rare. Their acquisition was a coup. Whatever their reasons, the sale buoyed Shapira. In England, he wrote letters home "in the most exuberant spirits." On his return he brought with him trunkloads of gifts. Myriam was thrilled; Rosette was horrified by the extravagance. Concerned with appearances and eager to prove that her mate was a good Protestant, she fretted, "What would the Bishop's wife think of me?"

Shapira, on the other hand, seemed a new man. Having concluded his sale to the museum, Harry recalled, "he had never been more even-tempered or more contented to remain quietly at home."

But he did not stay home for long. Over the next six years he traveled extensively, collecting Hebrew manuscripts throughout the Middle East and establishing himself as perhaps the British Museum's top purveyor of such works. The Department of Oriental Manuscripts regarded his first sale as one of the "most important collections" among the institution's Near Eastern holdings at the time. Shapira seized on his relationship with the museum as an opportunity to billow his flagging reputation, hanging a sign in his shop's window announcing to the world that he had moved on: once a simple shopkeeper—and the subject of scandal—he was now M. W. Shapira, agent to the British Museum.

It was then, as a reenergized Shapira sought to shake the odor of the pottery scandal, that he claimed to have first laid eyes on the Deuteronomy scrolls.

In Shapira's telling, it happened in July 1878, nearly five years to the day before his fateful performance for London's scholarati. At the time, he'd been home in Jerusalem, a world away from the tony Victorian confines of the PEF. Waiting on the treacherous road between Bethany and the Fountain of the Apostles, Shapira knew little of the unsavory fixer he was shortly due to meet, save what he had picked up a few days earlier at the home of his friend Sheikh Mahmoud al Arakat. The courier's name, the sheikh had said, was Salim (not al Kari)—and he was the sort of man who would "steal his mother-in-law for a few beshliks."* The comment had the zing of a one-liner, but under the circumstances it was more like a compliment—a selling point for the business at hand.

The locale was unsettling, plunked at the edge of the brutish desert along the road east to Jericho, two miles outside the protective embrace of Jerusalem's stone walls. Years later, in a letter to the German scholar Hermann Strack, Shapira would note that Salim had insisted on this spot, unwilling to risk a meeting in town, where Shapira guessed he was wanted for robbery or murder. Shapira had traveled this route before, though it was always an artery leading elsewhere, a landscape to hurry through as he exited Jerusalem at the start of expeditions east of the Jordan. During these difficult crossings, Shapira, like other Europeans who came this way, took precautions. He had established solid relationships with a number

---

*A beshlik was an Ottoman-era coin.

of Bedouin headmen, among them Sheikh Arakat and Ali Diab of the Adwan tribe. On prior outings, Shapira had engaged these men to protect him from those who might kidnap and extort travelers, as they had done several years earlier to Ginsburg. Now here he was, lingering alone on this very road to rendezvous with precisely such a man.

As a Christian, Shapira knew that Bethany—el Azariyeh to its Arab inhabitants—was the site at which Jesus miraculously raised Lazarus from the dead. Perhaps it was in hopes of a similar miracle that he'd set aside concerns and sought out this meeting. If Salim's parcel contained anything like what Shapira imagined it might, such a marvel could yet complete the resurrection of his career.

All he knew were the tantalizing tidbits he'd gathered a few days earlier at Sheikh Arakat's home in the village of Abu Dis. Shapira— who would tell this story several times, with slight variations, in letters and newspapers and in conversation—had been chatting with the sheikh and several Bedouin guests when the subject turned to ancient inscriptions, and one of the guests told a story. About a dozen years before, he said, a few tribesmen on the run from Ottoman authorities had taken refuge inside a cave hewn high in an embankment overlooking Wadi Mujib, that gorge in Jordan where I'd hiked in neck-high water. Hiding in that cave just east of Dhiban, the ancient Moabite city that had yielded King Mesha's victory stone, the men chanced upon several bundles of very old rugs. Hoping to find a stash of long-hidden gold rolled within the carpets' linen folds, they peeled away several layers of material. To their disappointment, what they discovered was not gold. All they found was a bunch of old blackened leather strips, smelling of asphalt and covered in some sort of scrawl they could barely see, let alone read. When the Arabs departed the cave, the man told Shapira, they tossed aside the worthless strips. One of them, though, thinking better of so hasty a decision, snatched them up off the ground. A good career move, as it turned out: the man had since gone from privation to comfort, and now commanded a large flock of sheep that allowed him to keep his family clothed and fed.

Shapira was unsure what to make of the story. It was undeniably alluring. Ancient leather scrolls, covered in weird writing, ferreted away in cliffside caves, wrapped in linen and discovered by Bedouin on the lam. But he had already been burned by the Bedouin and the stories they had told him, and anyway, all this was hearsay more than a decade old.

And yet the halo of truth hung about the report. Since biblical days, Moab had been known as a place of refuge. Before he was anointed king of Israel, David hid his parents there to protect them from a murderous Saul. Before that, Moses had established three "cities of refuge" east of the Jordan, where accidental killers sought sanctuary from victims' blood-avenging families. More recently, Shapira and Almkvist, his friend from Uppsala, had made an expedition to the very area the Bedouin man had described. In his letter to Strack, Shapira described kicking up what appeared to be lumps of embalmed corpses along the way. At the time, he believed they had strayed into an ancient burial ground, and he marveled aloud that land this arid could preserve documents of extreme age. He had been thinking of papyrus—like discoveries earlier that century in Egypt. Now Shapira wondered if leather, too, could survive in such conditions.

At once skeptical and curious, he inquired whether or not he might see a few of these strips as proof the man's story was true. That idea was swiftly rejected. Ornaments of this sort conferred blessings on the region in which they were found, the storyteller explained.

"Every Bedouin who delivers old charms or talismans to Europeans has to be driven out from among his people because he delivers the blessings of his country to others," he said. This did not bode well. Then another guest jumped in—he thought he could convince the strips' owner to part with them. Sheikh Arakat floated Salim as a suitable middleman, one who not only would kidnap his own mother-in-law but, more important, would "rob or steal away any antiquities of his country without caring a bit for their blessedness."

And so there was Shapira, awaiting the arrival of this shady functionary. As Salim approached that July afternoon, he may have been greeted by a man in flowing robes, meant to make him feel at ease among his own. Or perhaps Shapira wore his English gentleman's costume, the one he's wearing in the only photograph of him that has survived—the dark overcoat and the muted pants, the leather shoes and pith helmet—to emphasize his cultural superiority, or that he had money to burn. Shapira was a man of many costumes, a "good actor," in Besant's recollection.

Labeling someone a good actor is not a compliment unless that person is, in fact, an actor. Otherwise it implies vanity, self-importance, and the ability to lie with an air of honesty. This was not the first—or the last—time someone attached the label to Shapira. His own daughter implied as much, describing her father as a man who constantly altered his appearance as though he were a player moving through scenes in a revue. "[He] assumed various disguises, just like the Emirs in fairy tales," she wrote.

Sometimes he appeared like an ordinary Roomi so scantily clad that Ourda [her maidservant], scandalized, would avert her eyes. In this guise he would go into the city at regular hours, and always returned home looking more or less worried and careworn. At other times Mr. Benedictus [Harry's fictionalized name for Shapira] would wrap himself in a flowing silk "simarra" like an

Arab chief, and would lie full length with bare feet on the divan
in the arched alcove and smoke his "narghileh," the rose petals
dancing merrily in its ample bowl. . . .

But the child retained the remembrance of one wonderful
night (the incidents connected with which never faded from her
memory) when she awoke to see her father standing by her crib.
He was wearing a golden band round his forehead, and his dark
hair was covered with a long silken veil with hanging tassels.

Where the actor's work ends at the proscenium, Shapira's extended into the audience, the lobby, the world. He shifted constantly, from one day to the next, one meeting to the next, one minute to the next—all part of an effort to belong. He was a searcher: a man with no real country and shifting religious beliefs. Adrift, he had spent the past three decades trying on different ensembles to see what fit; working to sink roots, to establish himself as a man of consequence, a man of note, a serious man with a reliable reputation as a purveyor of rare and important antiquities—a reputation that was now imperiled.

When at last Salim arrived, Shapira said, he handed over a small strip of road-black leather, creased and slimy. The strip had been generously oiled—its former owner's effort to protect it from the extremes of desert life. Taking a closer look, Shapira reported, he was able to make out a few faded ancient Hebrew letters inscribed on the strip in some manner of ink or dye.

When Salim handed over the first segments of the scrolls that day, Shapira's mind was certainly attuned to all the inherent possibilities in the bandit's delivery: ancient Hebrew was the alphabet in which the Moabite Stone had been inscribed sometime in the late ninth century BCE. If these leather strips were anywhere near as old as their writing suggested, they would not only be unique, they would be incalculably valuable—far more so than any manuscript he had yet acquired.

Whatever means Salim had employed to come by this sample, he had done well. Shapira recalled handing him a few beshliks (winning at least a temporary reprieve for the man's poor mother-in-law) and informing him that there was more where that came from should he secure the rest of the manuscript. Salim grunted his assent and departed. Shapira, meanwhile, went home and waited, wondering if he had just stumbled across the discovery that would change his life.

OVER THE NEXT five weeks, Shapira wrote, he met the Bedouin thief on four subsequent occasions. Each time, Salim brought along a bit more of the manuscript, until one day he informed Shapira that there was nothing more to be had of the blessed tribesman's charm.

Salim took his money and departed, never to be heard from again. Not long afterward, Shapira claimed, Sheikh Arakat—his only link to Salim—died, and with him any hint of the manuscript's specific provenance. "Every trace of its history was lost to me, and is still so," Shapira explained years later as he prepared to take his document to Europe. In other words, he was telling Strack, there was no way to find out where, exactly, the fragments had come from.

Once he had the full cache in hand, Shapira went to work, quietly. He had certainly studied the Old Testament as a young man and was intimate with biblical Hebrew. He had also become familiar with other scripts over the course of years in the antiquities trade. But he was not a trained scholar. In correspondence with men of greater formal education, he was comfortable setting forth his observations on manuscripts he had obtained, demonstrating a real depth of learning regarding their content, textual characteristics, and value as artifacts. At the same time, he remained deferential, often seeking the approval of his interlocutors, in hopes, perhaps, that they would see him as a sober-thinking man, intelligent, educated—and aware of his place in scholarship's hierarchy. In such correspondence he could come off as a son seeking approval from his father. But once he had secured Salim's collection, Shapira did not immediately contact the scholars he often consulted on such matters. Maybe this was because he had been betrayed before, badly, by such Bedouin intermediaries and could not afford another embarrassment. Perhaps he had other motives. Whatever the reason, he elected to keep his discovery to himself for the time being.

Here's how Shapira described what happened next: he brought the leathers to his office, where he struggled mightily to decipher them. There were fifteen pieces in all, he told Strack, and they were folded, not rolled. Most were black as the cave from which they were reported to have come, covered in a layer of something like asphalt. The leather itself was decayed, eaten away by insects or saltpeter, both abundant in the caves overlooking Wadi Mujib. The opaque grime must have taken hundreds, maybe thousands, of years to set. It was impossible for Shapira to know whether anything significant lay beneath—and if so, whether he would ever be able to retrieve it. Still, he tried. Laying a strip flat on his table, he sprinkled some water onto the leather and gradually a few letters began to emerge.

"But this was only the case for a moment," Shapira recalled. "Soon the leather became weet & I could see nothing more."

He waited for the document to dry and tried again—to no avail. What's worse, as anyone who's worn new shoes in a rainstorm knows, water and leather don't mix, and Shapira's experiment "nearly spoiled the peace." The document, hidden away so many years in a cave, would not let go of its secrets so easily.

So, Shapira reported, he tried again—this time with spirits. It was a risk. If the ink was composed of organic materials, the alcohol might easily degrade it, erasing forever the author's intent. Shapira splashed a bit onto the scroll, rubbed it gently into the leather, and leaned in to gauge the effect. When he did, the haze began to dissipate and words, phrases, sentences, buried beneath the detritus of centuries, emerged—visible for an extended moment before disappearing back behind their asphalt shroud. Over and over Shapira doused and read, each effort rewarding him with a quick glimpse of the scrolls' text before the spirits evaporated and the words again vanished. The Lord giveth, and the Lord taketh away.

After several such tries, something else became clear: these strips, unlike his "Moabite" pottery, contained more than a random dump of symbols. They were, in fact, inscribed with ancient Hebrew letters, nearly identical to those found on the Moabite Stone. Shapira had handled ancient parchment before, but he'd never seen leather manuscripts three thousand years old. No one had. Some similarly ancient sheets of papyrus had been discovered in Egypt, but until now all indications had been that parchment could not have survived so long in the peculiarly damp climate on the eastern shores of the Dead Sea.

As the rest of the text emerged slowly from the darkness, Shapira began to read:

Eleh hadevarim asher diber Moshe al pi Adonai el kol b'nei Yisrael bamidbar b'ever haYarden ba'Aravah. "These are the words that Moses spoke according to the word of Jehovah unto all the Children of Israel in the wilderness on the other side of the Jordan in the Aravah."

The text was familiar.

Elohim eloheinu diber eleinu b'Horev lemor. Rav lachem shevet ba-

har hazeh. "God our God spoke unto us at Horev, saying: You have dwelt long enough at this mountain."

This was not the first time Shapira was seeing these words—but something was off.

P'nu u'se'u lachem, uvo'u har ha'Emori v'el kol sh'cheino baArava ba-har uvash'feilah uv'chof ha-yam. "Turn and take your journey and go to the Mount of the Amorites and to all the places near it, in the Aravah, in the hills, and in the valley, and by the seaside."

This was the Book of Deuteronomy. The fifth and final book of the Torah. The book in which Moses addresses the Children of Israel before they cross into Canaan, not too far from where Shapira sat now. But what odd changes. He opened a traditional Bible to the first page of Deuteronomy and began to read.

Eleh ha-devarim asher diber Moshe el kol Yisrael b'ever haYarden, bamidbar baAravah, mol Suf. "These are the words that Moses spoke unto all Israel on the other side of the Jordan in the wilderness in the Aravah, across from Suf."

The similarities were obvious—but there were differences: some words missing, others added. Shapira's scroll began with a rendition of the traditional text's first verse, but then it skipped to verses 6 and 7. That was followed by verse 19. Verses 20 and 21 came next—and they were followed, in turn, by 26, 27, and 34. It was wonderful. This was Deuteronomy, sure as day—but such a strange rendering.

When he had read the entire first strip, Shapira pushed it aside and went to work on the next fragments—wetting them with spirits, reading quickly before they dried, and writing each word down as a full transcript slowly took shape. The slips, he was amazed to discover, contained three different manuscripts. The first two were near-identical texts of the altered Deuteronomy—much shorter than the traditional rendition and interspersed occasionally with verses from elsewhere in the Pentateuch. Some of the differences stemmed from abridgments and a slight reordering of words. Elsewhere, the conventional words were replaced with synonyms. Sometimes the scribe used selected or partial verses that preserved the flow of the narrative, or lines taken from passages in Numbers (and, in one case, Exodus) that narrate the same episodes, or episodes that Deuteronomy alludes to but does not fully recount. Shapira's scrolls also omitted chapters 12 to 26, in which Moses presents an exhaustive list of statutes by which the Children of Israel will be expected to live once they cross into Canaan—from animal sacrifices to avoiding swine to smiting Hittites, Jebusites, and Canaanites.

These revisions alone were extremely unusual. Remarkably, though, the most extensive and creative variations were found in the book's most famous passage: the Ten Commandments. Shapira's Decalogue, as these laws are known to scholars, was markedly different from the version with which the world was familiar. Imagine taking the Declaration of Independence's pronouncement that all men are created equal, adding to it language from the First Amendment's prohibition on abridging the freedom of the press, moving the new hybrid law two-thirds of the way down the document, and replacing it at the top with the Constitution's rules on presidential power, and you'll have a sense of the radical changes underpinning Shapira's Ten Commandments. These laws form the foundation of the Judeo-Christian ethic, which shapes the worldview of nearly a third of the planet's population. Any changes to the text were shocking. But if the Ten Commandments could be altered, moved around, and added to, everything else would seem fair game.

In Shapira's version, the exhortations against worshipping other gods and crafting idols are melded into a single edict, reducing the traditional Ten Commandments to nine. The scrolls' author then adds a new final commandment, borrowed from another biblical book entirely: Leviticus's well-known exhortation not to "hate thy brother in thy heart." The punitive portion of the commandment against idols, in which God vows to visit vengeance on the descendants of idolaters, is plucked from its traditional spot in commandment two and moved to number seven, which now threatens such retribution for the progeny of those who make false oaths.

The Book of Leviticus, which includes a section conspicuously similar to the traditional Ten Commandments, was a ripe source for the author of Shapira's scroll. The commandment that forbids taking God's name in vain is replaced with a synonymous phrase from Leviticus 19. The Decalogue's trio of two-word commandments is expanded by phrases from elsewhere in the Torah. The statute against adultery includes a line from Leviticus 20. Now, instead of the time-honored "Do not commit adultery," the law reads, "Do not commit adultery with your fellow's wife." "Don't murder" becomes "Don't murder the life of your brother." "Don't steal" is rendered here as "Don't steal the wealth of your fellow."

The command to mark the Sabbath is replaced with the version of that commandment from Exodus (in which the Ten Commandments also appear), but where Deuteronomy orders the Children of Israel to "observe" the Sabbath, and Exodus insists they "remember" it, Shapira's version exhorts the Israelites to "sanctify" the holy day.

The combination of age, novelty, and text meshing was highly unusual—maybe even unique. The very fact that it differed from what was believed to be the immutable text handed down from God to Moses raised myriad historical and theological questions. If these scrolls were as old as their script indicated, they would have been written many years closer to the Bible's original composition than the printed editions Shapira sold in the front room of his shop, or even the older manuscripts he kept stowed away in the back. And if this was true, they were more likely to represent God's original intent. What Shapira's scrolls meant, in other words, was that the text that had been read and revered in churches and synagogues for thousands of years, the text from which he and his friends at Christ Church would quote once again come Sunday, was, in this way, a fraud.

Shapira worked on the scrolls for the next month. The task alternately distracted him from his responsibilities as a family man and inspired great bursts of enthusiasm. In *The Little Daughter of Jerusalem*, a young Myriam falls for an older boy, a Jew in the process of converting. When she rushes home to tell her father about her new love, he doesn't hear a word of what she says. "You'll never guess what I've discovered this very afternoon," he says.

> *"Look at those parchments! For weeks I've been trying to clean them, and only think of it! if they are really and genuinely authentic, do you know what they will be worth?"*
>
> *"But, papa, his name is Casimir Krakowitch—"*
>
> *"They will make my reputation and your fortune, Siona."*
>
> *"And though he is still a Jew he is being prepared for baptism, and—"*
>
> *"Just think, Siona, I verily believe that these parchments are the original book of Deuteronomy."* ...
>
> *"I do assure you, papa, if I don't marry Casimir—"*
>
> *"Well, I'm very glad you've come back, my child, for after we've left those parchments to soak a little longer, you'll help me to copy my reports. But just think, Siona," persisted Mr. Benedictus, "if we can establish their authenticity, which I am pretty sure we can, they will turn out to be the very oldest MSS. in the whole world, actually the original, Mosaic Deuteronomy!"*

When Myriam fell ill, Shapira read the manuscript by her bedside, comforting her as he worked. Other times he recited passages aloud as he transcribed. Increasingly, he began to see the scrolls as the key to his own and his family's future. Later, sitting with his daughter in the yard, "he would speak at intervals, whilst drawing on his long Turkish pipe, of his grand discovery, his Deuteronomy parchment, and would dilate on all his hopes for [his daughter's] future which he founded on this marvelous prize," Harry would write. "He was going to make her so wealthy, so prosperous!"

By September 24, 1878, Shapira had finished his transcription of the scrolls. He grabbed a pen and paper and began furiously to scribble a copy of the transcript he'd been laboring over for the past month. The next phase of his life was about to begin—and he would start by breaking his self-imposed silence. Gathering his pages now, Shapira posted a copy of the transcription to Schlottmann. Although their relationship had faltered, Shapira once again found himself awaiting the German theologian's verdict.

The French had their Moabite Stone, the Brits their Rosetta Stone. Had Shapira bested them all? Had he discovered the original book of Deuteronomy?

SCHLOTTMANN DID NOT dally in responding—and he did not mince words. In a crushing rebuke, the German dismissed the discovery out of hand, calling Shapira's judgment into question and insisting the manuscript was a pathetic sham and nothing more. Later, Shapira would recall Schlottmann's censure.

"How I dare call this forgery the Old Test[ament]?" the scholar scolded. "Could I suppose even for a moment that it is older than our unquestionable genuine Ten Commandments?"

Schlottmann's logic here is circular, and based strictly in faith. The Ten Commandments, he was arguing, were unquestionably genuine. Because Shapira's scrolls called that genuineness into question, they could not themselves be genuine. The argument is weak. His other evidence was more substantial.

The scrolls, Schlottmann said, "contradicted" the traditional text of the Bible. He was referring here to the unusual way Shapira's document referred to the Almighty. In the standard version of Deuteronomy, God is referred to overwhelmingly as YHWH (Jehovah), the proper name of the Israelite deity. In Shapira's text, this name is used only twice, once at the beginning and again at the end. Elsewhere, the Lord is referred to as Elohim (God), which can function as both a title and a name. This leads to the repeated use of the awkward and redundant phrase "I am God, your God"—a clear sign, in Schlottmann's view, of fraud.

As if this were not bad enough, Schlottmann went on, whoever wrote this manuscript was ignorant of biblical genealogy, labeling the nation of Ammon as descendants of Esau, Isaac's hunter son and father of the Edomite nation, rather than the progeny of Lot.

Schlottmann leveled two further criticisms based on unusual phrases in Shapira's Ten Commandments. In the first verse of the Decalogue, the text employs an extremely odd verb, *hecheraticha*, to describe God's freeing of the Children of Israel from Egyptian bondage. This word, Schlottmann informed Shapira, was not only different from the one used in the traditional text, it was not even Hebrew—it was Aramaic. Finally, and to Schlottmann most damning, God's admonition that a father's sins will be revisited on his sons is laced with an embarrassing mistake: the correct word for "fathers," *avot*, is replaced with the grammatically incorrect *avim*.

Given his facility with the Bible and its language, it seems strange that such oddities had escaped Shapira's notice. Whatever the reason, Schlottmann's rebuke shook his confidence.

"I confess, that when getting prof. S letter I begin to totter in my opinion," Shapira later told Strack. "Not so much from the last reasons as for the general reason the prof. gives, that it contradic's our Bible ... The [s]trong reverence I always had for our Bible which did not agree with the narative of our M.S.S. made, still the M.S.S. some what doubtful in my eyes."

Shapira said that he returned to his transcription to check it against the manuscript itself. Ping-ponging between the two documents, he realized that he had made a number of errors in transcribing that accounted for Schlottmann's concerns. He quickly noticed, for example, that he had accidentally written "Esau" where the text actually said "Lot," rendering Schlottmann's second "proof" moot. Another critique—*avot* versus *avim*—was also based on a small error in copying. Finally, the verb *hecheraticha* may have been Aramaic, but its root was Hebrew, so his reading had not been as wild as Schlottmann implied.

Surely the Moabite pottery scandal was at the forefront of Shapira's mind as he absorbed Schlottmann's reprimand, alternately accepting and rejecting the scrolls. It was certainly on Schlottmann's mind. Not trusting that his admonishment would slow Shapira, the German wrote urgently to Münchhausen in Jerusalem to insist that he stop the merchant from taking his scrolls to market.

Shapira had hoped that the document from Salim would remake his career, finally overtaking the pottery as the matter for which he was best known. Now it risked plunging him into a new controversy.

Once again, Shapira kept quiet. He took the manuscript and stashed it away in a bank vault for safekeeping. But he never forgot about it.

TERRA INCOGNITA

In the wake of Schlottmann's gruff brush-off, Shapira departed on a second trek into Yemen, a four-month ordeal he hoped would bolster his reputation as a manuscript dealer—and, in so doing, help win back the respect of his own family. "You see if I don't make you proud of your old father and of all the grand things I mean to accomplish," he told Myriam before his departure.

Broadly speaking, nineteenth-century Yemen was terra incognita, so much so that Shapira believed he was the first European ever to set foot in the country. He was, certainly, a rarity, though as early as the mid-eighteenth century a handful of Europeans had trekked into the heart of Arabia Felix, as it was then known, and the British Crown administered a small area in the south. Nevertheless, much of the country was yet to be explored, let alone mapped, by Westerners. Shapira's primary goal was to procure rare manuscripts from Yemen's isolated Jewish community. Aware also that his observations along the way could prove useful to cartographers, he donned yet another costume for the journey—that of the desert explorer.

By necessity, many mapmakers of Shapira's day worked blind, gathering observations from travelers and sketching these details into maps of regions they themselves had never visited. Thinking himself a pioneer, Shapira stocked up on equipment that would allow him to gauge temperatures and elevations on his route. Although incomplete, his readings proved remarkably accurate.

On reaching Aden, Shapira engaged a local guide and two camels and, on June 11, 1879, headed north along the deserted plain near the coast. He had arrived during one of the country's two rainy seasons. The downpour, however, did not offer respite from the extreme summer heat. On the very first day of his journey, Shapira traveled in temperatures rising to 102 degrees—passing many merciless hours without the benefit of trees for shade. Nor was the weather the worst of his concerns. Aneroid barometer in tow, Shapira was navigating through hostile territory prowled by some of the region's "most savage and fantastical tribes."

That first day's weather was a taste of what was to come. Over the course of the next three months, Shapira pushed north into Yemen's interior, traveling up to eleven hours a day through the heat and hammering rain. He hacked his way through grass tall as a grown man, ascended narrow mountain paths edging on vertiginous drops, and forged serpentine rivers with so many switchbacks he found himself crossing the same waterway repeatedly in the course of a single day. Often he camped near wells—some of which leaked, spawning unlikely patches of greenery. He saw three-and-a-half-foot hay and indigo plants local women plucked and used for bathing. He encountered, he said, thousands of baboons. And he chewed on qat leaves, which contain an amphetamine-like stimulant that helped locals fight sleep during night hikes and guard duty. Shapira was more impressed by the price of the leaf than its narcotic effect.

"They are the dearest leaves I ever met," he reported in the *Athenaeum*. "A small bundle of wet leaves, not more than about four hundred grammes weight, costs two shillings. It is to [the Yemenis] the most delicious thing in the world—no paradise without it. . . . I could find little taste in it."

After an unforgiving nine-hour climb on his second day in the field, Shapira blundered into a trap similar to one that had befallen other Westerners who traveled in the Near East during that period. As he summited the mountain, he was taken hostage at the castle of Sultan Ali el Mahari. El Mahari, he said, led the most infamous band of thieves in southern Arabia—an impressive distinction—and held him for two days as negotiations dragged on over how much money would buy the sultan's permission to sally forth. Shapira offered no further details of his incarceration. All we know is that ultimately he was freed, a little lighter in the pocket but lucky not to have been forcibly unburdened of his entire travel fund or any vital organs.

Several days later, Shapira missed another near meeting with his maker when a violent rebellion broke out in the ancient town of Dhamar. According to Shapira, some three thousand Jews lived alongside seven thousand Muslims in this city, once a hub for politics and trade and a center of both Islamic and scientific learning. As Shapira's visit was nearing its end, he reported, a local militia rose up against its Ottoman overlords, accusing the Turks of withholding pay. During the course of the next five days, Shapira wrote, the prosperous city was plundered—buildings, fortresses, and all. He made it out just before the violence erupted.

Upon departing Yemen, Shapira met with the German cartographer Heinrich Kiepert and passed along his measurements and observations. Kiepert later published an account of the meeting as evidence of what amateur explorers and professional cartographers could accomplish when working in unison. He recalled that Shapira had kept his diary of the journey in Hebrew, though it was only then being reborn after millennia as a strictly religious tongue.

Shapira published details of his journey in the *Athenaeum*, in which he apologized for "trespass[ing] with the following notes on your space," then listed elevations for eight distinct mountains. It is worth noting here how the aneroid barometer functions. As elevations rise, air pressure drops. The barometer measures atmospheric pressure; elevation can then be inferred as a corollary. The sensitive instrument can respond to differences corresponding to just a few feet in elevation. All of which is to say that in order to take accurate measurements on the above-mentioned mountains, Shapira had to climb them.

THESE SCIENTIFIC ENDEAVORS that so impressed Kiepert were a side note to the true purpose of Shapira's journey: procuring manuscripts. Later, in an introductory essay he included with a catalog listing the 126 texts he'd managed to acquire, Shapira described encountering a Jewish community under pressure—scattered, superstitious, and persecuted by their neighbors.

Some ten thousand Jewish families lived in Yemen at the time, Shapira reported, most in a series of about fifty different towns. The majority worked as craftsmen—weavers, tanners, and potters—and were ministered to by rabbis, or so-called Maris who functioned at once as prayer leaders and ritual slaughterers/circumcisers (one hopes they never mixed up their tool kits).

The smaller towns, Shapira said, were infertile ground for manuscript hunting. They were poor, and the production of handwritten texts was an expensive undertaking. More ominously, Yemen's Jews were well known by their neighbors as ardent lovers of their books and were "subjected rather too often to the pillage and plunder" of manuscripts. Raiders frequently robbed religious volumes from Yemen's Jewish communities, secure in the knowledge that the People of the Book would rather pay exorbitant sums to ransom their texts than allow them to be "polluted by unclean people." By the time Shapira arrived, the situation had become so bad that, to prevent books from being stolen, Jews sometimes destroyed them.

While collecting books sounds altogether relaxing next to kidnapping and desert trekking, persuading Yemen's Jews to part with their prized holy books proved the most potent challenge of Shapira's sojourn in South Arabia.

"The amount of difficulties to get these books?" he complained in the introduction to his catalog, "& how I managed to destroy the curses and bans, lying since centuries upon them? And how I was enabled to overcome the supperstishness of this people is of course out of place in a Catalogue."

Neither in his introduction nor in his *Athenaeum* article did Shapira specify how he had managed to surmount these obstacles and secure so many manuscripts from his reluctant Yemenite hosts. His methods would be exposed only later, once Shapira had departed on another, more fateful journey.

While he was off being celebrated in London, his Deuteronomy scrolls making headlines, several elders of Jerusalem's Yemenite Jewish community approached Horatio Spafford, founder of the city's American Colony, and requested his help. In Yemen, they told the Chicago expat, a man calling himself Rabbi Moses had some years earlier arrived in their town.

"He lived among them when he was in Yemen, joining them in prayers in their synagogue until he had won their confidence," Spafford's daughter, Bertha Spafford Vester, would later recall in her memoir of the period.

Then "Rabbi Moses" inquired whether the community had any old manuscripts. They acknowledged that they did, but said they only brought them out on a particular holiday. At hearing this, Rabbi Moses decided to stick around for a while.

"When the Temanite [Yemenite] Scroll was uncovered he saw, with his experienced and practiced eye, how old and valuable it was," Spafford Vester recounted. "He offered to buy it, but they said they would rather part with their eyes or their lives than with their beloved manuscript."

Unmoved, Rabbi Moses approached the Ottoman governor and negotiated a deal. He returned a short while later, this time backed by a contingent of Turkish soldiers. He led them to the village synagogue, where he "forcibly took the Temanite Scroll, leaving a nominal sum of money."

More recently, the elders told Spafford, they had been shocked to spot this Rabbi Moses walking freely in the streets of Jerusalem. The so-called rabbi was, of course, Shapira—and now, the elders said, they wanted their Torah back. The problem, Spafford Vester reported, was that before her father could initiate any action, Shapira had slipped away to England to sell his Deuteronomy manuscript to the same institution where he'd probably pawned the elders' special scroll.

Nils Lind, a Swedish member of the American Colony, told a similar story. Lind dates the encounter to 1891, by which time Shapira was long dead and could not have been seen wandering the streets of Jerusalem. He also has a certain Yemenite rabbi called Shuni donning a prayer shawl and phylacteries to tell his sad tale. And in Lind's version, the visitor does not claim to be a rabbi, but rather introduces himself as Mordecai Shapira, a Jew from Jerusalem. Even so, the Swede's story ends the same way as Spafford Vester's: with Shapira essentially stealing the community's prized Torah scroll.

A third version of this story exists, this one told by the Yemenite rabbi Yihye Kafach, in his book *Milhamot Hashem* (*Wars of God*). Beseeching his readers to treat religious texts with due respect, he cites a litany of Hebrew books that Shapira took from Yemen's Jews.

> *And many of our multitudes sold old books that they had inherited from their ancestors to uncircumcised people who came to Yemen, such as Moshe ben Netanel [Shapira] who dwelt in the house of our master and teacher Avraham Salah. He himself sold him a Taj of the Nevi'im [Prophets] and Ketuvim [Writings] with the Targum of Yonatan ben Uzziel on Nevi'im, and R. Saadia Gaon's Arabic translation of Isaiah and the Ketuvim. Also a Mishnah, Seder Kodashim, with the Rambam's [Maimonides's] commentary in Arabic in a beautiful script, including drawings of our holy and glorious Temple and its holy vessels, in Massekhet Middot. I saw it in his hands with my own eyes, I and my/our master and teacher Yihye Korah z"l [may his memory be a blessing]. And we were powerless to take it away from him. To this day we do not have Seder Kodashim and Nashim in the manuscript of the Mishnah with the commentary of the Rambam z"l. And those aren't the only things they sold him. Many books in ancient manuscripts were sold to him and others cheaply.*

Whether Shapira stole these books or removed them for a pittance, the mission to Yemen was, from his standpoint, a triumph. In December 1879, three months after his return, Shapira made his second manuscript sale to the British Museum. Included in that transaction were a number of biblical texts, and rare works by the medieval philosopher-physician Moses Maimonides. Two further sales followed, in 1880 and 1881, and in 1882 the museum bought his collection of 145 manuscripts written by Karaites, a community that adheres to Jewish law as presented in the Bible, eschewing any fealty to the rabbinic doctrine that followed. Shapira obtained these texts in Iraq and Egypt and, coinciding with the sale, published an article in the *Athenaeum*. In it he described the manuscripts and delved into Karaite doctrine, but balked at explaining how he got them.

"As the sellers of the MSS. wished their names not to be mentioned," he wrote, "and as there are in general only one or two in each place I visited who possess MSS., I think the reader will excuse my not mentioning names and places."

Shapira's methods in Yemen render this defense less than convincing.

THINGS WERE LOOKING up for Shapira. The British Museum was a frequent client, its imprimatur conferring an air of import, respectability, and seriousness on him and his business—attributes he had nearly lost in the fallout from the Moabite pottery affair. If the British Museum still trusted him, why should anyone else have an issue?

Shapira gained further courage, he would later tell Strack, when he made a discovery that called Schlottmann's brusque dismissal into question and pointed to the authenticity of his Deuteronomy scrolls.

Whereas people of faith had long believed that Moses himself wrote the Torah, the late nineteenth century saw a growing chorus of European scholars beginning to challenge that claim, undertaking systematic investigations into the Bible's origins. Moving beyond the assumption that the Torah was handed down in its current form from God to Moses on Mount Sinai, these investigators took to reading the scriptures not strictly as believers, but as historians and literary critics. They began to pose fundamental questions about the Bible. Who wrote it? Why? When? And in what historical context?

Germany was biblical criticism's intellectual hub, and in 1883 Shapira encountered the groundbreaking work being done there when he received a copy of *Einleitung in das Alte Testament* (*Introduction to the Old Testament*) by Friedrich Bleek. A Christian academic who had once studied for the ministry, Bleek maintained his faith even as he launched a scientific inquiry into the genesis of the holy book he held so dear. As early as 1877, Shapira had taken note of the "many many variations" from the traditional biblical text in manuscripts he had brought back from Yemen. Reading Bleek's *Introduction* gave name to these observations.

Bleek had not emerged in a vacuum. Centuries before these German scholars began to weave a full-blown hypothesis about the Bible's true authors, close readers had also noticed inconsistencies.

"[The Bible] would report events in a particular order, and later it would say that those same events happened in a different order," Richard Elliott Friedman explains in his highly regarded exploration of the Torah's origins, *Who Wrote the Bible?* "It would say that there were two of something, and elsewhere it would say that there were fourteen of that same thing. It would say that the Moabites did something, and later it would say that it was the Midianites who did it. It would describe Moses as going to a Tabernacle in a chapter before Moses builds the Tabernacle."

The Torah's report of Moses's death seemed to be among the most glaring irregularities. Here it is, from the final chapter of Deuteronomy: "So Moses the servant of the Lord died there, in the land of Moab, at the command of the Lord. He buried him in the valley in the land of Moab, near Beth-peor; and no one knows his burial place to this day."

But if Moses wrote the Pentateuch, how, exactly, did the 120-year-old prophet manage to record his own death and burial? For centuries, believers simply rationalized away the apparent problem. Moses was a prophet, they would say. God must have dictated that passage to him before he died. Another tradition held that Joshua, Moses's successor as the Israelite chieftain, had taken over for the last few lines.

The possibility of Joshua's involvement, along with other discrepancies, raised a radical proposition: that the Five Books of Moses were not written entirely by the eponymous author. For those who embraced this theory, Moses remained the primary writer; Joshua's contribution would have been minimal.

But there were other problems: a list of kings who reigned after Moses had died, references to Moses in the third person, anachronistic language. Most authorities rejected the earliest expressions of these concerns, explaining them away through tortuous interpretation. Some scholars noted the issues but urged their readers to keep silent. Others mocked the authors of such blasphemy; some burned their books.

None of the detractors was able to kill the questions. Although the supposition that Joshua wrote the final verses of the Torah still allowed for Moses's composition of the vast majority of the Pentateuch, as time passed, scholars began to ascribe less and less of the text to the prophet. By the time Shapira said he grew wise to the field of biblical criticism, its proponents gave Moses very little credit for writing the books that bear his name.

The first person to claim outright that the majority of the Torah was not written by Moses was none other than Thomas Hobbes. Among his observations, the English philosopher noted the Torah's occasional use of the phrase "to this day." On the face of it, these three words seem innocent enough. In the context of a document purportedly reporting on contemporary events, however, it is problematic. The traditional text of Deuteronomy, for example, tells us that "Jair son of Manasseh received the whole Argob district (that is, Bashan) as far as the boundary of the Geshurites and the Maacathites, and named it after himself: Havvoth Jair—to this day." In noting that the region in question is called Havvoth Jair "to this day," the Bible betrays the fact that a significant amount of time has passed between Jair naming the district and the Bible's reportage.

Similarly, after announcing Moses's death, Deuteronomy tells us that "no one knows his burial place to this day." In other words, it has been a while since Moses died, and *still* no one knows where he was interred.

These arguments made a case for who did *not* write the Bible. Eighteenth-century scholars, following on earlier work by the philosopher Benedict Spinoza—who was excommunicated from the Jewish community—began to explore who *did* write it. Anyone who read the Torah with even cursory attention would have noticed its tendency to tell the same story twice: Genesis includes two different versions of the creation of man and animals; two episodes where Abraham passes off his wife as his sister (and a third where Isaac does the same); two places where Beersheba is given its name—and two different explanations for why. Jacob's name is changed to Israel twice. God reveals his name, Jehovah, once in the burning bush at Mount Sinai, and once again in Egypt.

As they did with oddities like Moses's death, traditionalists rationalized these doublets, explaining, for example, that by including contradictory versions of the same story, Moses was simply trying to teach his readers one lesson or another. But investigators, unsatisfied with such easy answers, dug deeper, and in so doing noticed something interesting about these doublets: each time the Torah repeated a story, one version referred to God as Jehovah, while the other always called him Elohim (the Hebrew word for God). And it went further than that. The Jehovah half of the doublets used other words and phrases that did not appear in the Elohim portions, while the Elohim sections were consistent in their use of terms not in the Jehovah segments. Researchers began to put two and two together—or, more accurately, to take two and two apart—and as they did, they came to an interesting conclusion: the Jehovah stories must have been written by one author, while the Elohim stories were written by someone else entirely. The Torah, in other words, had two different authors—which meant at least one of them was not Moses.

In the nineteenth century, Bible scholars pushed this "documentary hypothesis" even further. They began to notice that some of the Elohim stories, and many of the Torah's laws, tended to focus heavily on subjects of interest to priests—and so, researchers deduced, were probably written by a third author, this one hailing from the Israelites' priestly class.

It didn't end there; just as two became three, three quickly turned to four when a German scholar named W. M. L. De Wette noticed that, while traces of the Jehovist, Elohist, and Priestly versions could be found in the first four books of the Bible, most of the fifth book, Deuteronomy, was written in a style all its own. This observation pointed to a fourth author, the Deuteronomist. As the number of biblical authors grew, Moses's assumed role in writing the Torah diminished. While early Bible critics believed certain inconsistencies could be explained by the supposition that Moses had access to a number of different sources when putting the Torah together, by the time De Wette posited a fourth author, most biblical critics believed the book had in fact been assembled after Moses's death.

In the 1870s and '80s, the biblical scholar Julius Wellhausen published a series of books and articles giving the documentary hypothesis its classic formulation, based on the theory that the Torah was composed by four different authors: the Jehovist, the Elohist, a Priestly writer, and the Deuteronomist—known colloquially as J, E, P, and D. This expression of the Pentateuch's development persists, more or less, to this day. Building on the work of his predecessors, Wellhausen argued that the Torah was an amalgam of these four separate, shorter documents, none of them written by Moses. Later, unidentified editors gathered these texts and wove them together, eventually forming the Pentateuch. Going through the entire text, Wellhausen spelled out exactly which verses belonged to which source.

Among the work Wellhausen had undertaken along the way to developing his unified theory was editing Bleek's *Introduction*. Bleek, for his part, had been a student of De Wette, the father of Deuteronomy criticism. Bleek's book, published in 1869, gave voice to his theories on the origins of the Hebrew Bible. Shapira received a copy and devoured it. After sitting, disappointed, on his Deuteronomy scrolls for close to five years, he said, "What a change came over my mind after studeing the above book."

Bleek's work would have been interesting to anyone curious about the Bible, but Shapira said that reading the book was more than interesting—it changed how he thought about the Old Testament. Bleek, he told Strack, convinced him that Schlottmann's angry dismissal of his Deuteronomy fragments had been too hasty.

WHAT SHAPIRA ENCOUNTERED in Bleek's work was a view of the Pentateuch as a living organism that began its life as a series of shorter books and grew in length over the course of centuries as these disparate texts were incorporated. Bleek was uncompromising in his belief that the Book of Deuteronomy, specifically, could not have been written by Moses and was certainly the work of a later author.

After studying Bleek's book, Shapira said, he was startled to realize that the phrase "to this day" was missing entirely from his copy of

Deuteronomy. So was an account of Moses's burial. And there were a number of other significant omissions, too. A central theme of the traditional Deuteronomy is the prohibition against worshipping at sites other than the Holy Temple in Jerusalem. Critical scholars believe that this prohibition was a late addition to the book—and it, too, was missing from Shapira's copy.

If Bleek and his fellow Bible critics were to be believed, these omissions were not, as Schlottmann seemed to think, proof that Shapira's scrolls were fake. Quite the contrary: if the Torah with which the modern world was familiar was made up of several shorter texts, then Shapira's abridged copy—lacking, as it was, these post-Moses tells—might actually have been the original copy of the book, the one written by "D" before later editors began their work.

Buoyed by his new insight, Shapira called on Prof. Paul Schroeder, a specialist in ancient Semitic epigraphy then visiting Jerusalem from his post as German consul in Beirut. Schroeder, unlike his countryman Schlottmann, took one look at the manuscript and pronounced it unquestionably genuine.

This confirmation seemed to lend Shapira the courage of his convictions. Equipped with the professor's endorsement, he was certain his reputation would be repaired beyond question and that his discovery would raise him at last from the ranks of Jerusalem's merchant class to the tony halls of the academy.

"Now, at last, he would be free to shed his humble bookseller's garb," Harry would recall. "No more need to spend long days in the stuffy shop, engraving texts on olive-wood covers for prayerbooks and albums! Good heavens, no!—he would sell off the whole stock. . . . And then he would travel, travel to the ends of the earth and explore all its beauty, all its wealth; and he would be given a chair in some European university as an Orientalist; and last, but by no means least, he would score a victory over that insolent drag-oman" Ganneau. Anticipating a long period away from the shop, he hired another assistant and, Harry wrote, bought her a pony.

Flush with Schroeder's approval, Shapira dashed off his letter to Strack, the German Orientalist, who that same year had established an organization aimed at converting Jews to Christianity. Shapira knew Strack from prior business, and perhaps he hoped that their ac-quaintance, and Strack's penchant for converted Jews, would soften his stance in the aftermath of the Moabite pottery scandal. The let-ter brimmed with Shapira's typical deference to educated men and his meticulous attention to textual detail. Although he suggested that the manuscript could be as ancient as the sixth century BCE, he also took pains to point out its various defects.

After offering condolences on the recent death of Strack's father, Shapira wrote: "I am going to surprise you with a notice and a short description of a curious manuscript written in old Hebrew or Phoe-nician letters upon small strips of embalmed leather and seems to be a short unorthodoxical book of the last speech of Moses in the plain of Moab."

He regaled Strack with details of his meeting several years earlier at Sheikh Arakat's home in Abu Dis, where a number of Bedouin men first told him the story of an inscrutable talisman discovered in a Moab cave. He described his furtive encounters with Salim on the desolate road between Bethany and the Foun-tain of the Apostles, explaining that this fugitive had liberated the whole of the ancient document from its once-blessed owner over the course of several exciting weeks. Shapira told Strack about de-ciphering the scrolls: how he'd plied them with water and spirits to break through the sea-black patina to the ancient letters beneath. How he soon discovered that the old strips contained an exotic and abridged version of Deuteronomy. How he wrote to Schlott-mann, and how Schlottmann wrote back, enraged. And then he told him about reading Bleek.

"I see now that the most of the varreations between our M.S.S. & the (traditional) Bible are of such a character, as are, already used by many eminent scholars, as a prove that our [traditional] Deut was not written by Moses or about his time. All such passages are not to be found in our M.S.S."

While Shapira was clearly excited at the prospect of his manuscript proving important, his letter to Strack was measured. Adopting the lingo of the Bible critics with whom he had just become acquainted, Shapira began to lay out some of the difficulties the text presented. For one, he returned to Schlottmann's observation that, unlike the traditional Deuteronomy, his scrolls referred to God almost exclusively as Elohim. Adding to Schlottmann's incredulity was the fact there were exactly two mentions of "Jehovah" in Shapira's manuscript—in the first and last verses. Odd, that these all-important verses would turn to God's proper name.

"Could we suppose," Shapira wondered, "that the first and last verse are adding by a Jehovistic scribe who copied an Elohistic M.S.? (perhaps from a tomb of an Elohistic believer) & put his own heading and closel form? I confess the last suggestion does not well satisfy me."

Shapira was equally circumspect about assigning a date to the manuscript. While he believed that the script used probably indicated that it was written hundreds of years before any known copy of the Bible, he acknowledged that there were other possibilities.

"You will ask me dear Prof. what I suppose to be the date of our M.S.S.," he wrote. "To this I will say, judging from the form of the letters, one will be inclined to give to this unorthodoxical manu-

script such an early time, as between the date of the Mesa stone &
and the Siloam inscription, or about the 6th century B.C."

"But one must be very cautious," Shapira warned.

It was just possible, he said, that some texts—those buried with
the dead, for example—were deliberately composed using old scripts
no longer in common use at the time of the scrolls' composition. If
his was such a text, he wrote, "the date may be very late." In any
event, he said, that determination "will of course be for scholars to
decide."

Along with his letter, Shapira sent Strack a Hebrew transcription of his manuscript.

"You will dear prof. be better able to find the faults and virtues
of [the manuscript] than I," he wrote. "I will also ask pardon for all
my daring suggestions & ask [you] to give me your candid opinion
about it should you or your friends find it so interesting as I flater
myself to be."

It is difficult to reconcile this Shapira with the pompous actor
of Besant's and Simpson's recollections. One easily could dismiss
such admiring entreaties as suspect—highlighting less an authentic reverence than calculated flattery meant to disarm a skeptical
scholar. But if that were the case, why would Shapira have ditched
the modesty act when he stood before a room full of such authorities, as he did when he unveiled the scrolls at the Palestine Exploration Fund? Did he simply determine that the meeting required
him to turn on the showman's charm? Was he by now so confident
of his manuscript that he could not contain his enthusiasm? Was
Shapira energized by an audience, but more circumspect when left
alone in a room with pen and paper? Were Besant and Simpson
simply mistaken in their recollections? Or was the answer "All of
the above"?

"You may send me a telegram with a few words upon my ex-pences," Shapira said in closing.

> I think to go soon in a few days for a short time to Egypt for
> examining some M.S.S. if possible & then G.W. [God willing]
> very soon to Berlin with my M.S. Excuse also my very bad writing
> done in great haste.
>
> Allow me to remain yours truly
> & obedient servant
> MW Shapira.

In late June or early July, Shapira headed to Germany. In light of the international embarrassment his pottery collections had inflicted on the nation and its scholars, to say nothing of Schlottmann's early rebuke, it seems odd that this was where he would choose to unveil his manuscript. But Germany was biblical criticism's capital, and he must have believed that scholars there would clamor for a document that spoke to their theories.

In Berlin, Halle, and Leipzig, he deliberately sought out opin-ions from biblical savants whose approaches to interpretation dif-fered one from the next. Although they disagreed on much, the scholars were unanimous in their verdict—the scrolls, they said, were forgeries.

Shapira seems to have taken the rejection quietly. Unbowed, he left Germany to try his luck elsewhere. Arriving in London in late July, Shapira headed to the offices of the Palestine Exploration Fund, where he displayed his scrolls for Walter Besant and the cream of London's biblical savants.

11

SYDNEY

It was 5:45 on the morning of Sunday, May 25, 2014, when Delta flight 417 began its initial descent into Sydney. My new plan— rudimentary though it was—was now in place. I knew very little about Matthew Hamilton, the elusive Australian who had contacted me eight months earlier, announced that he'd discovered who bought Shapira's scrolls from Bernard Quaritch, and then disappeared. I had his email address, though he'd been ignoring my messages for months. And I had a home address thirty miles outside Sydney—but it was six years old and, even then, had belonged to someone named Gary Matthew Hamilton. Beyond that, all I knew was that at one point he had probably worked in the library at Moore Theological College, a small Anglican school in Sydney. I'd called a few weeks earlier in hopes he was still there—or, if he'd moved on, that someone at the school might know to where. The lady I spoke to put me on hold, checked with her colleagues, and then informed me that Hamilton had once been employed by the library. "But it was years ago," she said. "No one's seen him since then."

At the time, this conversation had not seemed particularly helpful. But in reviewing the private detective's dossier on the plane, I realized that I'd learned something on that call: Hamilton had, indeed, worked at Moore. This was now confirmed. And that seemed to me a fairly solid indication that he was Anglican. And where's the best place to find an Anglican on Sunday morning? Church.

Hamilton was not interested in talking to me, but if I approached him in the pews, he would at least have to play nice. There would be no door for him to shut in my face. It was another long shot, but if it failed, I could always try the home address.

I rushed off the plane and through customs, grabbed my bag from the carousel, and got in the taxi line. It was just after seven now, the weather was mild, and church, I imagined, would begin around nine. The line was long. Assuming it took twenty minutes to get a cab, forty-five minutes to get to my hotel, and ten minutes to check in, that would leave another three-quarters of an hour to shower, pinpoint the Anglican church closest to the address I had for Hamilton, and find my way there.

Nearby, a woman in an Andre the Giant T-shirt had begun to act funny—repeatedly leaning over, then shooting upright. I looked around to see if anyone had noticed, but she and I seemed to be the only solo travelers around and everyone else was engaged in conversation. We moved forward slowly through the line's roped-off switchbacks until the woman jolted up once again and took off running—ducking under the ropes as she made a break for the side-walk. My eyes shifted quickly to her suitcase, which she'd left behind, right by my feet. Having spent a significant amount of time living in and reporting on Israel, I was immediately concerned—over there, abandoned parcels merited a special name: *hefetz hashud*, a suspicious object. Too often, such packages ended up detonating. That's why, while everyone else watched her mad dash, I was busy staring at the lady's bag, hoping it didn't start ticking. It didn't. Instead I heard retching. Turning toward the sound, I caught a glimpse of the woman hunched over a trash can. She wasn't a terrorist; it appeared she was in her first trimester. I was relieved, though I had to pass the trash can three times as the taxi line snaked forward.

The ride from the airport was remarkable only for how unremarkable it was. I had landed halfway around the world on a continent once home to massive numbers of English convicts, and still I could as easily have been driving from Philadelphia International Airport to my parents' house in the city's suburbs. The highways were well maintained and lined with deciduous trees and flowers. Road signs were green and white. The only real differences were speed limits posted in kilometers per hour and cars moving by on the wrong side of the road. A few minutes after eight, the taxi dropped me at the Novotel Sydney Rooty Hill, a neighborhood over from Tregear, where I believed Hamilton had once—and, I hoped, still—lived. The hotel was located at the far end of a massive parking lot abutting a casino, a bowling alley, and a Domino's Pizza. My room was on the fourth floor, and after dropping my bags, I opened my MacBook and did a Google search for "Anglican church" and "Tregear." A single name came up: All Saints Anglican Church, on Ellsworth Drive. I scribbled the address in my notebook and called the concierge for a cab. Then I dialed the church. It rang and rang.

After a quick shower, I threw on a tie and tossed a camera, notebook, and digital recorder into a small backpack. I had also brought over a couple of gifts for Hamilton, peace offerings, as I had come to think of them: a copy of my father's book on Deuteronomy and the Hebrew edition of Myriam Harry's *Little Daughter of Jerusalem*.

My driver took me out the back route, past the casino, and turned onto a small street that ran parallel to some train tracks. A double-decker train huffed by, and I began to feel the jet lag creeping in. My ears were warm, my neck tight. I closed my eyes and wondered what time it was back home, but opened them quickly: over the next few hours I would learn whether this insane journey had been a colossal waste—whether my quest to find Shapira's scrolls would be granted new life or would run into its final brick wall.

I got out at a corner half a block from the church to avoid drawing attention to myself. Then, tightening my tie, I crossed the street (reminding myself to look right first, then left) and headed toward the rainbow sign that announced the church to passersby: MOUNT DRUITT INDIGENOUS CHURCH. This was odd. I double-checked the address in my notebook—I was in the right place. What had happened to All Saints Anglican? My plan, like so many before it, seemed to have failed before it had begun.

A car turned into the church parking lot and I trotted in after it. "Excuse me," I said as the driver emerged. She was a middle-aged woman and not indigenous, which offered hope that the sign out front was somehow misleading. "I'm trying to find All Saints Anglican Church. Is this it?"

"Oh," she said, surprised. "It was. It's indigenous now—has been for ten years."

"Really," I said. Then, to say something, "Do you know a guy named Matthew Hamilton?"

The lady shook her head. A van full of children arrived now, and she opened her trunk as they filed out. "I'm sorry." She removed a few bags of groceries from the car and headed toward the chapel. The kids ran around to the rear of the church, and I walked in a circle considering my options. I could go inside and ask around. Or I could just head over to the old home address the private eye had given me for Hamilton.

"There's a Presbyterian church." The lady had set her groceries down and pointed in the direction from which I'd come.

"Sorry?"

"It's just up the block," she said. "This side of the road."

In Australia barely an hour and already I was grasping at straws.

I wasn't holding out much hope—one doesn't go looking for an Anglican at a Presbyterian church.

The neighborhood was downtrodden. Broken beer bottles and bird excrement painted the sidewalk. Shapira would have gotten a kick out of the fact that my search for his scrolls had taken this nice Jewish boy to more churches in more countries than the papal nuncio. As I approached the small brick building housing the Tregear Presbyterian Community Church, I felt the buzz of a walking bass line. When I entered, the joyous roar of rock and roll came at me with force. The lobby was little, hardly a lobby at all, and, building up my courage, I opened the chapel door a crack to peer inside. About thirty people swayed in narrow pews to music emanating from the multi-piece electronic church band on the pulpit. There was some singing, some clapping. I tried to make out the words, but the chapel door swung open and I backed out of the way. An older woman in pleated pants and a beige cardigan emerged with a stack of brochures.

"Welcome," she said, handing me a thin pamphlet. "Can I help you?"

"I'm actually looking for someone who may go to church here," I said. "Matthew Hamilton?"

"Matthew Hamilton," she said. "Yes. He used to come here. But I haven't seen him in twenty years."

"Do you happen to know where he lives?" I was waiting for her to ask me why I wanted to know. It was a little odd, after all, for a foreigner to show up in the middle of the church service asking to speak with a onetime parishioner. But she didn't ask. "I have this address," I said, showing it to her. She shook her head.

"I don't think that's right," she said. "Wait a minute. Let me see who's here."

The music came roaring out again as she opened the chapel

door and slipped back inside. This was promising. Hamilton was not here, but he had attended this church. I was getting closer. I glanced through the church bulletin and peeked at the books on the shelves. I was making my best effort to appear as studious and harmless as possible when she returned five minutes later with a white-haired gentleman in tow.

"Paul Beringer," he said, extending his hand. "So, you're looking for Matthew Hamilton, are you?"

Beringer had attentive blue eyes, an honest smile, and what he would later refer to as a "Buddhist haircut," received on a recent trip to Thailand. "He worshipped here when I was pastor, but I haven't seen him in twenty years."

Beringer touched his chin and considered. He had been Hamilton's pastor. If I managed to find him through this man's auspices, Hamilton would have to at least hear me out. It was beginning to feel like my shitty plan was working.

"Do you think he still lives around here?" I asked. "I have an address."

Beringer looked at the jotting in my notebook.

"I don't think so," he said. "It's been a very long time. What's this regarding, if you don't mind my asking?"

Over the past couple of weeks I'd been rehearsing what to say to Hamilton if I found him. I hadn't thought through what to tell anyone else.

"I'm writing a book about an ancient Bible that's gone missing."

"Mmmm," Beringer said, nodding.

"Matthew and I were in touch a few months back," I said, wielding Hamilton's first name to imply an intimacy that did not exist. "But I've been having trouble reaching him."

"It's really been years," Beringer said. Then something occurred to him. "Did you come by car?"

"Taxi," I said.

Beringer shook his head. "They really get you on taxi fares in Australia," he said.

"Matthew has a daughter—she goes to church about a mile away. Come on, my car's right across the road."

"That's extremely kind," I said. "But I wouldn't want to take you from praying."

"No, no," he said. "This sounds important." I was starting to love this man.

Beringer led me out to his maroon Nissan and let me in. As he began to roll forward, a man with a giant white beard sped through the crosswalk in an electric wheelchair. Beringer hit the brakes.

"G'day!" he shouted from his window. The man nodded back. "One of our local people," Beringer said.

Beringer had left the community church twenty years earlier to take a post in rural Australia. He and his wife, Jenny, had returned here to retire a year and a half before my visit. He remained involved in local charity work and still preached occasionally, but he wasn't particularly involved in that day's service and so had time to shuttle me around. He was a remarkably open man: he spoke honestly about his health, his family, his education, his career in the ministry. He had initially planned to study with the Presbyterian Church of Australia but changed his mind when he learned of its theological liberalism. Instead he did four years at Moore College, where Matthew Hamilton had once worked as a librarian. I mentioned this to him and asked if Hamilton had any formal training in manuscripts or archaeology. Beringer didn't think so. That made me uneasy— could Hamilton really have discovered the information he claimed to have discovered?

After about fifteen minutes, I began to notice the scenery repeating. When we passed the same row of houses a third time, I knew we'd made a wrong turn. Beringer drove on unperturbed. I got the sense that he was after a little adventure in his retirement, and searching for Hamilton with a foreign writer was scratching that itch. When eventually we pulled into the parking lot next to Multi-cultural Bible Ministries, I once again heard strains of rock: electric guitars, bass, drums. Beringer led the way past several well-dressed people chatting and enjoying the midmorning sun. He pointed to one man who had a stage microphone running along his cheek, like Madonna. He was the pastor, the child of Maltese immigrants who had converted from Catholicism.

We stepped inside, and the lady at the door greeted Beringer warmly. In the distance I saw the band rocking out inside a very large auditorium for a few hundred worshippers.

"Have you seen Jessica Hamilton?" Beringer asked now. "Is she here today?"

The usher hadn't seen Jessica.

"What about Ernestine?"

The usher hadn't seen Ernestine, either. Beringer glanced around briefly, sizing things up, and then bounded outside. "Back in the car," he said, and I obeyed.

While Beringer backed out of his parking spot, I belted up and asked who Ernestine was. "She's a good friend of Jessica's," he said, stomping the brakes to avoid a churchgoer. "She'll know where Jessica is."

"Where is Ernestine?"

"I don't know," he said.

There was another wrong turn as we navigated through a neighborhood of modest single-story homes fronted by nicely kept yards. Oddly, the lawns and streets were largely devoid of people. Were they all at church? When we reached Ernestine's place, Beringer parked in the driveway beside a large tree in which an enormous spiderweb had trapped a rugby side's worth of small bugs. He nearly leaped from the car, flung open the screen door, and rang the bell. I joined him on the porch. And then: nothing. No one answered for one minute, then two. Beringer rang again, and again we waited in silence. After several minutes of this, it was clear no one was home. By this time I was back at the car, leaning against the hood and wondering what Beringer would do next. Would he drive me somewhere else? Wish me luck and send me on my way? Hit another groovy church? I looked up at the porch. He was still there, waiting, but I could sense—in his posture, the slowing of his movements—a dimming of enthusiasm. We exchanged disappointed glances as he let the screen door slam shut. And that's when we heard a small voice calling from inside. "Hello . . . Just a moment, please."

I hopped back up onto the porch as a little woman swung open the front door, squinted out into the day, and said, "Oh, hello, Paul."

"Hello, Pamela!"

Pamela was in her late fifties or early sixties and about five foot two. She wore wire-rimmed glasses and was draped in a floral housecoat. "I'm sorry," she said, inviting us in. "I was about to have a shower."

The house was dim and short on air, and there were books and board games piled along wall-to-wall carpeting. A very thin cat stalked the living room, glaring at us. On the far wall, by the adjoining kitchen, hung a painting of Uluru, the gorgeous sandstone formation that juts like a camel's hump from the flatlands of Australia's Northern Territory. Nearby, a stuffed bear peered out from a shelf.

"How are you, Paul?" Pamela asked, falling into a recliner. She was taking our sudden intrusion in stride.

"I'm fine, Pamela," he said. "Listen, this good man here is a professor from San Francisco and he's come all the way over here just this morning looking for Matthew Hamilton."

"Matthew Hamilton," she said, scrunching her lips. "I don't think I've seen him in twenty years."

I was beginning to get a sense that my flight had arrived two decades late.

"What about Jessica?" Beringer asked.

"You'd have to ask Ernestine."

Pamela went off looking for her cell phone but couldn't find it. She circled the living room and the kitchen. "This isn't like me," she called from the next room. She emerged a moment later with her landline in hand and dialed her own cell number. We all heard a buzz coming from inside the living room.

"Oh, my," Pamela said now, reaching into her brassiere. She removed the vibrating phone and made a funny face. To keep from laughing, I silently recited Talmudic passages I'd had to memorize as a kid. When I glanced over at Paul, he was doing a pastorly job of keeping it together. Pamela dialed Ernestine, but there was no answer.

"I've got a town directory somewhere," Pamela said. She turned back toward the kitchen. "It's old, but . . ."

Pamela was flipping through a stapled directory from 2001 when she came back into the living room. "Hamilton, Hamilton, Hamilton," she murmured as her finger ran down the list of names. "Here," she said. "Matthew Hamilton."

"Where is he?" Beringer asked.

Pamela read the address. It was the same one I already had.

The old Hamilton address was a ten-minute ride from Pamela's place. I'd already explained that Hamilton had some information I needed to complete a book, but on our way over, Beringer pressed me for details. I told him about Deuteronomy and the British Museum, about Shapira's scrolls and their disappearance. And I told him that Hamilton had somehow discovered who bought them from Quaritch. Again I worried that the discussion was headed toward the question I didn't yet want to answer: *Why couldn't you just ask him over the phone?* But the story had only further amped the curious pastor.

"I'm loving this!" he said. "If we don't find him, I'm calling in ASIO!"—the Australian Security Intelligence Organization.

We had pulled onto a quiet residential block with no sidewalks. The homes were not fancy, but they were well kept—lawns trim and green, roofs and driveways in good repair. We crept forward, scanning for house numbers, and located Hamilton's two blocks off the main road. "Here we are," Beringer said, and then, spotting something as though on safari: "Look!"

He pulled quickly to the side of the road, threw the car into park, and pushed open his door. Ahead of him, a white SUV was leaving the curb. Beringer hopped out and took off after it, waving his arms above his head like a castaway who had spotted a passing plane. He didn't stop even as the vehicle turned the corner. A moment later, the car slowed and the front window came down. Beringer leaned in and began talking to the driver. By this time I had caught up, and Beringer, head still inside the SUV, grabbed my shoulder and said, "Just arrived this morning to see Matthew. His name is—"

Here he turned to me, kindly allowing me to invoke my own name—difficult to pronounce outside the Fertile Crescent, surely more so with an Australian accent. But I hesitated a moment before opening my mouth. I looked in at the driver, a woman in very big sunglasses. I didn't know who she was, exactly, but clearly she knew Hamilton. And if she knew Hamilton, it was possible she'd heard of me—the American writer who was stalking him. And if she'd heard of me, she'd know Hamilton did not want to talk.

"Chanan," I said finally. "Hi."

My name didn't register.

"He's inside," she said. "Go ahead in."

She pulled away and Beringer sprang to the front door.

"Who was that?" I asked.

"That was Toni," he said. Leaping onto the porch, Beringer knocked confidently on the front door. "Matthew's wife."

A moment later, the front door swung open. It opened toward me, so I was able to hide behind it for a moment while the two men greeted each other after many years. I couldn't believe my luck. I'd gone to church that morning hoping to find Hamilton in a public place where he would have to hear me out. Instead, not four hours after landing in Australia, here I was at his front door with his former pastor making introductions. Beringer and Hamilton shook hands and spoke affectionately for a few moments while I stayed put behind the door. I still hadn't seen Hamilton and wondered what he looked like, and what he'd do when I emerged. Eventually Beringer turned toward me.

"Listen, Matthew, this guy here has come an awfully long way to see you," he said.

I leaned over, poking my head into the doorway.

"Matthew," I said. "Chanan Tigay. The Shapira guy from the U.S." Hamilton was taller than I am, about six feet. He looked about thirty-five, though in fact he was fifty-one. He had thick brown hair with patches of white at the temples and a thin mustache that didn't so much as twitch as he shook my hand and invited me inside.

"Ah, yes," he said, friendly as can be. "Come in, come in."

It was as though he'd been expecting I would show up sooner or later. Over the past eight months I had thought of Hamilton every day. I had spent hours in front of my computer searching for him, agonizing over his disappearance, imagining what he looked like, parsing his silence, divining his motives. Most of all, I had won-

dered who had bought Shapira's scrolls—and how had Hamilton
found out? But Hamilton, it now occurred to me, hadn't thought
much about me at all. Every couple of weeks, maybe, and then only
to decide whether to skim, skip, or delete my latest email intrusion.

Hamilton led us through a small living room, past the kitchen,
and around a corner into the narrow hallway that led to the rear of
the house. Before we had even reached his office—which doubled as
the room where clothing was ironed—Hamilton, smiling pleasantly,
drew a line in the sand.

"I can talk about a lot of things relating to Shapira—but I can't
tell you the Name," he said.

The Name, of course, was exactly why I had come. I was happy
to talk about anything relating to Shapira; my wife might say that
was all I ever did. But I hadn't laid down several thousand dollars
and flown halfway around the world to chat about Shapira. In advance of the trip, simply finding Hamilton had loomed large in my
mind as the biggest hurdle. I now realized that, having tracked him
down, the real work was only just beginning. I smiled now at his
declaration.

"I thought you might say that," I said. "I'm hoping to convince
you otherwise."

Now Hamilton laughed. "I thought *you* might say *that*."

We entered his office. It reminded me of my own: piles of books
and documents populated his desk like little Ulurus in the plain, the
neon screen of his computer casting its faint moonglow over the
bookish clutter. Hamilton pointed out a bookcase packed tightly
with what must have been a dozen or more blue loose-leaf folders labeled SHAPIRA. Somewhere stuffed in one of those piles, or
clipped into one of those binders, or embedded in an email on that
computer, was the Name. I felt like I had as a kid when my parents
took my brother and me to our favorite baseball card shop: I wanted

to rush the desk, tear open the folders, and go to town. Instead I unzipped my backpack and offered Hamilton my gifts. Beringer excused himself and said he'd call later to arrange lunch. When he'd gone, Hamilton set my dad's book down on his desk.

"I knew you were serious when I saw who your father was," he said.

Hamilton grew up in Parramatta, the second city established in all of Australia. The son of a nurseryman, he had bounced around this corner of New South Wales most of his life before settling in Tregear. As a child, he had a photographic memory. That recall no longer comes quite as easily, but his IQ hovers in rarefied Einstein-like digits. In the late 1970s, while taking the test to gain membership in Mensa, he discovered an error. Hamilton became interested in Hebrew and other biblical manuscripts in the mid-1980s, when a coworker showed him a documentary called *Jesus: The Evidence.* Instantly fascinated, he has worked on the Bible (both testaments) and the Dead Sea Scrolls ever since. He keeps a hundred thousand photocopied documents relating to this research—research through which he'd encountered my father—stored in a shed out back, where his pet pig, Oliver, roams.

We spent the next hour dissecting aspects of the Shapira story. It was a cordial and interesting conversation, tempered by an underlying tension. Neither one of us sat down the entire time, as though doing so would indicate—or precipitate—a letting down of our guard. For the duration of our conversation, Hamilton had a little smile on his face. Whatever tension we felt, he was enjoying himself.

He spoke extremely fast, and everything he said I interpreted through the filter of the Name. He must have assumed as much, because whatever he told me seemed calculated to offer no tip-offs. He delivered a mind-bogglingly thorough analysis of Shapira-related scholarship from the 1880s through the 1960s. Each time he cited a new book or article, I wondered whether that had been where he'd discovered the buyer's name. He offered an articulate dismantling of the Nicholson theory—and I wondered if his work on the English-Australian nobleman had led him to the discovery. He mentioned the Quaritch General Catalogue, and I wondered if somehow I'd missed a vital clue back in England. Finally I just asked him how he'd found it.

"I can't tell you that," he said. There was a moment of silence. "What I can say is that he was an Englishman."

Now we were getting somewhere.

"So they didn't get too far from Quaritch," I said.

"Well," Hamilton said, "he was from northern England."

I was briefly excited by this divulgence. If Hamilton did not give me the Name—and all indications pointed, depressingly, to his remaining steadfastly silent on this point—this would at least allow me to narrow my search to a single country. But beyond that, it was of little value. I wouldn't get far googling "man AND Northern England AND Shapira."

"Anything else you want to tell me about him?" I asked in that half-joking, half-serious way that indicated that I was pushing him in a direction he didn't want to go, and knew it.

"I think I've said enough," Hamilton answered.

"If you don't mind my asking," I said, "why is that?"

"Ah," he said. "Well, you recall that when I first wrote, I told you that I'd only given the Name to one other person."

"I do," I said.

"And that person was Yoram Sabo."

I HAD SUSPECTED Sabo for months. All the same, the news took me aback. There's something bracing about learning that you're not just being paranoid. And yet, in a search that had thus far yielded many more questions than answers, it was a relief to definitively solve one of the mysteries that had vexed me. At long last I knew for certain why Hamilton had been stonewalling me, and it was oddly satisfying to have my suspicions confirmed. What's more, I couldn't really blame Sabo. I'd probably have done the same thing.

None of which meant I was prepared to stop trying.

The discovery of the Name, Hamilton told me now, had been his own, but by dint of his decades in the field, Sabo had earned the right to reveal it in his documentary. The film's release would then clear the way for Hamilton to publish an article addressing the more circumscribed subject of Nicholson's supposed involvement. Sabo, at any rate, had orchestrated Hamilton's unexplained silence.

As I processed this, the front door opened and Beringer hurried into the room.

"You didn't answer your phone," he said.

I apologized and told him it had been turned off while Hamilton and I were speaking.

"Come on—my wife wants to have you over for lunch," he said.

"Ah," I said. It was all I could come up with. I was in no way prepared to leave. As long as I could keep Hamilton talking, there was still hope. I had gained access to the lion's den and did not know if I'd ever be allowed back in. But Beringer had been so kind, so helpful, so authentic, that refusing this latest kindness seemed rude.

"That sounds great," I said, and then, to Hamilton, "Can we continue this later?"

"Of course," he said. "How's about dinner tomorrow?"

This was progress. He was willing to continue talking.

"Do you like spaghetti Bolognese?" he asked.

Two free meals proffered in two minutes—I was starting to like it here. But I had a feeling Hamilton would be more likely to open up away from his own turf. Somewhere I could buy him a drink or three to lubricate his persistent misgivings.

"Please," I said. "Let me take you to dinner."

We made arrangements to meet the following night at my hotel. Then I left for Beringer's house where, over a lovely lunch in his backyard, strewn with toys left behind by his grandchildren, Beringer said grace: he thanked God for our chance encounter, acknowledged how far my journey had come, and offered a blessing for the successful resolution of my search.

I'm no Christian, but that was a prayer I could get behind.

That evening back at the hotel, I lay down at last, exhausted. Sydney was seventeen hours ahead of San Francisco, so I sent my wife the requisite "greetings from the future" email and began making notes about the day's events. It had been epic. After eight months trying to find him, it had taken just four hours to gain entry to Hamilton's study. He had welcomed me into his home and offered to break bread. I had the distinct sense that, although Hamilton wasn't intending to give me the information I'd come for, he felt bad that I'd traveled so far and would leave disappointed. I could work with that. He was some kind of genius, and I wasn't going to outsmart him. He had maintained a steadfast silence for months, so pressuring him seemed unlikely to suddenly succeed. Ultimately, I decided as I drifted off to sleep, the best path forward was simply to appeal to his humanity. And if that didn't work? At least I could tell my friends I'd been to Tregear.

The next day, I read through the materials again in case anything Hamilton had told me—he was an Englishman, from northern England—now rang a new bell. Nothing did.

That evening, Hamilton called up to my room right on time, and I found him in the lobby. We walked together to the near-empty hotel restaurant and were seated immediately. In a black sweater, black pants, and glasses, he appeared studious, a look enhanced by the two blue loose-leaf binders under his arm. The waiter came by and handed us a drinks menu.

"It's on me," I said.

"Nothing, thanks," Hamilton said.

"Nothing? You're sure? A beer?"

He explained that he didn't like beer. On occasion, he told me, he'd order a ginger beer. I had discovered a very rare breed—the one Australian who did not drink beer. I thought back to my meeting with Lowell Bergman: "What's your plan?" he'd asked me then. Beyond appealing to Hamilton's humanity, my plan for this evening included only one other essential component: having a few drinks with this guy in hopes he'd open up. That plan was now crushed like so many empty cans of Tooheys. The waiter went off to fetch dinner menus and bread.

"This is for you," Hamilton said. He slid one of the binders across the table. I opened it and began to flip through. It contained fifty-nine pages of his research notes on Shapira. Printed in a tiny font, the material had been divided into twelve sections, including an extensive bibliography. Chapters included headings like "Shapira—Biographical Information," "The Manuscript—General Information," "Timeline of Events," "Bibliographic Review of the 'Shapira Affair,'" "Genuineness," and "What Happened to the Manuscript After 1883." Each section was methodically detailed, heavily footnoted, and laid out with forethought and clarity. There were charts, photographs, and diagrams. One figure, meant to illustrate how information had passed from one scholar to another, looked more like schematics for the Airbus A380 than anything to do with the Bible. Hamilton, it seemed to me, had missed nothing. Enthralled by his thoroughness as I paged through the document, I began to notice that certain lines and passages were blacked out—just a few at first, until, toward the end, entire pages were obscured.

"You'll notice I redacted any mention of the Name," Hamilton said. He had been as thorough in his redaction as in the compilation of this amazing file. Whether it appeared in the text, a chart, or a footnote, every reference to the Name, or anything that might lead me to it, had been covered over. He hadn't simply taken a black pen to these references, but, in an effort to make certain I could not peek through from the back of the page, for example, or attempt to read them beneath some special light, he had used his word-processing program to black out each reference. I think I made a joke about plying the pages with spirits, as Shapira had done to his scrolls so many years earlier.

Hamilton ordered the prawn curry. I have absolutely no recollection of what I ate. For the next three hours we talked around the issue. He was generous with his research—aside from the Name, he was willing to divulge and elaborate on everything he had discovered over the course of years investigating Shapira. The details of what he said were familiar to me, but his analysis was impressive. His familiarity with the literature on Shapira had allowed him to trace how bits of misinformation had come down to modern investigators, like us, as received wisdom. He had spent uncountable hours transcribing long articles in German into Google Translate—then passed endless days making sense of the mangled English that had emerged. I didn't push him to divulge anything more than he was willing. Instead I expressed genuine astonishment at what he'd accomplished.

We finished our entrées, and the waitstaff bused our plates. As we continued talking over the empty table, Hamilton began to let slip little details about the circumstances of his discovery. He had come upon the Name, he told me, during a Google search. He began by entering an enormous variety of search terms, and combinations thereof: *buyer, collector, auction, auctions, manuscript, purchase, Shapira, Schapira, Shappira.* And hundreds, maybe thousands, more, combined and recombined. Then he read through the results—all of them. Rather than stopping after the first page of Google hits, at which point the relevance of the links typically tapers off, he continued reading. He proceeded this way, carefully, methodically, for hours until finally, one night in November 2011, an intriguing hit popped up in Google Books. It was an obituary that had appeared in an obscure journal having nothing at all to do with the Bible or archaeology. But all Hamilton could see was the brief abstract describing the article—not the article itself. And so he deepened his search, trolling through a mountain of online information for the actual publication to determine if he'd discovered what he thought he'd discovered. At four in the morning, he found it. And, Hamilton told me, it said exactly what he'd hoped it would say: "The Name became the eventual possessor of the notorious 'Shapira' manuscript."

I was stunned. Scholars had been searching for this information for decades. I had traveled ceaselessly to find it. Sabo had been at it for thirty years. And Hamilton had found it sitting in the comfort of his chair, thirty miles outside Sydney and eight feet from his ironing board. This, it seemed to me, was a testament to the power of the Internet—and to this man's dogged skills as a researcher. I hadn't been taking notes during dinner because I didn't want to risk spooking him—I had long ago learned that subjects reluctant to give you the information you want are allergic to notebooks and tape recorders. But I did not want to forget a single thing Hamilton was telling me. I was hopeful that, with all this information, I could return to my room when he'd left and begin to plug a host of new search terms into Google that would lead me where they'd led him.

I excused myself and headed for the bathroom. On the way, I

snatched a few cocktail napkins from the bar and locked myself inside a stall. There, I furiously wrote down everything Hamilton had just told me: *Obituary. Google Books. Obscure journal. Notorious Shapira manuscript.* I was in there awhile, and some poor guy was knocking repeatedly at the door, desperate to get in. I was afraid that if I relinquished the stall I'd lose my train of thought, and much of what Hamilton had said would disappear. So I kept writing. When I was done, I flushed and opened the door. A young kid pushed by me without making eye contact, head and shoulders bowed like he was walking into the wind. I stuffed the napkins into my back pocket and sat down at the table.

"So," Hamilton said. "Was it worth it, coming all the way to Australia?"

I didn't want to be rude. He'd just spent three hours with me, had made me a copy of his research, answered all of my questions. He'd been less forthcoming than I'd hoped, and more than I reasonably could have expected. Also, I was growing increasingly convinced that maybe, just maybe, he'd already told me enough. So I demurred, mumbling something about how nice it was to finally meet him and to see his copious research firsthand. Then Hamilton excused himself to use the restroom.

As he rose from the table and walked toward the back of the room, I noticed that he had left his own, unredacted research folder on the table, not ten inches from my hand. My eyes shot up, searching the room. My heart kicked at my ribs. I felt like a pickpocket who'd spotted a rich lady's purse on a lunch counter. I couldn't believe he'd just left it sitting there. Maybe my earnest approach had worked—I had earned his trust and he now felt comfortable enough to leave the binder behind. But what good was this trust if I didn't then use it to my advantage? Maybe he just didn't want to bring a binder into the bathroom. Or was this something else—something, frankly, biblical? Maybe, I thought, Hamilton was testing me. I glanced around the room again to see if he was peeking at me from behind the wall by the bathroom. He wasn't.

Now I had a decision to make. Opening the binder was unquestionably the wrong thing to do—nothing short of stealing. And if I was to succeed in this search, I did not want to feel that the achievement was tainted. But I also knew that opening Hamilton's book could save me. I needed the Name, and there it was, inches away. Salvation was at hand and I was dithering. I knew—*knew*—that if I didn't grab the book, I would kick myself for days, weeks, forever. This was my job. To let it go to waste would be irresponsible. If I waited any longer, Hamilton would be back and the decision would be made for me. I was left with only my gut to guide me.

Hamilton returned a couple of minutes later. Sitting back down, he set his hand gently on the binder's cover. I don't know if he was assessing its location or just using it for balance—but it hadn't moved. I hadn't touched it.

But something in Hamilton's demeanor had changed. Now he began asking *me* questions: *If you had the Name, what would you do with it? When is the book due? When will it be published?* I answered to the best of my ability. The truth was, the answers had much to do with him. If he gave me the Name, my publisher might push back my deadline, allowing me time to track down leads. I wasn't entirely sure what he was getting at with this new line of inquiry, but my answers satisfied.

Because then, three and a half hours after we sat down to eat, thirty-six hours after I'd landed in Australia, and about 5,832 hours after he had first sent me an email inquiring into my research, Hamilton simply blurted it out.

"Philip Brookes Mason." He said it loud and fast. It was like he was trying to generate momentum that he couldn't stop even if he wanted to.

"Sorry?" I said.

"That's the Name. Philip Brookes Mason."

I ripped the napkins from my pocket and quickly wrote it down. No need to be coy now.

"That's it?" I said.

"That's it," he said.

"Wow." I was stunned. "That's it. That's the Name. Thank you."

So then. Moses Wilhelm Shapira. Christian David Ginsburg. Charles Clermont Ganneau. And now: Philip Brookes Mason. With their tripartite names, our cast of characters sounded like a roll call of famous assassins.

Hamilton smiled a little. He seemed relieved.

"Come over here," he said. He waved me to his side of the table, pulled out a chair, and opened his binder to the first page. Then he asked me to open mine.

"So," he said, and began to read. "'With Crown's hypothesis shown in this report as wrong it is now possible to re-commence the search for the manuscript, and in contrast to the early 1950s–mid-1960s, we now have the name of the person who acquired the MS from Quaritch.' And under the black line there where I redacted it, the word is Philip Brookes Mason. Next . . ."

For half an hour, the two of us sitting side by side, Hamilton proceeded through the file, reading aloud the blacked-out sections, giving shape to the life of a man who just a moment earlier had barely even been a name.

Mason was a successful physician, born and bred in the English Midlands in a city called Burton-on-Trent. No one had ever before connected his name to Shapira's. As a leading member of the Burton Natural History and Archaeological Society in the late nineteenth and early twentieth centuries, he had amassed a world-class collection of stuffed birds and a near-complete British herbarium. He dabbled in other areas of natural history, too. But aside from his association with a group that included "archaeology" in its name, his interest in matters archaeological was minimal. The obituary in which Hamilton had discovered his connection appeared in the October 1904 edition of the *Journal of Conchology*, published by the Conchological Society of Great Britain and Ireland. For nearly seventy years, those tracking Shapira had pursued his scrolls in the British Museum, at Sotheby's, in the stately offices of Bernard Quaritch Ltd. All the while, the key to the manuscripts' whereabouts, and my sixth clue, was hiding in plain sight—on page 104 of an old magazine about seashells.

WHEN HE MET Sabo, Hamilton did not initially give him Mason's name. He had held off, much as he'd done with me. But then he got to thinking.

"What if I get hit by a bus?" he said. "No one will know."

I thanked Hamilton profusely and we said our goodbyes. When I returned to my room, I pulled the cocktail napkins from my pocket and entered the search terms I'd scratched out earlier in the bathroom stall. The third snippet to pop up in the Google window was the *Journal of Conchology*.

I took Hamilton's binder to bed with me. Shutting off all the lights but the one on the nightstand, I started reading. I hadn't noticed at dinner that the very first page was, in fact, a letter, written to me.

"I do not see the results of my research, in the long term, as mine," Hamilton wrote. "They belong to God as I serve with my research. Please consider this as you use what I release now and what will most probably be released later this year. My hope is the [Sabo] documentary comes this year and I then release an article on Nicholson and his Shapira MSS. At that point I can share all the redacted parts below."

Arriving at dinner that night, Hamilton had no intention of divulging Mason's name. But some spirit had moved him to do so—and it appeared I had God to thank. The Name belonged to Him. And to Hamilton. And to Sabo. Now it belonged to me. And I was off to England again to find the scrolls Mason had purchased, though he knew them to be fakes.

But were they really?

12

LONDON CALLING

It was already a very good week for Ginsburg. Esteemed among Bible scholars, he'd gotten another boost to his public profile shortly before Shapira's arrival in London. Prime Minister Gladstone had awarded him a grant of five hundred pounds to pursue his seminal work on the Massorah, an enormous compendium of notes on the writing and pronunciation of biblical Hebrew. Now the United Kingdom, through the agency of its national museum, had taken a serious interest in acquiring Shapira's manuscript, and Ginsburg had been deputized as the venerable institution's steward.

He was a natural choice. Several years earlier, Ginsburg had established himself as an authority on the Moabite Stone, publishing a thorough evaluation of the pillar whose script so closely matched that of the Shapira Deuteronomy. And Shapira, for his part, had expressed a willingness to work with him after their acquaintance of more than a decade.

Scrolls in hand, Ginsburg departed the meeting at which Shapira had unveiled them and headed to the British Museum, about a mile and a half from the PEF's Adam Street headquarters. There he set up shop in the manuscript room, a cavernous hall with a book-lined mezzanine overlooking the work floor. Sensing the work would be hard on his eyes, Ginsburg hired an Assyriologist named William St. Chad Boscawen to assist. Shapira, no doubt buoyant at his lively English reception, headed for his room at the Cannon Street Hotel to await news.

On July 28, E. A. Bond, the museum's principal librarian, informed the institution's trustees of Shapira's arrival. Already known to them through prior manuscript sales, Shapira's latest coup was greeted with excitement—although one would hardly have guessed it reading the meeting's minutes:

> *The principal Librarian informed the Trustees of an offer by Mr. M. W. Shapira of fragments of the book of Deuteronomy written in Phoenician [ancient Hebrew] characters on leather, and stated to have been found in the neighbourhood of the river Arnon, and to be of a date before the Christian era.*

It was not long before the British press learned of the discovery. All at once, the papers exploded with wall-to-wall Shapira coverage. Suddenly the "little merchant of Jerusalem" was garnering headlines at a rate that today might rival coverage of a celebrity divorce. Newspapers began publishing lengthy descriptions of the scrolls, translations of their content, and excited speculation about their origins. Although many papers hedged, noting that until Ginsburg rendered a verdict on the strips the jury was still out, excitement at even the possibility that they were authentic was electric.

While acknowledging that Shapira had in past years become "almost too well-known," the *Liverpool Daily Post* of August 9, 1883, marveled at the putative import of his find. Because Jews had passed down their holy book with "unimpaired rigidity," the editorialist wrote, the traditional text with which the world was familiar had remained strikingly static over millennia. But the discovery of a more original version of the Hebrew Bible "would be of unspeakable interest and value."

A correspondent in the *Athenaeum* reflected on the "marvelous" notion that sheepskin could be preserved for thousands of years outside of Egypt's sand-dry environment. Ginsburg, well aware of the interest swelling around the fragments, wrote in regularly to offer updates on his progress and to note interesting discoveries he'd made in the course of his work. Shapira, too, took to the pages of the English press to expound on, among other subjects, exactly how he had managed to obtain the scrolls in the first place. That story itself became a fulcrum separating the growing ranks of believers and skeptics. For the doubters, it was all a bit improbable: Desperado Bedouin hiding out in a cave had just happened to make the greatest-ever manuscript discovery? Really? And the sheikh who had introduced Shapira to Salim the thief—he just happened to die shortly after the affair and so could not be interrogated? That was what Shapira wanted them to believe? It all sounded awfully convenient.

Others were more sanguine. After suggesting that the manuscript could date from the eighth century BCE or earlier—easily making it the oldest Bible ever discovered—the *Saturday Review* pooh-poohed any thought that such a discovery was "antecedently improbable."

"The ancient Israelites were noted scribes and it was difficult to believe that nothing of their writing remained," the paper reported. "Mr. Shapira is a well-known collector of curiosities. Few of the hundreds of English travelers who visit Jerusalem annually but have had some dealing with him, great or small. Living where he does, and being well known among the tribes of the desert, familiar with their ways and language, it is not surprising that he should hear of, and succeed in obtaining, anything strange or ancient that they might have found."

Or, as another paper more economically put it, "Truth is sometimes stranger than fiction."

Once in print, Shapira's version of the scrolls' discovery took on a life of its own. Claude Conder, the PEF agent who, along with Ginsburg, had been one of two men initially invited by Shapira to see the scrolls, reported that the fragments "are said to have been found with a mummy." A terrific story, were it only true. Alas, Shapira never made any such claim.

Other men whose preferred head garb could only have been of the tinfoil-hat variety, chimed in, too. On August 11, one Fred. W. P. Jago wrote in to the *Western Morning News* to suggest that Shapira's manuscript bore some resemblance to the Cornish version of the Ten Commandments.

Solemn and ridiculous alike, in the aftermath of the Moabite pottery scandal and his recent rejection in Germany, all the attention must have been beyond satisfying for Shapira. Here he was, a decade out from the Moabitica affair, garnering excited attention from the press, hobnobbing with London's elite, being taken *seriously*. He visited and corresponded frequently with Ginsburg, a world-renowned scholar. Back home among his fellow congregants at Christ Church, folks who didn't always see him quite as he saw himself, his legend grew. He wrote home frequently with news of his exploits—the meetings with bigwigs, the excited newspaper coverage.

Then, on August 13, the biggest vote of confidence yet: Prime Minister William Ewart Gladstone, the profoundly religious son of a slave-owning sugar baron, paid a special visit to the museum to view the ballyhooed manuscripts and shake the hand of the man who had brought them to London. With his friend Ginsburg looking on, Gladstone peppered his honored guest with deeply informed questions. Shapira, very much in his element, regaled the prime minister with a lively rendition of the scrolls' discovery. Gladstone completed a careful inspection and, astonished, noted the similarities between their script and that of the Moabite Stone. Even more amazing than Gladstone's knowledge of Near Eastern epigraphy is the fact that as Ginsburg's work progressed, a number of English-language newspapers published substantial sections of the Shapira manuscript—*in Hebrew*. The Bible sensation then sweeping England no doubt led Shapira to believe London would prove fertile ground for a sale. Many Englishmen had studied the Holy Tongue alongside Greek and Latin—and knowledge of Hebrew, in its turn, certainly fed fascination with archaeology among well-heeled men like Gladstone. Several papers covered his visit to the museum that day. As soon as he departed, rumors quickly sprouted. The prime minister, observers whispered, was so impressed by what he'd seen that he had already earmarked several hundred thousand pounds of government cash to help secure the pricey scrolls. The museum's treasurer, an anonymous functionary if ever there was one, suddenly learned the price of celebrity—interested parties organized a stakeout, keeping a close eye on him whenever he departed the museum for the treasury, which he did frequently in the course of his usual business. Once, after this poor man was spotted leaving a government building in a manner that seemed somehow secretive, word got out that he had been inside finalizing a large payment for the museum's important guest from Jerusalem.

Meanwhile, Ginsburg kept quiet on the major question of the day: were they or weren't they the real deal? A scholar's scholar, he refused to announce a verdict before his work was complete. "May I suggest that those scholars who may wish to take part in the discussion on the nature and character of these fragments should first inspect them before they commit themselves to any strong opinion?"

Ginsburg implored in the *Athenaeum* following his transcription there of Shapira's Ten Commandments.

Of course, no one paid his admonition any mind and, as in any good media frenzy, even his caution became the subject of gossip and speculation. On August 16, the *Liverpool Daily Post* noted that while Ginsburg remained engaged at the museum deciphering the scrolls, with Shapira occasionally there by his side, his "reticence leads many to put faith in the original assertion, that these scraps of leather are hundreds of years older than the Christian era."

As Ginsburg's work extended from days to weeks, his reluctance to pronounce judgment, coupled with the prime minister's overt enthusiasm, conveyed to many observers the clear impression that the United Kingdom was preparing to fork over the largest sum ever paid for an archaeological relic. The transaction would redeem England, which had missed out on the Mesha stele, solidifying the British Museum's reputation as perhaps the world's greatest repository for valuable manuscripts from the Near East. It also would save Shapira—restoring his name and making him famous for all the right reasons—not to mention establishing him as one of the wealthiest men in Jerusalem. In another country, and another era, Shapira's story would have been held out as evidence of the American dream: a young immigrant journeys alone to a new country, where, battling illness, prejudice, and bad luck, he manages—through equal parts hard work, ingenuity, and good fortune—to overcome the odds and transform himself into the richest guy in town.

NEWS OF SHAPIRA'S coup traveled across Europe and the Mediterranean. In Palestine, the chatty merchant's family was suddenly treated like royalty. Now, when Myriam and Rosette went to church on Sundays (Augusta was off at boarding school in Berlin), "everyone bowed to them." During the week, Harry recalled, an endless column of visitors turned up at the Villa Rachid to offer their "aigre-douce [sweet and sour] congratulations." Beggars and cripples arrived in limping regiments, seeking handouts from the important ladies. Salesmen—shoulders laden with packages of cooking ware, fragrant soaps, dining finery—hauled out to the house, braving Shapira's moody ostrich for a chance to entice his wife and daughter into a purchase or two. Myriam took to the attention with "reckless extravagance." She bought whatever she desired from every honey-tongued merchant who showed up, donated freely to all comers, and borrowed easily from a friendly German banker. When no cash was at hand, she blew large sums on credit extended by local shopkeepers all too happy to please the good Queen Shapira and her adorable princess.

Shapira himself continued to write home with tales of increasingly wondrous exploits. Not surprisingly, all the good news helped stoke the family's excitement and further fuel their exuberant spending. In one letter, Shapira told them of his meeting with Gladstone—the prime minister of England!—and suggested that a private individual was now prepared to pay a million pounds for his scrolls. Upon reading the letter, Myriam exclaimed: "Why, with all that money we really could buy up the whole of Judea!"

Given her feelings about the Moabite pottery, it's easy to imagine Rosette's anxiety over this latest escapade, though there's no record of her response. Indeed, laudatory as Shapira's initial reception had been, the stench of the pottery affair, predictably, resurfaced. One after another, the papers turned to his prior miscues.

Even as it praised his "extraordinary" find, for example, proclaiming that "the surprises of archaeology are magnificent and apparently inexhaustible," the *Times* was certain to remind readers that the Moabite pottery had turned a light on Shapira "not altogether creditable to his sagacity." This sort of dig touched a very raw nerve for Shapira, who moved quickly into damage-control mode. Sitting alone in his posh hotel room, he dashed off a four-page letter to Ginsburg, relitigating the whole pottery affair in an effort to ensure it didn't come to color the work of the scholar of record. "Dear Dr!" the letter began.

> The known article of the 4th of August mention again the sad business of the Moabite pottery & I think it will be right to let you know dear sir how little I am to be blamed even if the pottery should be unquestionable forgeries. . . . Now you will understand dear Dr why my greatest enemies M. Ganneau & [German Bible critic Emil] Kautzsch could write nothing against my honesty.

Here he was, standing at the precipice of a comeback, about to achieve his dream, and the damned Moabite pottery, a scandal that was not only entirely out of his control but was by now a decade old, was being regurgitated by some in the press. And for what? To sell papers? To perpetuate the ancient canard about Jews (even converted ones) being unsavory businessmen? Implicit in Shapira's letter is not only the persistent sense that he was, once again, being savaged for a hoax of which he himself was the victim, but also grave concern for his economic well-being, which was now riding exclusively on Ginsburg's verdict.

Shapira had invested heavily in the Moabitica, fully expecting that Germany would buy up his third collection. When public opinion soured, he was left, quite literally, holding the bag. The affair was a major financial shock, he told Ginsburg. He had lost more money on unsold pieces than he'd earned on everything he'd managed to move.

Back home, meanwhile, expenses swelled: there was the villa

he'd rented outside the city walls, employees who demanded their salaries, cabinets full of Moabite pottery no one wanted, and one daughter off at private school in Berlin while the other splurged.

As his concerns percolated, Shapira offered the museum a list of pros and cons for the manuscript's authenticity. "My reasons for doubting the genuineness of this M.S. for a long time have been as follows," he began. Then, in parallel columns titled "Against it" and "For it," he enumerated eleven arguments against the scrolls' authenticity, beside each of which he included possible explanations. Much of the "Against" column echoed Schlottmann's reasoning, although No. 10 stands out as uniquely Shapira's:

Against it	For it
It is too good to be true & too surprising?	So it is & maked me also irresolute very often

In hindsight, this chart is interesting not so much because of the arguments it advances, whether pro or con, but because it seems to have been written by a man with a solid grasp of public relations. None of Shapira's arguments against authenticity was new—a scholar of Ginsburg's stature would already have noted everything included here in short order. Whatever Ginsburg's position at the time, then, the list was unlikely to push him any further toward a determination of forgery. On the other hand, if the scrolls were found to be inauthentic, this list established a paper trail that would allow Shapira to claim that he never attempted to pull the wool over Ginsburg's eyes—that he had been an honest broker all along.

Shapira and Ginsburg stayed in close contact, meeting now and again and corresponding by letter. Ginsburg's work was painstaking. The scroll was nearly impossible to read when Shapira had first shown it off at the PEF and, through frequent rubbing with spirits,

its condition had since been degraded further. Moreover, a whole nation was now paying attention. Journalists were watching desperately for any reportable nugget, and eager scholars were clamoring for a verdict. Working quickly and under the frenzied attentions of a hungry public, his efforts, understandably, were not perfect—and his errors provided excellent material for hawkeyed reporters out to prove their smarts.

"With some of [Ginsburg's] observations we concur," the *Record* conceded. "But it appears to us that a good deal more remains to be noted which he has not as yet found time to touch, and that there is room for a little more accuracy than appears at present either in his translation or in his remarks."

In his column the previous week, Ginsburg had suggested that the use of "God, thy God" in Shapira's Ten Commandments was especially notable because it was unique: the construction, he said, did not appear anywhere else in the Old Testament. The *Record*, however, seemed pleased to point out that Ginsburg was mistaken—this very phrase, supposedly distinctive, in fact occurs in the Book of Psalms: "Pay heed, My people, and I will speak, O Israel, and I will arraign. I am God, your God." In a subsequent column, Ginsburg acknowledged his error, and then proceeded to one-up his challengers. The *Record*'s researchers, it turns out, had not scoured their Bibles quite studiously enough. The phrase "God, thy God," Ginsburg reported, actually appears *twice*: once in Psalm 50 and again in number 45.

On August 15, 1883, while studying the scrolls alongside Ginsburg, Shapira received a most unwelcome shock. None other than his "greatest enemy," Charles Clermont-Ganneau, bounded through the doors of the manuscript room, greeted those in attendance, and asked if he might have a look at the scrolls.

In the fifteen years since the Moabite Stone's discovery, Ganneau had continued his diplomatic work, filling posts in Jerusalem,

Constantinople, and Jaffa. But it was his success as an archaeologist that had earned him renown. Working as a representative of both the PEF and the French government, Ganneau had documented his discoveries in a series of articles and books with titles like "A Stele of the Temple of Jerusalem" and "Studies in Oriental Archaeology." By the time he burst in on Shapira and Ginsburg, Ganneau had been named a Knight of the Legion of Honor. As he racked up a record of significant achievements and awards, he built on his early work debunking Shapira's pottery and became, according to one remembrance, "the top expert in matters of archaeological frauds."

It was a role he embraced with brio and a soldier's sense of duty. With archaeological forgeries proliferating in the Near East, the fledgling field's credibility was at stake. If someone did not step in to stem the tide, these fakes threatened to undermine true science in the eyes of laymen. Ganneau, gushed one Moabite Stone scholar, was just the man, a "pitiless and irrefutable denouncer of the apocrypha."

Shapira, who had already suffered the sting of Ganneau's pitiless denouncing, became livid at the French archaeologist's sudden intrusion into the Department of Oriental Manuscripts. Even after Ganneau had almost single-handedly thrown Shapira's career and reputation into disrepair, here he was, at the very hour of Shapira's return to the limelight, claiming to have been sent by France's minister of public instruction to get "acquainted" with the scrolls. It's even possible that Ganneau, having arrived from France that very morning, had been authorized to make an offer for the manuscripts if, after examining them, he still thought it prudent. Shapira wanted no part of it. He doubtless suspected what Ganneau himself would soon acknowledge—that getting "acquainted" with the documents meant blasting them as frauds.

A few days after alighting in London, Ganneau wrote in the

Times that he had "entertained, in advance, most serious doubts as to [the fragments'] authenticity, and that I came here in order to settle these doubts."

Years later he would admit that "the sole fact of Mr. Shapira's intervention in this affair could only confirm the impression of defiance that I had felt . . . upon the announcement of this unlikely find."

When Ganneau arrived at the British Museum, Ginsburg initially allowed him a quick glance at two or three of the scrolls, but he soon backtracked, asking the Frenchman to leave and return another time. Soon Ginsburg withdrew even that offer, suggesting to Ganneau that he might not be permitted to see any further fragments at all. It is possible that this was payback for the scene in Jerusalem eleven years earlier when Ganneau had refused him access to the Moabite Stone. Maybe there was lingering tension after Ginsburg scolded Ganneau for his behavior in obtaining the stone.

By the end of Ganneau's visit to the museum that day, Ginsburg's offer was this: *Come back Friday and we'll let you know.* Ganneau departed for accommodations at 42 Great Russell Street, a townhouse situated so nearby that, sitting by the front, one could almost look in through the windows of the manuscripts department.

While he awaited a decision, Shapira put to rest all questions about whether his nemesis would be allowed a preview of the manuscript. The answer, he informed Ginsburg and Bond, the museum's principal librarian, was a firm no.

When Ganneau returned on Friday, he was turned away. He departed, he would report, full of despair. And that, Shapira hoped, had put an end to that.

FROM PARIS WITH DOUBTS

When Shapira next heard from Ganneau, it was not in the form of another visit to the museum but in a lengthy hatchet job in the pages of the London press. In it, he reported that when he had approached Bond as agreed that Friday, the museum's top librarian explained that "he could not, to his great regret, submit the fragments to me; their owner, Mr. Shapira, having expressly refused his consent."

"There was nothing to be said against this," Ganneau explained in the *Times*. "The owner was free to act as he pleased. It was his strict right, but it is also my right to record publicly this refusal, quite personal to me; and this, to some extent is the cause of this communication. I leave to public opinion the business of explaining this refusal. I will confine myself to recalling one fact, without comment. It was Mr. Shapira who sold the spurious Moabite potteries to Germany; and it was M. Clermont-Ganneau who, 10 years ago, discovered and established the apocryphal nature of them."

Shapira's refusal was undeniably personal. And Ganneau's gloating only goes to show how right Shapira had been in his wariness of the strident linguist. But his summary dismissal from the Department of Oriental Manuscripts had not dampened Ganneau's eagerness to get at the manuscripts. Insulted by Shapira's rejection, he did not repair to a nearby pub to drown his sorrows. Instead he gathered his pride, took leave of Bond, and joined what seemed like the rest of London in the museum's Kings Library, where Ginsburg had recently ordered that two of the fragments be put on display. There Ganneau launched his own rogue inquiry, spending the next two days jostling with the mass of plebes who, like him, had come to see the scrolls for themselves. The rest of Friday and again on Saturday, he struggled to gain a foothold near the glass display case, around which waves of visitors had packed themselves. The light was very poor. The task was "unpleasant." And yet Ganneau's work yielded what he called, a bit disingenuously, an "unhoped-for result."

"The fragments," he concluded, "are the work of a modern forger."

Ganneau was a difficult man, but his scholarship was—and remains—widely respected. His reasoning, as ever, was lawyerly, clever, and, ultimately, simple.

Despite the subpar working conditions, Ganneau explained, he was able to see enough of the scrolls through the glass to discern that, between each column of writing, a vertical crease ran through the leather, from top to bottom. Next he noticed that two parallel vertical lines, "almost invisible but indelible," had been etched into the leather to the left and right of each crease, using some sort of hard point—a stylus, perhaps. These lines, Ganneau surmised, had been scored to guide the scribe, indicating the borders over which his writing ought not stray. But he then noticed something interesting: the writer seemed to have ignored these guidelines, his calligraphy frequently jutting over the boundaries both left and right. This struck him as odd—why would a scribe make the effort to scratch in borders if he was simply going to pretend they did not exist?

The answer, Ganneau deduced, was—like answers to so many of life's big questions—to be found in the Torah. More precisely, it could be located in the way Jewish scribes, known in Hebrew as *sof-*

rim, prepare the parchment on which they inscribe the scrolls Jews read aloud in synagogues four times each week. These *sifrei Torah,* which can measure well over a hundred feet in length before they are rolled up like carpets and affixed to wooden posts, are, like Shapira's scrolls, written in columns. And the columns are ruled—single vertical lines scored top to bottom between columns of writing and horizontal lines scored between them, one for each line of text. The effect looks something like a piece of loose-leaf paper. Above and below the writing are blank margins. While these margins typically are not scored horizontally, the vertical line is often scratched all the way from the top of the upper margin to the bottom of the lower one. Such scoring was evident on Shapira's scrolls, which for Ganneau was a telling clue. From it he deduced that the forger had simply acquired an old synagogue scroll and sliced off its lower margin.

"He obtained in this way some narrow strips of leather with an appearance of comparative antiquity, which was still further heightened by the use of the proper chemical agents," he wrote. "On these strips of leather he wrote with ink, making use of the alphabet of the Moabite Stone, and introducing such 'various readings' as fancy dictated the passages from Deuteronomy which have been deciphered and translated by M. Ginsburg, with patience and learning worthy of better employment."

Ganneau's theory seemed plausible, not least because Shapira had bought and sold dozens of Torah scrolls of the variety that could have been desecrated for such a project. Was it so difficult to imagine the prime actor in the Moabite pottery scandal putting one of his holy scrolls to such unholy use? The only remaining question, Ganneau said, was whether "the forger" had the gall to sell the marred Torah scroll after performing his diabolical surgery, thereby leaving behind evidence of his crime.

"Nothing is more easy than to effect the experimental examination which I suggest," Ganneau crowed. "Let there be given to me a synagogue roll, two or three centuries old, with permission to cut it up. I engage to procure from it strips in every respect similar to the Moabitish strips, and to transcribe upon them in archaic characters the text of Leviticus, for example, or of Numbers. This would make a fitting sequel to the Deuteronomy of Mr. Shapira, but would have the slight advantage over it of not costing quite a million sterling."

In rushing his essay into print, Ganneau had scooped Ginsburg—who had yet to issue his own conclusions—and had poisoned the well for Shapira. His report now set the course of public opinion. Where earlier Shapira's discovery had prompted excitement, it now invited scorn. He could only hope that, having conducted a more thorough examination than Ganneau's, Ginsburg might come to a more favorable conclusion.

While he awaited Ginsburg's answer, a number of other outlets took aim. For those predisposed to believe in the strips' authenticity, the similarities to the Moabite Stone pointed to its ancientness. But for others, the resemblance was evidence of a ruse. Rev. C. H. Waller fell squarely into the latter category. Presumably working off Ginsburg's published transcriptions, Waller counted up the number of words that occur in both Shapira's scroll and the Moabite Stone, arriving at a figure of forty. But these repetitions didn't just occur, he insisted. They occurred in a highly "peculiar manner." In addition to a number of awkward words whose use in Shapira's document, he noted, seemed forced, he pointed out that certain place names—Moab, Ara'ir, Arnon, Jahaz—appeared in Shapira's text as well as on the Moabite Stone. But other place-names that appear in the traditional text of Deuteronomy are absent from the Shapira manuscript. Tellingly, he said, these missing names also do not show up on the Moabite Stone. All this, Waller postulated, pointed to the fact that whoever wrote Shapira's document was working with the Mesha stele in front of him, deliberately copying words from its text to present the appearance of kinship between the two, thus making the scrolls appear much older than they actually were. A similar argument had been used to condemn the Moabite pottery, whose letters were akin to those chiseled into the stone.

Taking up Ganneau's repudiation with delight, a number of newspapers now claimed to have known all along that the slips were nothing more than an elaborate hoax. Among them was the *Standard*, which pronounced the affair a "solemn farce."

"Our only wonder has always been how a fraud so transparent could for a single hour have imposed on the credulity of the experts who for the last three weeks have been wasting their learned leisure in discussing the authenticity of these scraps of dingy leather," the paper scolded. "So barefaced, indeed, is the attempt to impose on the world scraps of leather a few centuries old, covered with Moabitish characters of recent date, as a manuscript of Deuteronomy, written in the Ninth Century before the Christian Era, that we did not consider it necessary to occupy space which could be utilized with more authentic chronicles by extensive quotations from this rough travesty of the Pentateuch."

These are harsh words—and utterly self-serving. Because what the *Standard* did not mention here, for obvious reasons, is that just eight days earlier it had published a column about Gladstone's visit with Shapira, "occupying space" with a debate not over whether the manuscript was real or fake, but exactly when it had been written: eighth century BCE? The period of the captivity? The Maccabean period?

The *Times,* for its part, took pains to demonstrate that it, too, had been skeptical. Belatedly diminishing the affair to which it had devoted so much prime real estate to an "interesting and amusing" curio, the paper reported that, "in first calling attention to the subject we poluted out the strong antecedent presumption against the genuineness of the fragments, a presumption resting upon the extreme improbability that leather should be found in excellent preservation after the lapse of twenty-seven centuries."

If the *Times'* editorial staff had early on "poluted out" the scrolls' fraudulence, as they proudly declared on August 21, why then did they bother to publish the final installment of Ginsburg's translation the very next day?

Nevertheless, the unlikelihood of leather surviving so long in the relatively damp climate around the eastern shores of the Dead Sea was a common refrain among Shapira's doubters. The *Standard*, in its underhanded effort to disavow the manuscripts, made a similar point—as did the *Academy*, where the British orientalist A. H. Sayce argued that ascribing such staying power to animal hides was "really demanding too much of Western credulity."

Although the proliferation of voices condemning his scrolls can't have pleased Shapira, he must have taken heart from the fact that next to none of those men who had thus far issued verdicts on the manuscripts had, in fact, laid eyes on anything more than the two poorly lit scrolls exhibited under glass. Rather, these scholars and enthusiasts were relying on hearsay, speculation, reports in the papers by still others who had yet to see the full coterie of fragments, and Ginsburg's piecemeal publication of his transcriptions. In fact, it sometimes felt as if the only person in London not holding forth on the authenticity of Shapira's scrolls was the one man who had standing to do so—Christian David Ginsburg.

This imbalance did not go unnoticed by some of the day's more restrained observers. Blasting the "egotism of the learned world," one journalist opined that, whatever Ginsburg ultimately concluded, there were those scholars who, ignoring the "true spirit of criticism or scholarship," seemed altogether too eager to stigmatize the manuscripts as forgeries.

"The flippant offer of a French archaeologist to provide us with an entire Pentateuch of similar apparent antiquity," he wrote, "is about equal in value to Dr. Lardner's promise that he would swallow the first steamship that succeeded in traversing the Atlantic."

Ganneau's theory, while plausible and well argued, reflected as much about his methods as it did about the scrolls. To begin with, when he first appeared at the museum, Ginsburg allowed him access to just two or three of the strips, and for what he himself acknowledged was only a "few minutes." This was scantly sufficient time, or material, for a thorough review. The bulk of his thesis, he said, emerged after examining only two further scrolls as he battled to stay at the front of a rapacious crowd. It was clever—but the willingness to go public with the theory on so little evidence was reckless. Unless, of course, Ganneau's story about developing his theory at the public display had been concocted to hide an uncomfortable truth: that he had come by his ideas less honestly. It would not have been the first time.

ON AUGUST 22, Ginsburg handed his report to Bond. Having enjoyed the benefit of a month with the scrolls, he offered a more complete testimony than Ganneau's. He investigated not only the physical characteristics of the strips but also the "internal" evidence imparted by their writing. He was thorough. He was, it seemed, objective. And he wasted no time getting to the point.

"Dear Mr. Bond," his statement began. "The manuscript of Deuteronomy which Mr. Shapira submitted to us for examination is a forgery."

Ginsburg condemns the strips on ten basic points, beginning

with much the same argument Ganneau had made in the *Times*. The fragments, he said, were sliced from the margins of a Torah scroll. Taking it a step further, Ginsburg suggested which specific Torah scroll might have been the source of the slips. In November 1877, he recalled, Shapira had sold a number of such scrolls to the British Museum. Among them, he reported, was one cataloged by the museum as "Oriental, 1457." That manuscript, he said, had just such a cutoff slip fastened to the beginning of Genesis (Shapira had used it to label the document). "And this scroll was bought from Mr. Shapira in 1877, the very year in which he declares that he obtained the inscribed slips."

Shapira, in fact, claimed to have acquired the strips in the summer of 1878. Even so, this error does nothing to diminish the comment's underlying accusation: that someone not only *could*, but *did* remove a strip from an old scroll and affix it to Oriental 1457. Most damningly, circumstantial evidence pointed to who that person was: the man who had sold the manuscript to the museum—Moses Wilhelm Shapira.

Ginsburg went on to note, as Ganneau had done earlier, the presence of vertical lines, scored into the leather of the Deuteronomy fragments. More remarkable, he said, was that the uninscribed slip that had been appended to Oriental 1457 also was scored in this way, and its lines "correspond to the inscribed Shapira fragments."

Next Ginsburg pointed out that the upper and lower edges of the Torah scrolls in the museum's collection were rough and worn from years of use. Shapira's fragments, however, were worn only on their bottom edges; their top sides retained the smooth edge of a surgical cut. This indicated to Ginsburg that Shapira's fragments had only recently been sliced from their mother scroll.

In addition, Ginsburg argued that the fragments had been treated with chemical agents to infuse them with the appearance of antiquity. Noting that the edges were of a different color than the rest of the strips, he suggested that the forger had enclosed the scrolls in a frame to hold the chemicals as they acted on the leather.

Ginsburg's internal evidence was more technical. The conclusions he drew from it, however, do not require a Ph.D. in ancient Hebrew to understand. The scrolls, he reported, were forged by a gang of no fewer than four people: two scribes who did the writing, a chemist, and a "compiler"—the group's boss, who not only called the shots on what text was to be included, but orally dictated it to his scribes word for word. Even more remarkable, Ginsburg named both the geographic origin and religious faith of the compiler. He was, Ginsburg said, a Jew from Poland, Russia, or Germany, or one who had studied Hebrew in northern Europe. His thinking here signals Ginsburg's nimble mind. Working through the text, he spotted a number of curious spelling errors. In one case, the text spells the word *chevel* with the letter *kaph,* where in fact the letter *chet* would have been correct. In another, the phrase for "of their drink offerings" is written using *chet* where *kaph* was called for. Whoever wrote the manuscript, in other words, seemed to have used these two letters interchangeably. In speech, Ginsburg pointed out, northern European Jews did just that—when spoken, *chet* and *kaph* sounded the same. From this he infers that the Polish, German, or Russian Jewish compiler dictated these words aloud to one of his scribes, who simply wrote them down as he heard them—one indistinguishable from another. In doing so, he inserted a number of telling spelling mistakes.

Three decades later, on the day following Ginsburg's funeral at London's Southgate Cemetery, the *Times* published a short piece recounting his role in the Shapira affair. Several days after that, a Cambridge resident named, appropriately enough, Israel Abraham wrote in to correct the record: it was, in fact, Ganneau, Abraham insisted, who had been the "first public exposer" of Shapira's deception. Abraham's assertion did not sit well with Ginsburg's son, Benedict, a prominent barrister and secretary of the Royal Statistical Society. Just as the drama itself had unfolded years earlier in the *Times*, Ginsburg fils took to the paper's pages to defend his late father's rightful place as the exposer in chief. The story he told reads like something he had been waiting years to get off his chest.

When Ganneau entered the Department of Oriental Manuscripts all those years earlier, Benedict said, his father—days away from publishing his findings—had taken him for a "brother savant" and laid out his argument for forgery. Thus educated on the intricacies of a manuscript with which he had almost no prior contact, Ganneau "tried to anticipate the report and to claim credit for the exposure."

In a subsequent letter in the *Times*, the younger Ginsburg added the following:

> Dr. Ginsburg was drawn to his recognition of the source from which the parchments of the MSS. were obtained by his knowledge that the margins of certain synagogue rolls, purchased some time previously by the Museum from Shapira himself, had been tampered with. Ganneau could not have known this. I submit to you, Sir, that it is conclusive of the fact that in a moment of pardonable, if ill-placed, confidence, Dr. Ginsburg told Ganneau of his discovery, thus enabling the latter to anticipate the official report.

Given Ganneau's zeal to expose fraud wherever he caught a whiff, to say nothing of his alleged habit of co-opting other people's ideas as his own, this account rings true.

Whoever enjoyed the privilege of condemning the Deuteronomy manuscripts first, the verdict was the same—and its impact on Shapira was devastating. If Ganneau had fouled the well, Ginsburg exploded it altogether. Shapira had been holding out hope that the museum's report would contradict that of the Frenchman. Shortly after passing his report to Bond, Ginsburg met with Shapira and disabused him of any such notion. Shapira was crushed, and the following day sent the scholar a foreboding note.

> Dear Dr. Ginzberg!
>
> You have made a fool of me by publishing and exhibiting things that you believe them to be false. I do not think that I will be able to survive this shame. Although I am yet not convince that the MS is a forgery unless M. Ganneau did it.
>
> I will leave London in a day or two for Berlin.
>
> Yours truly,
> MW Shapira

Ginsburg—whether out of pique or concern we do not know—shared the note with other interested parties, who took it as nothing more than a stagy call for sympathy meant to guilt him into changing his mind. On the day Ginsburg's report appeared in the *Times*, the paper also ran this gibe:

"[Shapira] is so disappointed with the results of his bargain that he threatens to commit suicide. This, we venture to think, he will not do. He has survived the Moabite pottery fraud, and he will probably survive this new one."

14

PLAYING DEFENSE

Humiliated and threatening suicide, Shapira fled England for the Continent. It is possible he was headed to Berlin to see Augusta, who was enrolled in private school there. En route he stopped in Amsterdam, where he paused to compose a lively twelve-page letter to Bond arguing forcefully against Ginsburg's debunking.

Shapira seems to have regained a measure of composure in Amsterdam; this letter was far less desperate than his last. While the earlier note laid blame at Ganneau's feet, this one impugned Ginsburg's motives, taking particular issue with his contention that a Polish Jew was behind the production—a theory Shapira insisted had been arrived at in "great haste."* Among all Ginsburg's claims, Shapira viewed this one as the most dangerous. It was bad enough that Ginsburg indicted the manuscript as a forgery—but that alone might have allowed Shapira's career to survive. He may, again, have proved the bumbling victim, the fraud's first dupe, but that is something altogether less sinister than the underlying implication of the Polish Jew contention: that Shapira himself was the forger.

The irony of the argument is as bitter as its insinuation of guilt.

---

*Ginsburg also suggested that it may have been a Russian or German Jew.

By the time Ginsburg's report was published, Shapira had been a Christian for the better part of thirty years. And now here was Ginsburg, himself a convert, labeling Shapira a fraud precisely because of a linguistic tic he would have picked up studying Hebrew as a young Jewish student in Kamenets-Podolsk. No matter how far Shapira had come or how high he had climbed—no matter how many manuscripts he had sold or Our Fathers he had intoned—the world he had so strived to impress and in which he had tried so desperately to fit still saw him as a tricky little Jew from Poland. He had spent three decades evading his past; now it would prove to be his downfall.

"You will excuse my troubling you again with my bad English," Shapira began, "but the thing seems to me to be of such high importance that I dare to write again begging you to let the M.S. be examined by several scholars & archiologe's of different schools or doctarinns. The sin of beliving in a false document, is not much greater than disbiliving the truth. The tendency of showing great scholarship by detecting a forgery is rather great in our age."

Shapira's accusation against Ginsburg here is the mirror image of Ginsburg's charge against him. Whereas Shapira had been accused of scheming to get ahead through the deliberate creation and marketing of a fraud, Ginsburg, Shapira said, was puffing himself up by knocking down an authentic relic as fake. This puts a finer point on Shapira's earlier cri de coeur to Ginsburg: "You have made a fool of me," he had written in his anguished note a couple of days earlier, "by publishing and exhibiting things that you believe them to be false."

Why, Shapira was asking, would Ginsburg have put two of his fragments on public display if he had been convinced all along they were faked? If he had believed them frauds, why did he continue publishing excerpts in the papers? Shapira answered the question for himself. By setting the scrolls on a pedestal, he told Bond, Ginsburg could gain greater fame when he knocked them off. And with that, Shapira proceeded to hack away at Ginsburg's report.

> *If polish jews of Jerusalem would have any hand in such a forgery, we would have had since the time of 1878 many more of such kinds, even, the two table stones [of the Ten Commandments] & the thing would have a marked by an few Americans & Russians who are hunting for such relics, besides: the question would be for what purpose did they made that M.S. of Deut. the payment was too small to devide between them & the Arabs. no; the polish jews had had nothing to do with it.*

After presenting his counterarguments on this matter, Shapira showed that, despite it all, he still had a sense of humor, citing, of all things, an old Jewish joke. The story is premised on the biblical exhortation that Jews "redeem" their firstborn sons through a five-shekel payment.

"I confess Sir that my argument look to me after written them as comical as the 5 reasons that a jew gave, for not having redeemed his first born son with 5 shekels according to the law given by moses.— mentioned in the Rabinical book," Shapira wrote.

> *A prist asked him for the 5 shekels as his first born son is now 30 days old, he, the father, would not pay him the sum? Why? he now asked? because the father answered,*
> *1st I am myself a prist –*
> *2 my wife had a son before and this is not a first born.*
> *3 they are twins and not subjected to that law –*
> *4. It is not a boy, but they are girls*
> *5 they were born dead — — —*

Though not an instant classic, the joke still managed to make Shapira's point: he was well aware that, like the dissembling father of his story, he appeared to be summoning every excuse in the book. But whereas the joke, mercifully, ended, Shapira spent eight more pages pressing the manuscript's authenticity and explaining why, even if it was fraudulent, he assuredly was not its forger.

"But some one will ask did Shapira, not make it?" To this he responded by pointing to his own reported errors in transcribing the document, errors noted by the likes of Schlottmann, to whom he sent what he now described as his mistake-laden transcription in 1878. These errors, Shapira wrote, cast doubt on the manuscript's veracity from the very start. Shapira claimed that he later realized many of these mistakes were not errors in the text but rather in his transcription. Had he been the forger, he asked Bond, would he have included such suspicious errors when sending his copy to Schlottmann?

"So," he continued, "Shapira who read the M.S. often so bad as to make the M.S. very suspicious could not have been the author of it."

He also noted that he was neither a calligrapher nor a chemist, skills that would have been necessary to produce such a document. This explanation is unpersuasive, as Ginsburg himself believed the operation had been undertaken by a number of people, each possessing a unique set of skills.

On concerns raised by Ginsburg and many others about the feasibility of leather surviving in the damp climate east of the Dead Sea, Shapira demurred.

"Here I do not know what to say?" Shapira wrote. "Because, that are only guess work. as we do not know. how the things were keep & in what place & how. well covered. & how long used before they were buried."

Finally, he added, the lower edges of his scrolls were degraded because in the course of routine use, a reader naturally rubs up against the lower portions with greater frequency than the upper ones.

"That, Sir, are the reasons why I am not convinced that the MS are false," he concluded. "Nevertheless I do not wish to sell it even if the [illegible] buyer should take the ris[k] himself (I have such offers) unless to authorities."

ALTHOUGH HE PROFESSED himself "not convinced" that the scrolls were fraudulent, Shapira suggested who might be responsible if they were. Here, as in his brief letter to Ginsburg, Shapira implicated Ganneau, "who must have been very bitter" after Münchhausen published a letter in the *Athenaeum* suggesting that the Moabitica Ganneau so roundly dismissed could have been real. Seeking retribution, Shapira said, Ganneau could have forged the scrolls "to put a trap into me and the consul."

The Ganneau theory, while self-serving, cannot be dismissed outright. Like the firefighter moonlighting as an arsonist, is it not possible to imagine that the great, duty-bound fraud hunter himself had hatched a brilliant fake so as to ferret it out and expose it? And that, just as Ginsburg was about to take credit for discovering his deception, he swooped in to expose it himself? Perhaps Ganneau hadn't stolen Ginsburg's theory at all. Maybe he knew all the answers because he had written the questions. And what better dupe than Shapira—a man clearly out for a big score. A man who, even before showing up at the British Museum, fragments in hand, had become "almost too well known" as a purveyor of fakes.

In his *Times* takedown, Ganneau himself had laid out criteria for identifying the forger.

"Who is the forger?" he asked. "That is a question which it does not concern me to answer, nor even to raise. I will merely call attention to the fact that he can only be a person familiar with Hebrew, and who has had before his eyes exact copies of the Moabite Stone."

To these attributes I would add that the putative forger—if not Shapira—would have had to know, or know of, Shapira, and would have required contacts among the Arabs living in or near Jerusalem willing to pass the forgeries along to him. He also would have had to possess a background in Bible study. This would make for a fairly short list of candidates—and topping it would be a man who knew the Moabite Stone more intimately than any other, a man who had not only been first to transcribe and translate it but had, quite literally, rebuilt it: Ganneau himself. He knew Shapira, of course, and they did not get along. What's more, Ganneau's contacts with Arabs around Jerusalem were robust.

Here's another name that would surely appear near the head of the list: Christian David Ginsburg. That he was expert in ancient Hebrew is by now evident. He was also a recognized authority on the Moabite Stone. There were no hard feelings between Ginsburg and Shapira, and so spite or revenge are out as motives. But if the forger's goal was, as Shapira suggested, to gain fame debunking his own creation, Ginsburg could have done worse than saving the British Museum a million pounds sterling and substantial embarrassment.

Consider this: Ginsburg had met Shapira at his shop in 1872, during his journey in Palestine and Moab. As anyone passing through Jerusalem with even a glancing interest in Near Eastern antiquities knew, Shapira's store was ground zero for the collection and sale of ancient inscriptions. Ginsburg had experienced this firsthand, having examined there what he at first thought were missing fragments of the Moabite Stone. And then there was Ginsburg's appearance at the Palestine Exploration Fund meeting, where Shapira had so flamboyantly unveiled his scrolls. Recall that, although only a small number of people had been invited, Ginsburg arrived with "the whole of the

British Museum" and "all the Hebrew scholars in London" in tow. The large group of scholars, along with at least one member of the media (William Simpson of the *Illustrated London News*), would have exponentially increased the buzz orbiting the scrolls. So, too, did Ginsburg's periodic updates, transcriptions, and translations in the English press which, coupled with his reticence on the question of authenticity, had led many to believe he thought the scrolls were real. Additionally, Ginsburg had contacts with any number of Bedouin who, during his Near Eastern journey, had served as his guides, captors, and saviors. Finally, his suggestion that whoever had forged the Shapira scrolls was a Jew from Poland, Germany, or Russia is curious. Ginsburg himself was a Polish Jew, Warsaw-born, who had later converted to Christianity and emigrated to England. Was this suggestion a bit of reverse psychology ("Of course Ginsburg didn't do it—if he had, he wouldn't have blamed a Pole")?

Then there's this:

Not long after the Shapira affair, the prolific Russian Jewish writer, bibliographer, and book dealer Ephraim Deinard visited London to sell a number of items to the British Museum. Charles Rieu, who headed up the Oriental Manuscripts Department, asked Deinard to stick around and compile a catalog of the museum's Duke of Sussex manuscript collection. Deinard, an iconoclast with an impressive white goatee and a stinging distaste for Jews who convert out, accepted the invitation, but with a stipulation: he had to be permitted to work off-site. The museum, he complained, was too stuffy and, worse yet, forbade smoking. Rieu accepted Deinard's conditions and had the collection delivered to Virginia Water, Ginsburg's home in Surrey. There, Deinard reported, nestled in the attractive countryside beside his host's pleasant garden, he was given two rooms in which to breathe, smoke, and work. It was while doing so, he said, that he made a troubling discovery.

Among the manuscripts over which he toiled, he said, for eighteen hours each day, Deinard discovered a beautiful old copy of the Massorah, an ancient anthology of comments on the pronunciation and writing of the Hebrew Bible. In 1880, Ginsburg had begun publishing a multivolume critical edition of this book, a towering work that became his seminal contribution to biblical scholarship. Now, scrolling the first pages of this earlier publication, Deinard noted that its scribe, a native of Vilnius, had written the manuscript sometime between 1833 and 1834.

"At this point I checked *The Massorah* published by Ginsburg," Deinard remembered, "and lo and behold it was a transcription in every detail from this manuscript!"

"I feel myself under a sacred obligation to reveal to the scholarly world that the apostate, whom I knew to be a total ignoramus, was not the author," Deinard said.

Sure now that Ginsburg had stolen his masterwork from this older book, the feisty Deinard very deliberately left the manuscript open on his table to make sure that "the apostate should see it" upon his return.

He did.

"Towards evening, when he came in and saw the manuscript open, he realised I had uncovered a dangerous secret, and snatched it from the table and hid it," Deinard recalled. "I was never allowed to see the manuscript again."

This story comes with three attendant caveats. First, Deinard wrote it nearly four decades after the encounter allegedly took place, by which time he was into his seventies. Second, no one else witnessed the meeting, and by the time Deinard's book was published, Ginsburg, dead six years, could not respond. Finally, in the same book—a two-volume set of tales about Jewish life in Russia—Deinard included an animated and error-ridden recounting of the

Shapira affair. In his rendering, the Odessa-born merchant attempts to sell the original stone tablets containing the Ten Commandments for five million pounds. Shapira, of course, was born in Kamenets-Podolsk, and the sale he proposed to the British Museum was of a leather manuscript, and that at a mere one million pounds. Deinard's recollections, then, must be taken with a grain of salt.

Or they could be true.

Either way, his claim was cutting—that Ginsburg, among the most respected biblical scholars of his day, was nothing more than a rank plagiarist. Worse yet, his greatest work, the accomplishment for which he remains best known, was the very opus that he had allegedly stolen from a brilliant Vilnius sage. If Ginsburg had faked it once, the story suggests, certainly he could have done it again.

While many of Ginsburg's printed books were auctioned off by Sotheby's, much of his extensive manuscript library today resides at Cambridge University. Among these texts is a nineteenth-century manuscript of the Massorah by a writer named Simon Silberberg—a book the eminent bibliographer Brad Sabin Hill told me is "almost certainly" the one Deinard claimed was copied.

"It's clear from Ginsburg's own description, in his introduction to *The Massoretico-Critical Edition of the Hebrew Bible*, that this is an extraordinary manuscript, and Deinard could well be right, more or less, that it served as the basis for Ginsburg's own work," Hill told me. "But Ginsburg's description, though it doesn't say it outright, is not altogether disingenuous. He says: 'He [Silberberg] has laboured and I have entered into his labours.' That, I suppose, is as good an admission as one can get."

IN 1902, NINETEEN years after the Shapira affair, the writer, linguist, and rare-manuscript collector A. S. Yahuda visited Jerusalem.

Shortly after he arrived, Yahuda, who would go on to write a controversial book called *The Accuracy of the Bible*, was approached by an Arab who offered the visitor his services as a guide. He had access to unusual antiquities, the guide told Yahuda, and could secure specimens not available to anyone else. The man's name was Salim.

Yahuda, recalling the incident years later in the *Jewish Quarterly Review*, quickly realized that the old man was none other than Salim al Kari. A few days after their meeting, Salim showed up again, this time offering up a selection of "Moabite antiquities": pots, lamps, idols, and small clay lions.

"The sight of all these monstrous figures brought to my memory those Moabite antiques which had been acquired from Shapira by the Berlin Museum," Yahuda recalled.

Several weeks later, the two men got to talking. "He said to me, in a disconsolate mood, that he was growing old and tired of a world of falsehood and wickedness in which an honest man cannot earn his bread without making forgeries!" Yahuda said.

"'I swear by Allah, the Messiah and all the saints,'" Salim continued, "'that I feel much happier with the little money I made out of the coins and the few other things I sold to you, than with all the money I got for the Moabite antiques,—and it was a lot—, in spite of all the endeavors of that rogue of [*sic*] Shapira to rob me as much as he could.' Then he began to tell me some 'secrets' of his past: how he helped Shapira in the preparation of the leather strips which had been cut away from old Torah scrolls and then inscribed with portions of Deuteronomy; and how he taught Shapira to soak these strips in an oil lotion to make them appear much older."

It's hard to know what to make of Yahuda's recollections. Like Deinard, he was telling his story years after the alleged interaction. And even if his memory was perfect, who's to say whether Salim was telling the truth or trying to insert himself into a well-known story to impress a foreign guest.

That famous story, in any event, remained set well into the twentieth century: Shapira had forged the Deuteronomy manuscript, tried to sell it to the British Museum, and failed.

Then, sixty-four years later, a Bedouin shepherd grazing goats on a mountain overlooking the Dead Sea accidentally discovered a cliffside cave full of old Hebrew scrolls and changed everything.

IN LIGHT OF RECENT DISCOVERIES

With the discovery of the Dead Sea Scrolls, some in the learned world could not help but notice the similarities between these manuscripts and Shapira's Deuteronomy. Suddenly much of the evidence put forward to dismiss Shapira's slips as forgeries seemed far less convincing. To begin with, both sets of scrolls were uncovered by Bedouin exploring caves near the Dead Sea. Then there were the evident parallels between the scrolls themselves. There were abridgments. There were sections from one biblical book imported into another. There were unusual spellings. There were even differences in the Ten Commandments. Tellingly, there were more copies of Deuteronomy found at Qumran than almost any other book of the Bible. Perhaps most significant of all, the discovery of the Dead Sea Scrolls proved that leather manuscripts could, indeed, survive in that region. Were Shapira's scrolls, some wondered, the very first Dead Sea Scrolls, discovered seventy years before the rest?

In April 1956, the head of Israel's Antiquities Authority suggested that the Shapira manuscript merited a new look. When Professor Menahem Mansoor, then chairman of the Department of Hebrew and Semitic Studies at the University of Wisconsin, heard this proposal, he became so excited that he found himself unable to sleep. The Egyptian-born Mansoor, a meticulous scholar who had served with the British Ministry of Information during World War II, wondered if he might be the man for the job.

Very little was then known about Shapira. While contemporary sources referred to him either as Mr. Shapira or M. W. Shapira, by the time Mansoor stumbled onto his story, no one even knew what those initials stood for. With none of the central characters alive to answer questions, Mansoor had to dig—not in the sands Shapira once explored, but in the voluminous files of the British Museum. He planted himself in the manuscripts department, not far from where Shapira and Ginsburg had welcomed Prime Minister Gladstone—and snubbed Ganneau—all those years earlier.

In the summer of 1956, Mansoor passed a full month combing through the museum's records on Shapira, stored away in its dossier No. 41294. The more Mansoor read, the less impressed he became with the arguments that had brought Shapira down. Much of the evidence against the Shapira manuscript did not add up. This was not necessarily surprising—the men making the call, after all, were not privy to the archaeological discoveries and scientific advances that the twentieth century had brought with it. But Mansoor was. He had all the tools and all the education he would need to determine whether Shapira's scrolls were authentic.

In the summer of 1956, Mansoor gave an interview to the *New York Times* in which he proclaimed to the world that, seventy-two years after Shapira's untimely death, he had reopened the investigation into the scrolls' authenticity. Prominently treated on the paper's front page, the article opened with a lede ready-made for Hollywood, announcing that the case of a man dismissed seventy years earlier as a huckster "because of disbelief that he had discovered a Dead Sea scroll has been reopened at the British Museum by an American scholar."

Racing through elements of the Shapira affair and Mansoor's recent adventures in the British Museum, the article closed with the Wisconsin scholar's preliminary conclusions.

"I do not claim that Shapira's Deuteronomy is genuine," he told the *Times*. "I simply believe that, in the light of recent discoveries, the whole question must be carefully examined. My impression is that there is a good chance of this scroll emerging as a genuine one."

The article was reprinted internationally in several leading newspapers, and Mansoor himself was featured on the BBC. His call to reevaluate the scrolls reached a large audience already primed by the Dead Sea Scrolls to take an interest in ancient Bibles written in the region where the prophets and poets of scripture had once spread wisdom and broken bread. Like Mansoor, many readers and listeners were intrigued by the notion that a largely forgotten merchant from Jerusalem might have beaten Muhammad ad-Dibh to the first of the famous scrolls.

But before Mansoor had a chance to gather his thoughts and publish a thorough report on his work, he found himself taking fire in the pages of a number of respected journals. The situation was reminiscent of Shapira's own battles in the press. The first salvo came from Oscar K. Rabinowicz, a journalist, educator, and ardent Zionist.

"There is no mystery about the 'Biblical Scroll Mystery' which John Hillaby described in *The New York Times* of August 13," he began. "It has been solved as far back as August 1883—seventy-three years ago almost to the day."

This bleak assessment of Mansoor's project was followed by a rundown of the evidence offered decades earlier to condemn Shapira's manuscript. Rabinowicz quoted at length from Ginsburg's report, concluding that it was "incredible that it should be thought possible to arrive at different conclusions through a new investigation."

Amazingly, considering what we know today, Rabinowicz ended his piece by calling into question the authenticity not only of Shapira's scrolls, but of the Dead Sea Scrolls themselves.

"If it should be possible to prove—as is indicated in John Hillaby's report—that these fragments are textually similar to or in some parts even identical with certain scrolls discovered since 1947 in Qumran," he contended, "then a mystery of unparalleled importance would be woven round the latter, and thus justify to a great extent what Professor Zeitlin of Dropsie College Philadelphia has been claiming about the Dead Sea Scrolls based on internal evidence."

In other words, similarities between the Shapira manuscript and the Dead Sea Scrolls was not evidence that the Shapira scroll was real—instead, such analogies would simply indicate that the Dead Sea Scrolls were fakes.

In case readers did not fully grasp the gist of Rabinowicz's argument, Zeitlin himself added a postscript. "I believe the entire blame for the sensationalism in connection with the Shapira forgeries should not be placed on Mr. Hillaby for his dispatch published in *The New York Times* of August 13, 1956," he wrote. "Mr. Hillaby reported only what he had been told by Professor M. Mansoor."

Rabinowicz published two subsequent attacks, and was soon joined by the Hebrew University biblical philologist Moshe Goshen-Gottstein, who between the winter of 1956 and the following summer published a series of thoughtful, and highly technical, articles in the *Jewish Chronicle*, the *Journal of Jewish Studies*, and *Ha'aretz*, then the leading Israeli daily. The essays powerfully argued that a basic knowledge of Near Eastern paleography not only ruled out any connection between Shapira's manuscript and the Dead Sea Scrolls, but made blatantly clear that the former was a modern forgery.

The ancients, he noted, used different scripts for monuments (like the Moabite Stone) and documents (like the Dead Sea Scrolls).

Scholars did not know this until years after Shapira died. But for Goshen-Gottstein, the fact that Shapira's scrolls were written in the monumental script demonstrated that the forger—ignorant of the distinction—had probably dreamed up his Deuteronomy using the Moabite Stone as a manual. Even putting that aside, he said, the textual deviations of the Shapira scrolls had little in common with those from Qumran.

"Scholarship did not suffer any loss by the decision of the responsible authorities of the British Museum in those days not to acquire the Shapira fake," Goshen-Gottstein concluded. "Due attention having been given to Dr. Mansoor's suggestions, it will incur no loss at present if further discussion of the Qumran scrolls remains unhampered by memories of the unfortunate Shapira forgery."

But even as Goshen-Gottstein sought to put an end to further consideration of the issue, Mansoor refused to be silenced. In December 1956, he went before a group of some three hundred international Bible scholars and Semitists to refute the claims being made against him. Mansoor handed participants a sixteen-page mimeographed pamphlet that included a series of documents, quotations, and other sources supporting his contentions. He found a receptive audience. Addressing the gathering, Mansoor reported, J. Philip Hyatt, Old Testament scholar and then director of the Society of Biblical Literature and Exegesis, had expressed the belief that the Qumran discoveries might eventually lead to the authentication of the Shapira documents. Several other "eminent scholars," Mansoor said, subsequently urged him to continue his investigation.

Three months later, another scholar went a step further. Writing in the *Times Literary Supplement*, Cambridge University Jewish studies lecturer J. L. Teicher argued that "the benefit of new knowledge derived from the discovery of the Dead Sea Scrolls" led to "the inescapable conclusion that the Shapira manuscripts were genuine."

This went beyond anything even Mansoor had claimed—not only in exonerating Shapira and rehabilitating his scrolls, but in Teicher's controversial assessment of the scrolls' literary provenance. Suggesting that the manuscript dated from the second or third century, Teicher described it as a copy of Deuteronomy "re-drafted for liturgical and catechetic purposes, in the Jewish-Christian Church." In other words, Shapira's scrolls were not written by Shapira. They were written by some of the earliest Christians.

"The moral duty of endeavouring to rehabilitate Shapira and his manuscripts is inescapable," he concluded.

One can only imagine Shapira's glee had he ever learned that an Egyptian-born Jewish professor from Wisconsin and a leading Cambridge scholar had fervently taken up his cause. During his life, he had desperately sought the embrace of the international scholarly community. Now, in death, he was at last receiving it.

In April 1957, Mansoor again went before the Society of Biblical Literature and Exegesis—this time in Dubuque, Iowa—to follow up on his earlier paper. Then in 1958, after devoting more than a year to his investigation, he published a forty-three-page report (replete with 193 often lengthy footnotes) in the *Transactions of the Wisconsin Academy of Sciences, Arts and Letters*. The article did not go so far as Teicher had, though it took direct aim at Goshen-Gottstein—and at Rabinowicz, whom Mansoor accused of waging a "holy war" against him.

Mansoor began his defense with a withering attack on the evidence offered up in 1883. He pointed out the remarkable similarities between the story Shapira told about his scrolls' discovery and the more recent tale of Muhammad ad-Dibh. Held up against each other, he said, "only the goat and the jars" are missing.

Next he turned to the writing itself. Citing archaeological evidence from Masada, he undercut Goshen-Gottstein's claims about the absolute distinction between monumental and written scripts. Even so, he pointed out, the script on Shapira's manuscripts differed in several ways from that of the Mesha stone: seven Hebrew letters looked different, four had minor deviations, and three were of an entirely new character. To his mind, therefore, the claim that a forger had copied the Mesha stele was weak.

Rabinowicz and Goshen-Gottstein argued that several word usages in the Shapira scrolls had not entered the Hebrew lexicon until much later than the manuscripts were purportedly written, constituting clear evidence of fraud: only a relatively modern person would be familiar with such usages, and so, they argued, the scrolls must necessarily have been written in a much later period than alleged.

Mansoor's critics also pointed out a series of grammatical problems, and a particularly embarrassing instance of two letters switching places, a mistake that left God himself not "getting angry," as in the traditional text, but "committing adultery"—an error that can only leave one wondering, Who's the lucky lady?

Mansoor, however, listed numerous examples that seemed to shoot down the argument that these irregularities in Shapira's scrolls were definitive evidence of fraud. He cited dozens of unusual word usages, grammatically challenged passages, and transposed letters that appeared in the Dead Sea Scrolls, the Samaritan Pentateuch, and even the traditional text of the Bible itself.

The contention that Shapira's scrolls were the work of a Polish or Russian Jew was dismissed in similar fashion. In reality, Mansoor claimed, the very sort of mistakes that led Ginsburg to that conclusion in 1883 appear all over the Bible. Said Mansoor, with evident sarcasm: "Is Rabinowicz, who endorses Ginsburg's and Neubauer's views, prepared to condemn (*chalila!*)[God forbid!] several books of the Old Testament because of the following 'scribal errors,' also committed because of the similarity of their phonetic value?"

Mansoor's paper did not so much answer questions as raise them. The verdict rendered by Ginsburg and Ganneau had been presented as authoritative, shutting down most serious consideration of the matter. Now Mansoor had demonstrated that—at the very least—there remained room for debate. Some scholars agreed with him. Others refused to entertain the notion that any doubt lingered. Others still suggested that recent archaeological developments made abundantly clear that Shapira's scrolls were real.

What, then, to believe?

In the end, all of these arguments—Mansoor's, Rabinowicz's, Goshen-Gottstein's—were speculative. They relied on hearsay: decades-old conversations, newspaper reports, letters, sketches, and books by men who had seen the scrolls late in the previous century. They were like detectives investigating a murder where no body has been found: it's clear someone was killed, but all the evidence—a spot of blood, a voice mail message, a neighbor who heard a faint thud—is circumstantial. Even if it all points in one direction, police can't be absolutely certain until they've found the corpse and performed an autopsy. There was simply no way, then, to answer the million-pound question—were the scrolls real or not?—without actually examining them, using modern techniques and technologies to establish exactly what they were, or were not.

Mansoor had initially hoped to do just that when he arrived at the British Museum in the summer of 1956. He searched the dossier on Shapira but did not find the scrolls there, and museum officials insisted they did not have them. It was their belief, they told him, that they had been returned to Shapira's family. But Mansoor found "no written record in the dossier to this effect."

About a year after Mansoor's summer sojourn in the Department of Oriental Manuscripts, he received an interesting "private communication" from Dr. Cecil Roth, a renowned expert in Jewish history at Oxford. Roth's note contained a suggestive nugget regarding where the scrolls might have landed in the years after Shapira's death. In 1887, Roth explained, a well-known London bookseller by the name of Bernard Quaritch had exhibited the strips at the Royal Albert Hall as part of a convention known as the Anglo-Jewish Historical Exhibition.

Mansoor followed the lead but "failed to produce further results as to the whereabouts of the document." He had asked a series of questions suggesting that Shapira's scrolls could have been authentic, undertook to find them in the museum, and failed.

How could a set of famous scrolls—even fraudulent ones—just disappear? If they had remained in the British Museum, as Mansoor initially thought, surely a thorough search would have turned them up. If they had landed among the stock of Bernard Quaritch, there had to be a record of their eventual sale.

But there wasn't.

Once the scrolls appeared in the Quaritch catalogs, their scent faded. No living person had the vaguest idea what became of them. Did Quaritch find a buyer? Did he keep them for himself? Give them away? Destroy them? The most honest answer anyone could offer to these questions was a resigned shrug. Mansoor tried. So did others. But some seven decades after they had captivated the English press, public, and prime minister, Shapira's scrolls had simply disappeared.

16

BURTON-ON-TRENT

On November 9, 1903, hundreds of townspeople poured into the streets of Burton-on-Trent, England, to pay final respects to one of the city's most prominent sons. Dr. Philip Brookes Mason, an esteemed old Burtonian, respected physician, and internationally known naturalist, had died four days earlier after a sudden "attack" proved too much for a body already wrecked by three years of deteriorating health.

The *Lancet* eulogized Mason as "a man of sterling qualities and excellent intellectual gifts." The Linnean Society, an exclusive caucus of natural historians to which Mason had been elected in 1872, added in its obituary that "only those who knew him intimately can bear testimony to the simple geniality of his character and his true kindliness of heart." At a meeting of the Burton Natural History and Archaeological Society (BNHAS), which Mason had helped found, a call went out to extend sympathies to Mason's widow, Annie—an appeal quickly seconded by a certain Mr. Moxon, who praised Mason's personal museum as "one of the finest in the country." Before commencing daily business at the Borough Police Court, Burton's mayor publicly expressed deep sorrow at the "great loss" of Mason's death.

When he died, Mason was one of the most popular physicians in the Midland counties and "the most intriguing character ever" to walk through the doors of the town's municipal hospital. But it was his vast collections of natural history specimens that earned him renown beyond the Midlands. "Shells, birds, insects of all descriptions—nothing came amiss to him, and his collections increased year by year," his friend the Reverend C. F. Thornewill wrote in the *Journal of Conchology* remembrance that Matthew Hamilton discovered in 2011.

As the years passed, Mason's collections grew to number some thirteen thousand items, far too many to be stored in his study, far too valuable to be hidden away in his basement. Seeking more space, and sensing the collections' educational import, Mason built a private museum in an annex to his well-appointed Burton home. In spacious rooms overlooking the water, sun coming in through louvered skylights, Mason's stuffed birds and mounted bugs and infinite plant specimens dwelled, lifelike, in glass cases, a silent Noah's Ark moored along the River Trent.

Mason's interest in the natural world is evident. Near Eastern archaeology, however, ranked very low—if at all—among his concerns. True, the Burton Natural History and Archaeological Society, where he served three terms as president, hosted the rare lecture on some Near Eastern theme. But the group concerned itself almost exclusively with hyperlocal archaeology focused on the occasional excavation of sites—churches, cemeteries, and the like—in Burton and its environs. And yet, if Thornewill was to be believed, Mason somehow ended up with the missing Shapira scrolls.

"It is not generally known that Mr. Mason became the eventual possessor of the notorious 'Shapira' manuscript, which for a time deceived some of the most experienced authorities on such matters, but was at length discovered to be a remarkably clever forgery," Thornewill wrote in his obituary.

Shortly after I returned home from Australia, a question had begun to nag: was Hamilton right? The Thornewill obituary seemed a solid indicator, but as I've seen time and again, people err and they exaggerate. Their memories falter. They invent. The more I thought about it, the less likely the whole thing seemed. How, exactly, did a man with no evident interest in the Near East, archaeology, or forgeries end up with Shapira's Deuteronomy? As I prepared to travel to Burton, what had begun as a small question grew—the innocuous spot on a man's foot that morphs into gangrene. Was the small-town English doctor on whose shoulders I was now resting all my hopes just a red herring of the variety that might have been stuffed and mounted in his museum?

On the night of June 25, 2014, I arrived in Burton-on-Trent hoping I might answer these questions.

My hotel, the Three Queens, on Bridge Street, was built in the 1700s, and its lush green carpeting couldn't hide the charmingly sloped floors or dampen the creaking of its steep wooden stairs. The walls were decorated with framed cartoons in which Oliver Cromwell made bold pronouncements I didn't understand.

Jet lag awakened me the next morning at four thirty and I sat in bed writing emails for an hour. Once Hamilton had divulged Mason's name, I began to investigate the late doctor's life—and the dispersal of possessions that followed his death. His wife, Annie, had been the sole executor of his estate, and in the years after he died she would sell off most of what he'd collected to a variety of museums throughout England. Eventually, items would land at the Burton Museum, the Derby Museum and Art Gallery, the Burton Leisure Center, the Bass Museum, and the Chester Zoo, among other institutions. As late as 1921, eighteen years after Mason's death, Annie was still selling parts of her late husband's collection. In November of that year she made a two-hundred-pounds sale to the Burton Museum. Among the items the museum purchased from Mrs. Mason were 425 cases of her late husband's stuffed British birds, the head of a Chartley cow, and a set of Irish elk antlers.

I sent off a few emails to each of these institutions asking if perhaps, along with the birds and the bugs, they had also purchased a very old-looking Bible. At five thirty, I lay back down for a twenty-minute nap that lasted five hours.

When I awoke, I called the Lichfield Record Office to confirm my appointment there the following day. The archive held historical records for the Burton Natural History and Archaeology Society, and I hoped that somewhere in these files I would find confirmation that Mason had owned the scrolls. Then I left to find Mason's house. Once I'd located the place, I intended to approach the owner and request permission to search it, in case the scrolls had somehow been left behind—in a trunk or a chest in some basement or attic corner. This, I was aware, was another in a series of extreme long shots—especially because I did not yet know if Mason had ever really possessed the scrolls. Then again, convincing Hamilton to give me Mason's name had also been a long shot.

Mason's house was empty. Whatever rooms were visible through ground-floor windows were completely bare. The lot in the rear was devoid of cars, and a decent-size garage in the corner was locked. However, two thriving flowerpots hung above the street-facing windows, so it was clear someone was still looking after the property. I snapped a few photos and trudged back to the Three Queens to plan my next move.

When I returned, I had received replies to two of my earlier emails. The first came from Richard Stone, a local historian and member of the Burton Civic Society. The birds, he informed me now, along with a number of other natural history exhibits, had been a mainstay of the town museum until it closed in 1981. "I don't recall any mention of a Bible Scroll," he wrote, but "PBM's house still stands, now an extension of the Three Queens Hotel, and the glass roof over the top floor room that once housed his exhibits is visible from the street."

This was a surprise. If Stone was right, not only had I been snooping around the wrong building a few minutes earlier—I was actually staying in an extension of Mason's home.

The second message was from Dominic Farr, assistant librarian at the William Salt Library, in nearby Stafford. Farr informed me that the library—which houses the collection of its namesake, a nineteenth-century London banker—held nothing specifically related to Mason. But a search of the catalogs had turned up a reference to a stained-glass window, dedicated to Mason, hanging in Burton's Holy Trinity Church. It stood to reason, then, that Mason had worshipped at this church—and if he did, I thought, perhaps the scrolls had ended up there. Annie Mason, it was clear, had taken great care in disposing of her husband's natural history collections, biding her time over nearly two decades as she selected the appropriate destination for each group of items. If she had, likewise, sought a suitable home for Shapira's manuscript, it was certainly possible that their church was that institution. There were reasons to think this hadn't occurred, chiefly the fact that the scroll was, at that point, still considered a forgery, and donating a forgery to one's church may not have been viewed as especially kosher. But I was here to explore all possible angles.

THE NEXT MORNING, I caught a cab into Lichfield, a charming town about fourteen miles south of Burton. I got out at the foot of a long, shop-lined promenade. Squat brick buildings huddled up one against the next, housing pubs, restaurants, and banks whose chimneys gaped at the gray morning sky. I followed the redbrick commons out to the friary, where a large A-framed building housing the town library and the record office sat at a bend in the road.

The office held a great deal of material from the BNHAS, including press reports, correspondence, and minutes documenting the group's periodic meetings. I signed out two of these diaries, starting with the book for 1888, the last year Quaritch had advertised the scrolls in his sales catalog. It included announcements of new members elected, upcoming outings, and acquisitions for the group's library. But nothing about Shapira's scrolls. I turned to the minutes for 1889 and read through two months of similar entries: attendance tallies for its lecture series, reports from various subcommittees. Then I flipped to Friday, March 8, 1889. Glued to a blue-lined page facing the handwritten minutes was a printed notecard about the size of a lady's wallet. It read:

BURTON ON TRENT

Natural History and Archaeological

Society

***

SESSION 1888-89

***

PRESIDENT HORACE T. BROWN, ESQ., F.G.S., F.I.C.

THE FIFTH MONTHLY

GENERAL MEETING

WILL BE HELD ON

FRIDAY, MARCH 8TH, 1889

AT 8 P.M. IN THE

MASONIC HALL, UNION STREET

BUSINESS: —

To consider the Report of the Popular Lecture Committee,

AFTER WHICH.

P.B. MASON, ESQ., M.R.C.S., F.Z.S., F.R.M.S., F.L.S., &C.,

WILL EXHIBIT AND READ A PAPER ON

"THE FORGERY OF SHAPIRA"

AND

Mr. T. Gibbs will exhibit an Ancient Helmet

found at Hartshorne.

***

Coffee will be served at the close of the business

G. HARRIS MORRIS, Hon. Sec.

This was extremely close to the proof I was looking for, but the fact that an event is announced does not mean it ends up taking place. Speakers cancel. Weather intervenes. The caterer goes out of business. What seemed clear from this invitation was that Mason informed the society that he had the scrolls and intended to exhibit them. But what if he had only been planning to buy them? Or the transaction was in the works but never went through? Until I could place Mason and the scrolls together in a room, I wouldn't be fully confident.

I photographed the invitation, then turned my attention to the minutes for the day Mason had been scheduled to deliver his paper on Shapira. Only seventeen BNHAS members and two of their friends had attended the meeting. With Horace Brown, the group's president, presiding, G. Harris Morris read a report issued by the Public Lecture Committee recommending that these talks (topics included "The Scenery and Geology of the British Islands" and "Cremation!") be discontinued due to low turnout. Brown, Thornewill, and Mason all took part in the subsequent discussion of the report, whose recommendations were adopted. Turning the page, I began to read about the next portion of the evening.

"Mr. P. B. Mason then read a paper on 'The Forgery of Shapira,'" the minutes read, "and exhibited the documents in question."

There it was—Mason and Shapira's scrolls, seen together publicly in Burton-on-Trent's Masonic Hall on March 8, 1899, six months after Quaritch had last listed them. Although the BNHAS lecture series seems to have been box-office poison, a local newspaper article glued onto the following page explains one additional reason for the low turnout: it was, to borrow from fables, a dark and stormy night.

> *Not even the promise of a paper on the forgery of Shapira, whose alleged discovery of a manuscript of a portion of the Bible caused no little excitement some years back among biblical scholars, and for that matter of that [sic] the general public, could induce many members of the Natural History and Archaeological Society to brave the elements on Friday evening. But the few who ran the gauntlet were well rewarded for their courage.*

Mason began his presentation with an explanation of his "rather strange" decision to discuss the Shapira manuscript before this particular organization. One branch of the society's work focused on archaeology, he said, and this discipline lent itself to "deliberate attempts at the deception of others, for the sake of gain."

No better example of such chicanery existed, Mason went on, than the one he would be exhibiting that evening—"the fabrication of what purported to be a manuscript portion of the Bible, not less than twenty-seven centuries old, and one not only venerable for its antiquity, but more valuable in itself, as it would have settled for ever a burning question between two schools of critics of the biblical text."

Although Mason's talk that evening had been billed as a "paper," the remainder of his address in fact consisted of his reading out loud most of the articles and letters that had appeared in the *Times* during the summer of 1883. Once he had completed his reading, it was time for show-and-tell.

"Mr. Mason is possessed of the whole of the Shapira fragments," the newspaper report concludes, "and the audience, much to their delight, were afforded an opportunity of inspecting them."

I was desperate for the very same opportunity, and spent the next few days jealously searching the archive to see if somehow—through a bequest by Mason himself or by Annie, his wife and executor—the BNHAS had ended up with the scrolls. If they had, perhaps they were there in the archives, or had been sent along to the Burton Museum when the BNHAS disbanded. In October 1907, the society mounted an exhibit of "curios" loaned to them by locals; none of the exhibits was Shapira's scrolls. Early in 1912, Annie had donated several books to the BNHAS library, but all addressed topics in natural history. According to minutes from the committee meeting of March 1 of that year, the group's chairman proposed that Mrs. Mason be thanked for her donation. This was typical; most gifts to the society, even modest ones, were noted in the minutes. There is no such mention of Shapira's manuscripts.

CERTAIN, NOW, THAT Mason owned Shapira's scrolls, I returned to the Three Queens to speak with Julia Wheatcroft, the hotel's operations manager. When she emerged from a room in the back, smartly dressed in a blue pantsuit, black flats, and glasses, I inquired whether

Trent House, the portion of the building where the Masons had lived, was, in fact, part of the hotel. Yes, she said—as of late 2010, it was. I explained to Wheatcroft what I was doing in town and asked if I might search the hotel for the scrolls.

"I know it sounds a little crazy," I said, "but stranger things have happened."

"I suppose," she said.

She was friendly but understandably doubtful. The hotel had been renovated a number of times, so a general search of the premises wouldn't do me much good, she said. In the unlikely event the Masons had left anything behind, construction crews would have tossed it ages ago. And anyway, I couldn't just go around poking my head into other guests' rooms.

"What about Trent Terrace—the room under the skylights?" I asked.

Trent Terrace was the name given to the annex in which Mason's museum had been housed. Wheatcroft called up the hotel's room list on her computer. The room under the skylights was unoccupied.

"I can take you up there now if you like," she said.

We climbed two steep flights of stairs, steadying ourselves on original hand-carved wooden banisters. When we arrived at the door, Wheatcroft knocked and let me in. The room had clearly been updated more recently than mine. With royal red carpets, white drapes, and a fluorescent-lit bathroom, it was every bit a renovated hotel room—and no bit a museum. It was immediately clear that there was nothing to be found here but free soaps—and yet, so that Wheatcroft wouldn't feel I'd wasted her time, I strutted around the room like Hercule Poirot, glancing behind the TV and the bed and the nightstand until, satisfied that a thorough search had been completed, I nodded to the door. As we left the room, I spotted a panel in the hall ceiling. The board was sealed tight with screws at each corner and would have required a sizable ladder to approach.

"Can I get up there?" I asked. Wheatcroft craned her head, then shook it.

"Some construction guys were up there a few years back and all they found were dead pigeons."

"Because if there's an attic above that room, that could really be where they might have stored the scrolls."

"Sorry," she said.

"What about the basement?"

I was pushing it—Wheatcroft had a job to do, and this certainly was not it. She thought for a moment and said, "I'll have to stop back at the desk for the key."

A few minutes later she was leading the way down a narrow staircase into the cellar. An old boiler crouched along the far wall of the low-ceilinged room, and as I stepped toward it I noticed a very old metal trunk sitting off to the side on a dusty brick ledge. It was exactly the sort of thing I had long imagined might one day yield the vanished scrolls. This, after all, was the way things worked in the Indiana Jones movies, in *The Da Vinci Code*, in that movie with Nicolas Cage.

I stepped up to the ledge and searched the box. It was rusted and mangled—and absolutely empty. Wheatcroft pointed to a low-cut doorway in the wall. We stooped low to pass into the main room running beneath Trent House. The space was dark and the floor was covered in a thick layer of slippery silt. I powered up my iPhone for light and Wheatcroft did the same. This area was divided into three distinct rooms: one was large and empty, and the others were further subdivided into a series of two-tiered brick alcoves running along each wall like prison bunks. Shining my phone onto the ceiling, I noticed a series of extremely old hooks set deep in ancient wooden crossbeams.

"Well, there's definitely some old stuff down here!" I shouted to Wheatcroft, who was hanging around near the door.

"Yeah," she said. "The cobwebs." She got a good laugh out of this and, mood lightened, I began to elaborate on Shapira's story, culminating with the Mason connection. Now, unexpectedly, she got excited. Her searching became more spirited. We moved from room to room, peering into each alcove, scratching at holes in the walls, reaching into gaps in the ceiling.

But beyond the cobwebs and the dirt, there was nothing there. Ducking back into the first room, I was halfway to the steps before I noticed Wheatcroft double-checking the old trunk. It was still empty, but she was trying.

BACK IN MY room I cleaned the basement silt from my boots, disenchanted but not surprised. When I set them down to dry, I turned to finding whatever information I could on Holy Trinity Church, which had honored Mason with a stained-glass window and, I now believed, was a possible repository for Shapira's scrolls. It didn't take long to discover that the church had been shuttered in 1969 and demolished two years later. (At least it hadn't burned.) However, on closing, Holy Trinity had been merged with another church, this one called St. Modwen's. If these establishments had united, their belongings must have been joined, too.

I wrote to St. Modwen's and heard back from Margaret Duprey, secretary to the Parochial Church Council. "What a fascinating story!" she wrote. "We'll be happy to do anything that we can to help." We agreed to meet after the church service that Sunday.

In the meantime, I set out to learn all I could about the church. There wasn't much. First came the Wikipedia page, then one or two other sites of little value. Then I came upon an essay about the church's renovation, and saw this:

In 1889–90 William Tate of London directed the redecoration of the whole interior of the church and the re-ordering of the sanctuary, including a mosaic ceiling in the apse and fluting to the apse pilasters. New furnishings included an oak altar and a brass altar cross; a reredos [altarpiece] in alabaster and green marble, with carved panels showing Christ in glory flanked by various saints including St. Modwen, was given by the vicar, C. F. Thornewill, and his two brothers.

Charles Francis Thornewill rode in the lead carriage at Mason's funeral and eulogized him at the grave site and in the *Journal of Conchology*. Now it turned out that he had also been vicar of St. Modwen's. It remained possible that the scrolls had come to Modwen's through the merger with Holy Trinity. But, I began to suspect, they might have arrived there via a more direct route—the Reverend C. F. Thornewill.

Beyond their shared affinity for exploring the natural world, Thornewill was clearly taken with Shapira's scrolls. While Mason had been the subject of a good number of obituaries, only Thornewill had deemed his ownership of the manuscripts worth mentioning in summing up his late friend's life. This was particularly notable given that his remembrance was published in a journal not of theology or archaeology, but conchology. All this was a clear indication that Thornewill believed the manuscripts, and Mason's possession of them, were significant. If, then, Annie Mason sought an appropriate recipient for the Shapira scrolls, Thornewill would have been a prudent and amenable choice. Perhaps Thornewill, as vicar, brought the scrolls to St. Modwen's.

The following Sunday, I woke early and, as was becoming my wont, went to church. St. Modwen's is Burton's parish church, an imposing sandstone building whose purpose seems to be to make parishioners feel small in the presence of the Lord—to inspire rather than embrace. Though Anglican, the building and the service were more formal than anything I'd seen in Rotterdam or at Christ Church in Jerusalem—"high church" is how St. Modwen's warden later explained it to me. Worshippers there take Communion, and the vicar preaches from a multistory pulpit gazing down over the pews. That's what he was doing when I walked in and took a seat near the back. I'd arrived, I now learned, on the Feast of St. Peter— and from the pulpit came a sermon about the fisherman apostle's life. Peter, the preacher said, was first called Simon. Later, Christ himself changed that—bestowing on his young disciple a new name meaning "rock." So, the preacher said, building up a head of steam, when Jesus announced, "'On this rock I shall build my church,' Peter must have felt pretty good."

All the same, Peter was constantly botching things. There was the time, for instance, when Jesus tried to wash Peter's feet, offering such a compelling explanation for his actions that Peter asked Jesus to wash the rest of him. Though he could be a bit overenthusiastic, Peter always found a way to "dust himself down and get on with the work" of loving Jesus. In his frequent erring, the preacher said, Peter was human. But in his unending love, he "achieved his potential in the Holy Spirit."

"Jesus chose Peter," he said. "He saw his failures but never abandoned his rock."

When the service concluded, I stayed put in my pew as a queue of parishioners passed by, wishing each other, and me, "Peace be with you." At first I responded with "Thank you, same to you," but soon picked up on the correct response, which was "And with you." I was getting pretty good at it by the time Margaret Duprey, with her long skirt, glasses, and graying ponytail, stopped by.

She seemed happy to see me. She'd found my email intriguing, she said, and hoped she could help. But the man I really needed to talk to was the church warden.

"He's just there in the back," she said, pointing to the preacher who had given the sermon. "Robin," she said as we approached. "This is the fellow I was telling you about." The vicar, it turned out, was not a vicar. He was Dr. Robin Trotter, a dentist, who happened also to have been elected warden at St. Modwen's some years back.

"Ah, yes, yes, yes," he said extending his hand. "Well."

Trotter was fifty-eight and recently retired from his dental practice. He talked incredibly fast and had a flop of Hugh Grant hair dangling over his forehead. I told him about the Holy Trinity connection, and then about Thornewill.

"Well," Trotter said, taking it all in, "Thornewill was a bit of a menace, really."

As vicar, Thornewill had overseen the archaeological excavation of the original abbey on the site, possibly under the aegis of the Burton Natural History and Archaeological Society. His work, Trotter said, had been haphazard, and he had not recorded his findings. Whatever discoveries he'd made about the site's long history were now lost. Even here, archaeology had been a developing endeavor, and scientific practices were not yet perfected or standardized.

Thornewill, poor record keeper though he was, may still have left behind the particular record—that of Moses's last speech in Moab—I was looking for.

"If he did leave it with the church, is there somewhere here something like that might be kept?"

"Well," Trotter said, "there's the Parish Chest."

He rapped on the cover of a large, dark wooden trunk sitting behind the pews. Over the course of the past few years, I had imagined discovering the scrolls many times over. When I did, this was another version of what I'd pictured: a heavy old oaken box, the back of a church, some town no one had ever considered.

The chest was about six feet long, three feet high, and a foot and a half from front to back. It dated from the sixteenth century, or even earlier, when it was used to store significant documents and other important papers. Now I set my hand on the chest's smooth lid, trying to divine what lay beneath.

"Can I look?" I asked Trotter.

"I don't see why not," he said. "But first, lunch—and a little refreshment."

Lunch was pasta, beer, and Yorkshire pudding at a gastropub that, centuries earlier, had served as the abbey infirmary. Though modern in its luncheon fare and decor, the restaurant still boasted the original medieval roof and crossbeams. Trotter furnished me with this history as we waited for our meal to be served. He was such a genial man, and so eager to chat, that I felt guilty as I wondered: is there any chance we could talk about this *after* we've searched through the Parish Chest? I had, after all, traveled here from California to find scrolls I hoped might actually be inside it. Unlikely? Perhaps. But the scrolls were most certainly not in this pub.

Our food arrived. We ate leisurely. Rather, I should say, he ate leisurely. I just ate slowly. Trotter didn't object when I offered to pick up the tab—an old journalist's habit meant to avoid even the appearance that a reporter might be stuck in his source's pocket. As we waited for the bill, Trotter produced a slim volume with a colorful cover depicting St. Modwen herself. Standing at the foot of a river—the Trent, presumably—Modwen was clad in a neat blue habit, her hands clasped in prayer as two large geese stood admiringly at her feet. Below them, the title: *The Parish Church of Burton upon Trent (St. Modwen): A Short History of 250 Years.*

"This might be useful," Trotter said. He slid the book across the table.

When at last we returned to the church, Trotter ducked into the office, emerging a moment later with a comically large skeleton key. Once, four locks had kept the coffer sealed, and four feoffees of the town charities kept hold of the keys. Today only one lock remains, which Trotter unlatched with a labored turn.

The chest was filled with books, documents, and photographs—one could see that immediately upon hoisting open the heavy lid. As he tried to secure the lid in place, Trotter yanked a bit too hard and a piece of the ancient chest cracked off. We froze—until Trotter turned to me and said, "What have you done to us?" Then he started laughing, and I joined in. He managed to snap the piece back into place after a couple of good shoves, and for the next hour he and Duprey and I unloaded the trunk's entire contents.

Taken together, the items we found told the story of the church's long history. There were several very old, very heavy leatherbound copies of the New Testament dating back several hundred years. There was a detailed list of who sat where inside the ornate sanctuary—indicating who had enough cash to pay for seats in the pews. There were minutes from meetings of local clergy, meetings Thornewill had attended (and during which he did not make any mention of the Shapira manuscript). And there were photographs of other people rifling through this very same chest years earlier.

In the pictures, the chest appeared to be much fuller than it was now. Trotter headed back into the office to have a look in two safes where old documents were stored. In the meantime, I went through everything a second time, emptying the envelopes, rereading the minutes, fanning through pages of the Bibles in hopes the ancient strips would come fluttering out. They did not.

Several minutes later, Trotter returned from the office, empty-handed. He'd found some old documents, he told me, but they had to do with insurance issues. And there was the ancient ritual silver. Before I left, Trotter invited me up onto the pulpit and led me to the back, where, as a consolation prize, I suppose, he pointed out a small green fresco—the alabaster reredos that Thornewill and his brothers had donated. It was lovely, even if it was not the Thornewill donation I was seeking.

Later, I phoned Spencer Bailey at the Derby Museum and Art Gallery. A large number of items from the Burton Museum now resided there, and the curator of another museum had recently told me that, as of several years earlier, this material remained uncataloged and in boxes. When Bailey picked up, I suggested that Shapira's scrolls might be hidden away in one of those boxes. "Right, well most of the cataloging has been done," he told me. "We've done all the ethnographic stuff. What's left is just the natural history."

"You know," I said, "it's not exactly a scroll—I just use that as a kind of shorthand. It's really fifteen narrow leather fragments with ancient Hebrew writing."

Here Bailey paused. "When you describe it that way," he said, "we do have something."

My heart began thumping.

"Really?" I said.

"We didn't know what language it was written in. We thought

maybe it was Sri Lankan or something of that sort," Bailey said. "It was in a wooden box and threaded together."

Bailey jumped onto his computer as I waited at the end of the line, my breath heavy. This was the first time in more than three years of searching that any inquiry had produced a response so promising. As evidence that Shapira's scrolls had been sliced from the margins of a Torah scroll, Ganneau had mentioned that some showed signs of having been threaded together. And who was to say that they wouldn't now be stored in a wooden box. It felt very close.

The clacking of Bailey's keyboard went on for three or four minutes.

"Ah," he said at last. "No. It was two blocks of wood, and it was written on palm leaves, or very thinly sliced wood. Sorry." He laughed a little then. "Must have gotten your hopes up."

"Ha," I said, a little too loud.

Someone at the museum, he told me, had tried to get together an exhibit on Derby's Jews, but they couldn't find enough material. "Just a few, how do you call them, mimosas?"

"Mezuzahs?"

"Right."

However, Bailey added, the museum did have a valuation list of Mason's collection.

At the museum a few days later, I was reading through a list of Mason's bequests when I landed on an entry labeled "Hebrew Character." The listing offered no further details about the object to which it referred, and naturally I was curious. Could "Hebrew Character" be shorthand for a manuscript written in the Hebrew language? For the "most original" copy of Deuteronomy, written in the "primeval Hebrew character on strips of blackened leather," listed in the Quaritch sales catalog? Could it even refer to the original owner of the manuscript—who was, before his conversion, quite the Hebrew character? I interrupted Bailey, who was at work at another desk.

"Sorry," I said. "There's something here listed as 'Hebrew Character.' Any idea what that might be?"

It had been clear from the outset that Bailey thought my search a fool's errand. He was very polite about it, though, and welcomed me to his office on a Friday afternoon. When I asked him what this entry might refer to, he looked genuinely surprised.

"Let's see that," he said. I handed him the list, and he squinted at it awhile, his lower lip curled up beneath his red mustache. "Mmm-hmm."

Bailey set the list down, straightened his dark-framed glasses, and turned back to his computer. He typed a few words, scrolled around a little, peeked back at the list, then, at last, smiled.

"Sorry," he said, genuinely apologetic. "It's a moth."

The Hebrew Character was not a manuscript in the Holy Tongue, nor was it that manuscript's previous owner. Rather, the listing referred to *Orthosia gothica,* a species of moth whose forewing is emblazoned with a pattern that looks strikingly like the fourteenth letter of the Hebrew alphabet, *nun.*

"I guess that's not it," I said.

"Sadly, no."

Bailey walked me to the sidewalk and pointed out the nearest taxi stand. "If I happen to turn up an old Bible scroll," he said, "I'll be sure to let you know."

MR. SHARP-EYE-RA

For Rosette and Myriam, back home in Jerusalem, euphoria was quickly turning to concern. Amid the adulation and the exuberant spending, they received word of Ganneau's *Times* condemnation. It hit them as hard as it had Shapira.

Rosette "nearly fainted at the sound of that name."

"Only to think," Harry would recall, "that this bird of ill omen should cross her husband's path again—this fiend of a man, this ignorant dragoman, this spiteful, bigoted Catholic who was bent on their ruin."

Bad as Ganneau's attack was, Shapira's silence was worse. Without warning, his letters home had simply stopped—badly shaking young Myriam. "He's certain to send us a telegram," Rosette said, to comfort her daughter. "From what he said in his last letter, the MS. was to be offered for sale just about now and you may depend upon it, he is telegraphing the result, that we may hear it as quickly as possible."

But no telegram came.

"It's quite probable that the letter has gone astray," Rosette said the next day, "and we shall get two together, via Brindisi."

But neither did the Brindisi mail bring any tidings.

They waited for weeks, each day Myriam chanting quietly to herself, like a mantra: "I know I shall have a letter to-day, I *know* I shall."

Rosette saw a series of visitors—no longer the merchants and beggars who days earlier had arrived in droves looking to capitalize on her imminent wealth, but friends come to offer comfort and posit theories about her husband's sudden disappearance. Although no letter arrived from Shapira, they did get word from an agitated Augusta, who wrote home upset that her school tuition had been left unpaid. For Rosette, financial concerns had now joined her husband's silence atop the growing list of daily stressors. The store was barely operating in Shapira's absence, and money had grown scarce. She was forced to sell off the family's animals and dismiss most of the servants.

And still they waited for some sign of life. The uncertainty was agonizing. Myriam would stand on the balcony of the villa her family lived in but could no longer afford, her eye pressed up against Shapira's telescope, willing the horse-drawn mail cart to come rattling down Jaffa Road, its driver cracking his whip. When he rolled into view, she would dash off to the post office, hoping at last to receive word from her absentee father. But still, months on, nothing.

Then the family received another bit of unwelcome news, this time about Augusta, who had recently become engaged to the son of a respected German scholar. Shapira's future in-laws had sent word that they could no longer stomach the association.

"You will understand," the prospective groom's father told Rosette, "that if [Shapira] cannot disprove all the accusations brought against him, we cannot possibly receive [Augusta] into our family, with its irreproachable record."

The wedding was called off.

In September, *Punch,* a popular humor magazine, published a

"Fancy Portrait" cartoon depicting Shapira—in profile, of course, to accentuate the caricature's large, hooked nose and scraggly black beard—holding tight to his scrolls as a smiling Ginsburg (also a converted Jew, but depicted here with a button nose as cute as any on Nantucket) arrests him on the doorstep of the British Museum. Beneath the drawing is a caption:

MR. SHARP-EYE-RA.
SHOWING, IN VERY FANCIFUL PORTRAITURE,
HOW DETECTIVE GINSBURG
ACTUALLY DID MR. SHARP-EYE-RA OUT OF HIS SKIN.

For Shapira, the racist illustration can only have highlighted, yet again, that his status as a convert had landed him as an outsider among both Christians and Jews. To Jews like Deinard, he was a pathetic apostate. For Christians, he remained an oily Jew.

As the English satirists sharpened their pencils, the Germans whom Shapira had visited before heading off to England jumped into the fray, announcing that they had recognized the deception immediately, dismissing the fragments as forgeries after just ninety minutes. True, they admitted, they had offered to buy the document, but only to demonstrate what a clever forgery looks like.

Hermann Strack, whose opinion Shapira valued greatly, also chimed in. After reading Shapira's letter, Strack wrote to the *Times*, "I declared that it was not worth his while to bring such an evident forgery to Europe."

SHAPIRA FLED FROM a contemptuous England to Holland, where the next, and last, months of his life remain largely unaccounted for. What, exactly, he was doing there—and why he was doing it in the

Netherlands—is unclear. He was hiding, certainly. From the press. From his colleagues. From his family. Especially from his family—Myriam, whom he had always wanted to make proud; Rosette, who had long warned he was flying too close to the sun; and Augusta, whose school tuition he could no longer pay. Following the Moabite pottery scandal, Shapira had launched an animated defense in the press—writing letters, making excursions to Moab, enlisting the backing of prominent figures like the German consul in Jerusalem. This time, though, after writing to Bond, Shapira went quiet. Whereas the last imbroglio had energized him, spurring him to action, this one seems to have knocked the wind out of him. If he felt he'd been stabbed in the back, subsequent news coverage of the affair must have felt like a twist of the knife.

He stopped first in Amsterdam and over the next four months, as his money dwindled, lived between there and Bloemendaal, a town about fourteen miles northwest. Then, sometime around the New Year of 1884, he moved into a quick succession of down-and-out hotels in Rotterdam. Along the way he carried with him an assortment of at least twenty Hebrew manuscripts. Among them was a Yemenite prayer book, a fifteenth-century commentary on Exodus, a fourteenth-century medical text complete with botanical lexicon, and the book of Genesis with Arabic translation.

In need of money, a suffering Shapira continued doing business out of his suitcase—corresponding with professional associates if not with his agonized family. Amazingly, he found a receptive audience for his latest wares in an unlikely corner: the Department of Oriental Manuscripts at the British Museum.

On October 15, 1883, less than two months after Ginsburg issued his report to Bond, the oriental manuscripts chief, Dr. Charles Rieu, notified the museum's trustees that he had recently made contact with Shapira.

"Dr. Rieu has the honour of reporting to the Trustees that the following four Hebrew MSS. have been offered by Mr. Shapira for £25.00," the letter began, before listing the merchandise on offer. "The above MSS. have been selected as the most valuable of a lot of twenty offered by Mr. Shapira and, the price [unintelligible] being moderate, Dr. Rieu begs to recommend the purchase."

Nearly three months later, Rieu wrote again to the museum's executives, urging the purchase of an additional four manuscripts from Shapira—these at the yet cheaper asking price of twenty pounds. It is striking that so soon after the explosive Deuteronomy affair, the British Museum, and its manuscripts department, no less, should have considered making one, let alone two separate purchases from the disgraced Shapira. But while the public now viewed Shapira as a forger, among those at the museum who had worked with him over the previous six years he remained perhaps their most important purveyor of inarguably authentic Hebrew manuscripts. Shapira had been, and remained, an important and trusted partner. At this late date, Rieu's recommendation indicated that, in his opinion, either the Deuteronomy manuscript was not a forgery or Shapira had not played a role in the hoax. Or perhaps, as they had after the Moabitica, museum administrators were simply willing to look the other way in their race to acquire the best manuscripts the market had to offer.

Toward the end of 1883, they purchased the first four of these manuscripts. On January 12 of the following year, they bought the next lot. It was the last sale Shapira would ever make to the museum, and probably the last sale he ever made, period.

IN JANUARY 1884, the French minister of public education sent Ganneau back to England to catalog Holy Land antiquities held by the British Museum and the PEF. Though he had categorically rejected Shapira's manuscript, Ganneau nevertheless sought it out on his return. When he contacted Bond, he was told that the order to refuse him access still held.

A few days later, Bond changed his mind. Ganneau could see the manuscript, but only in the presence of a museum official. The following day, Ganneau arrived in Rieu's office to begin his examination anew. But Ginsburg, on receiving word of Ganneau's arrival, burst into the room, "suffering from visible agitation," and tried to put an immediate halt to Ganneau's investigation.

"He felt, it seems, the need to cast a last glance at them, right at the time when the favor of a first interview with them was granted to me," Ganneau reported. "They fortunately were successful in calming him down and making him understand that he would have the complete leisure, once my little inspection had been done, to come back if his heart desired, to these documents about which he had gone pale for long weeks."

Ganneau's explanation for Ginsburg's sudden tantrum is dubious. Did he really lose his cool because someone else was looking at the strips when he wanted to see them? Or did he remain upset with Ganneau, who he believed had stolen his ideas about the manuscripts and scooped him in the *Times*?

In Ginsburg's absence, Ganneau's "little inspection" proceeded—confirming, he claimed, all of his earlier suspicions.

MORE THAN THREE thousand miles away, a young student at the University of Pennsylvania had only recently visited a local library to see four or five Hebrew scrolls that a merchant named Shapira had sold to a wealthy Philadelphian. Cyrus Adler would go on to become a noted authority in Semitic languages, but even at this early stage of his scholarship, the scrolls felt off.

"They seemed of great age, were mottled here and there with a green substance which looked like mold, and bore a label which said that they were several thousand years old, together with a letter by the great New Testament Greek scholar, Tischendorf of Leipzig, testifying to their genuineness," Adler recalled in his 1941 memoir, *I Have Considered the Days.*

It was the writing, Adler said, that made him suspicious. It looked to him "very much as though it had been influenced by printing, and I had my doubts of its antiquity."

Adler invited a chemist to have a look. After inspecting the green substance under a microscope, the scientist told Adler that it was not mold—rather, it had been "produced by dropping acid on the leather." Next Adler asked a Philadelphia leather merchant to join him at the library. He, too, inspected the manuscripts and concluded that their dark brown color, which gave them the appearance of antiquity, had been artificially produced.

Adler told a respected Yale philologist named William Dwight Whitney about his discovery. "Greatly excited," Adler said, Whitney insisted that the budding scholar announce his findings to the American Philological Association.

"Professor Whitney thought that [the scrolls'] fraudulent character would soon be determined," Adler wrote, "and he did not want this done by a European scholar to shame the Americans."

Adler delivered his paper, sketched out on the back of an envelope, in 1884. When he was finished, one scholar in attendance praised his investigative methods.

"'Now if you'd been a German,'" Adler recalled the man saying, "'instead of getting a chemist and a leather merchant, you would have read the articles in the Encyclopaedia on Chemistry and Leather.'"

Competition among professors, it is apparent, did not end at the eastern shores of the Atlantic. Even more remarkable is the fact that Adler never mentioned either the Deuteronomy controversy or the Moabite pottery, as if, ensconced in the ivory tower an ocean away from London, he was utterly unaware that either had ever existed.

Shapira, meanwhile, could not forget. Holed up in the Netherlands, his mental health deteriorated. One day, local police stopped him as he walked along a street in Schiedam, on Rotterdam's outskirts. Suspecting he was insane, officers arrested him on the spot. What exactly he was doing that led authorities to this conclusion is unclear. A subsequent article in the *Leydse Courant* altered the initial account of the arrest. Shapira, the paper said, was not stopped for insanity. "The reason why he was asked to come to the police station was that he looked very much like a person whose description was spread by the police in Dordrecht, who had visited ladies in that city to check the authenticity of their banknotes, probably with dishonest intentions."

Whatever happened that day, Shapira must have felt like a hunted man—come to Holland to escape the scolds of England, only to be plucked from the street by law enforcement. It was not the last police would see of Shapira.

Later, after months of wandering aimlessly around the Netherlands—leaving behind a trail of luggage and unmailed letters—Shapira gathered what money he had left and booked a room at Rotterdam's Hotel Willemsbrug. He entered, set down his valise, and took a small revolver in hand. He cocked the gun, chambering a single round. Then, after a final glance at this world—at his suitcase, perhaps, or at his own hands, or at the black river burbling below—he raised the pistol to his head, curled a finger around the trigger, and squeezed.

ONE DAY, AFTER months of silence, Myriam was sitting in a tree outside her house when she saw three strangers approaching.

> *Climbing quickly down the tree, Siona [Myriam's alter ego] brought herself on a level with the dining room window and looked through it.*
>
> *As usual, her mother was sitting knitting in her armchair, but now Siona saw three men in black coats coming through the door with very solemn faces . . .*
>
> *Siona watched them, as each sat down on the edge of his chair, forming a half-circle round her mother. And she noted, too, how the knitting slipped from between Mrs. Benedictus's hands and how her anxious eyes seemed glued on the sinister faces surrounding her.*
>
> *Siona could not hear a word of what they were saying, they spoke in such low, subdued voices; and besides, Ourda was singing so loudly, and her sequins were rattling so noisily.*
>
> *All at once her mother gave a piercing cry, and all the men closed around her. As Siona jumped from the tree, they called to her, "Quick, quick! bring some water, and some vinegar too."*
>
> *But the next minute Mrs. Benedictus had recovered herself, and though her lips quivered in her deathly white face, she managed to dismiss her visitors with quiet dignity.*
>
> *"The [L]ord will strengthen me to bear this heavy blow," she said. "I thank you gentlemen for coming to see me."*

But as the three men filed out of the room, her mother pulled Siona toward her, and clasping her passionately in her arms, she sobbed out, "Your father is dead! Your father is dead!"

Myriam Harry laid the blame for her father's death squarely at the feet of Ganneau. The depth of her hatred is evident not only in her novel, but in private correspondence with the German scholar Julius Euting. Writing not long after Shapira's death, she told her pen pal, "I feel like screaming and crying."

"If I were a man I would go to fight Ganneau," she wrote. "What he says is vile. Alas, I am only a woman but as a woman I want to avenge myself and my vengeance would be nobler."

Later, she would write again to Euting, having set aside thoughts of revenge but still incurably sad.

I have not been able to get thoughts of Papa, his activities and his great misfortune out of my mind. I don't want to speak of the Deuteronomy here, which he himself considered bogus in the end. And that was also not his greatest sorrow, even though his pecuniary hopes rested on it; what cost him his life was the thought of being viewed, in the eyes of the world, not as the deceived but as the deceiver.

That this accusation robbed an honest man of his senses, a woman of her husband, children of their father and their homeland— what that did to the unscrupulous, cruel world! And there was also no one there to take up the defense. When I learned of my father's death, I swore—in a typical Mediterranean overreaction— "revenge." Now that I have entered real life, the bombastic, theatrical ideas are gone; but I feel an unspeakable pain when I think of my father's sorrows, and it seems to me to be my duty (I was his darling, after all, and his ideas were my world) to make every effort to save his honor in the eyes of the world.

Shapira's death left his family in financial ruin. On August 16, bankruptcy proceedings commenced at the German consulate in Jerusalem. Wilhelm Duisberg, who had accompanied Shapira on his first fact-finding mission to Moab, was appointed administrator of the estate. An inventory was made of Shapira's business assets and creditors. His belongings were auctioned. Home furnishings were sold off. So was his manuscript stock, much of which was purchased by Adolph Sutro.

Rosette took what little money remained and boarded a ship back to Germany, where she moved into the Stockhausen home of her relative August Weinberger. Myriam joined her sister in Berlin. So recently Jerusalem royalty, the remnants of the Shapira family had exited the Holy Land.

18

SAN FRANCISCO

During the 1880s, Adolf Sutro, mining tycoon and future mayor of San Francisco, launched an exceptional international book-buying spree. Deep pockets allowed him to purchase in bulk, and the German-Jewish immigrant, born the same year as Shapira, collected thousands of volumes on his way to amassing a library that included more than 250,000 books, manuscripts, and incunabula. By some estimates, Sutro's was the largest private library in America.

Shortly after Shapira's death, Sutro visited Jerusalem. While there a German diplomat informed him that Shapira's collection had hit the market, and Sutro was eager to snatch up so many texts in a single transaction. In short order, he and the banker Melville Bergheim, among those deputized to liquidate Shapira's estate, came to terms. Sutro paid Bergheim two hundred pounds, and the banker handed over a unique and wide-ranging collection of texts, the majority of which Shapira had brought over—some would say stolen—from Yemen.

Back at home, Sutro stockpiled his growing collection in a series of warehouses. In 1906, the Great Earthquake rolled San Francisco and fires leveled much of the city. More than half of Sutro's books were reduced to ash. Fire was once thought to have destroyed the

Shapira scrolls in Nicholson's manor. It did destroy the suitcase beside which Shapira died, and the house where his wife lived after his death. Thankfully, the remainder of Sutro's books, including Shapira's collection, were stored in a fireproofed building on Montgomery Street, and by what one newspaper later called an "act of providence," these texts survived. Today, by an improbable fluke, the library is located just a hundred yards from my office at San Francisco State University.

When I first learned of it, the Sutro collection was being moved and was inaccessible. In any event, I knew the scrolls were not there—Sutro had purchased his collection of Shapira material a year before the scrolls were consigned to Sotheby's for auction. More than that, the man who had alerted me to the collection, Adam Rosenthal, had already searched it, to no avail. I still wanted to see the manuscripts in hopes they would offer a better sense of what Shapira was working on prior to his death and, maybe, yield some clue. But the library's very proximity had allowed me to put off doing so every time something else came up—a trip to Australia or the English Midlands, for example—secure in the knowledge that I would get there eventually. When those efforts failed to turn up the scrolls, something else happened: I began to realize that the Sutro collection was my last chance—the final corner left to search. If it held no new information, I had nowhere left to go. And so I froze.

This lasted months. Any excuse to avoid visiting the library would do—work, laundry, taking the car in for an oil change. But as my book came due, I realized this couldn't go on forever. Early in 2015, with ten days remaining until my deadline, I left my desk in the Humanities building, passed the one-room museum housing an Egyptian mummy, and walked to the library across from the Cesar Chavez Student Center, with its murals of Chavez, Malcolm X, and Edward Said. When I arrived on the fifth floor, I swigged what remained of my coffee, stored my bag in a locker, and asked for the catalog listing the collection's contents.

Taken together, Shapira's manuscripts offered what the late Berkeley scholar William Brinner, in his introduction to the catalog, called a robust picture of the "intellectual and religious life of Yemenite Jewry." It is ironic that this overview should have been furnished by a convert hailing from the quintessentially Ashkenazic Pale of Settlement. But if, when he reached the pearly gates, there was any redemption for stealing holy books, perhaps this was it: Shapira, in bringing these manuscripts forth from terra incognita, had played a small role in connecting these two disparate corners of the Jewish Diaspora and making one side's texts, at least, a bit less incognita.

A librarian wheeled the first cart of material into the glass-walled room over the university commons and wished me luck. Stored in gray cardboard boxes held shut with Velcro, the collection included items dating back as far as the thirteenth century. There were dozens of biblical manuscripts, as well as several important works by Maimonides, tractates of the Talmud, kabbalistic texts, and poetry. There were several tomes on medicine and philosophy and a few mystical texts with complex diagrams reminiscent of astrological grids.

I went through every item, page by page, on what was clearly the very off chance that Rosenthal had been mistaken—that somehow, at some point in the past 130 years, someone, for some reason, had wedged some fragment from Shapira's Deuteronomy scrolls between pages of the nearly two hundred items Sutro had bought from the late antiquities dealer's estate. By now I was accustomed to off chances. There was a yard-long charm to aid childbirth. A nineteenth-century kabbalistic work in which the author, Matityahu ben Samuel Kohen Mizrahi, argued that his brother Abraham was the Messiah. And there was a collection of rabbinic commentaries known as the *Midrash HaGadol,* similar to one included in Shapira's first sale to the British Museum.

Then I opened the next gray box and made a discovery that stopped me in my tracks. Inside was a gorgeous book containing portions of Ezekiel and Jeremiah on bulky leather leaves. Flipping through the medieval codex, I reached a page on which the lower margin had been carefully sliced off.

It took a moment to register exactly what I was looking at. I thought of Ganneau, who had incriminated Shapira with his suggestion that the Jerusalem merchant had inscribed his falsified Deuteronomy on leather strips cut from the lower margins of a Torah scroll. Looking now at the deformed book before me, I began to wonder if Ganneau was right after all. And if he was, could this be the very manuscript from which Shapira had taken one of his leather strips?

I found a ruler and measured the missing section; any of Shapira's slips could easily have fit. Was this the proof I had been searching for? Had Shapira sliced the blank margins from holy books—*these* holy books—and used them to inscribe his own clever version of Deuteronomy?

I put the codex aside and continued examining the collection with renewed purpose, eager to see if there were any further manuscripts marred in this way. Over the next several hours, I discovered five more codices in which margins had been removed. Some were leather, others constructed of thick beige paper. The latter could not have been used in fashioning the scrolls, which all the contemporary accounts referred to as having been made of animal hides. But could Shapira have been using these for practice? As five o'clock approached, I photographed and measured each of the codices, then put them away for the night.

When I returned the following day, I discovered part of a Torah scroll containing eleven columns from the Book of Numbers.

The scroll had guidelines scored across and beside the columns, and creases between each—much as Ganneau had described the Shapira scrolls. And the entire lower margin, running to eighteen inches, had been sliced off with a sharp knife, taking with it the bottom edges of several words.

That evening, I sent an email to Jordan Penkower at Bar-Ilan University, near Tel Aviv. Penkower is one of the world's leading experts on Bible manuscripts. I wanted to know if removing margins from copies of the Torah was at any point common practice. If it had been, what I'd discovered in the library would not necessarily implicate Shapira—anyone who had possessed the scrolls might have cut them. I asked whether he had ever come across another Hebrew codex in which the lower margin of a page had been sliced off. At four o'clock that morning, I received a reply.

Medieval codices were sometimes cut up to supply parchment for Jewish ritual objects like phylacteries and mezuzahs, Penkower wrote. "I doubt if one can claim with certainty that the cuttings from the Shapira codices were done by Shapira for the purpose of falsification," he said.

But in the hierarchy of holiness, a biblical codex—which is a bound book used for study—ranks lower than the Torah scrolls used in synagogues. I could imagine impoverished Jews, like those from whom Shapira had taken these scrolls, mining precious books for their leather. Given how jealously they guarded their books, however, even this seemed unlikely. I told Penkower that I had also found part of a Torah scroll whose entire lower margin had been removed. Were the margins of actual Torah scrolls ever sliced off?

He responded in short order.

"As to Torah scrolls," he said, "I am unaware of such cases, and at first blush, it would seem unlikely that one would cut off a margin to use for tefillin [phylacteries] or mezuzot."

In fact, I would learn, doing so is expressly forbidden by Jewish law. So is cutting off margins from one scroll—even if damaged beyond use—to repair another Torah scroll. It was almost unthinkable that a Yemenite Jew would have defaced a Torah scroll in this way. And if one had, certainly he would not have been so careless as to slice off portions of the text itself. Shapira, in other words, could not have received the scroll in this condition. I saw the door to his innocence closing. But after years of searching obsessively for just this kind of evidence, I could not simply declare the Deuteronomy scrolls a forgery. Part of me couldn't believe that the answer had been hiding so close by. So I contacted several more experts—scholars and scribes in the United States and Israel, people who study and write Torah scrolls—to see if anyone could disabuse me of my growing suspicions. None could. Though each was able to conceive of reasons someone might remove such a large section from the lower margin of a Torah scroll, not a single one had ever seen it done.

Which left only one option: Shapira.

Recall that these manuscripts had been sold off by Shapira's executors after his death. He had not sold them himself—and it was entirely possible he never intended to. Doing so would have exposed him to just the sort of accusation I now found myself making.

After traveling to seven countries on four continents over the course of four long years, I had, at last, found the smoking gun. Remarkably, it came not in London or Jerusalem, nor Berlin, Halle, or Rotterdam. Instead I found it stored away in San Francisco, a million miles from Shapira—and a few steps from my poorly decorated office.

SEVEN MONTHS LATER, I returned to London to make sure I was right.

In his report to Bond, Ginsburg had cited one of the Torahs Shapira sold to the British Museum—Oriental 1457—as evidence of fraud. Attached to the beginning of Genesis, he said, was a leather strip about the height of Shapira's manuscripts. This slip, Ginsburg alleged, was scored like a Torah, indicating that Shapira had removed it from such a scroll—just as he'd done with his Deuteronomy.

Today, Oriental 1457 is stored in five sturdy green boxes. Genesis, the first book of the Torah, is kept bubble-wrapped inside the last box. It is made of red leather, glossy in parts, rough in others. Beside the opening panel, with the worn words that introduce the Pentateuch—*In the beginning, God created the heavens and the earth*—is the small strip Ginsburg described. The piece is shiny and brown and inscribed, in what is almost certainly Shapira's writing, with "No. 20"—the number he had assigned it in his catalog of Yemenite manuscripts.

I removed the scroll from the box and unrolled it, then leaned over to look at the slip with a magnifying glass. There they were: three vertical lines etched into the shiny leather in exactly the pattern one sees in Torah scrolls. If I had any doubts before, they were now gone. I had not only found a Shapira scroll from which the lower margin had been removed, but a piece of leather that he had removed from a Torah scroll and written on. There could be no more doubt. Shapira was our forger.

ON THE FACE of it, this discovery would have seemed cause for dejection. In fact, it was exhilarating. True, if his manuscript had proved authentic, then Shapira may well have located the first Dead Sea Scroll, decades before the rest were uncovered. And while this intriguing possibility would doubtless appeal to scholars eager to learn more about the Bible's development, it was not the most enticing of the options. If the manuscript had been real, Shapira's primary achievement would have been recognizing its value. Beyond this, he would simply have played the role of middleman.

If, however, it was fake, then Shapira was the mastermind behind the forgery. Which made me like him all the more. I respected his willingness to dare in the face of bad odds, to take a shot though the dangers were immense. Ultimately, it seemed to me, his motives had less to do with greed than respect and, given his humble origins, I was finding it difficult to fault him for that. Dismissed once for his role in the pottery fraud, Shapira came back with an even bolder "find," knowing full well that his reputation—to say nothing of the purgatory in which he lived between Judaism and Christianity—could easily doom him. Interestingly, one could read in Shapira's Deuteronomy an effort on the author's part to promote the authenticity of Christianity. The scrolls excised chapters full of legal material that appear in the traditional text. Christians often say that theirs is a religion of love while Judaism is a religion of laws. If the "original" Deuteronomy was devoid of these laws, it might bolster the notion that Christianity is a more genuine expression of God's will.

I had also begun to notice something else.

In the course of my search, I had interviewed numerous scholars, asking each if they believed the scrolls were authentic. Even those who came down on the side of fraud made sure to point out, as Ginsburg had done in 1883, that the manuscript was brilliant, clever, creative—the product of a learned and vibrant, if devious, mind. *Brilliant. Clever. Creative. Learned. Vibrant. Devious.* All this was eminently more attractive than *middleman*.

More than that, Shapira was prescient. Not only did his Deuteronomy look very little like editions of the book readily available in his day, but it anticipated the Dead Sea Scrolls, the greatest archaeological discovery of the twentieth century. In fact, Shapira's scrolls resembled nothing so much as a "rewritten Bible." Rewritten Bibles are characterized by additions, paraphrases, and interpretations not present in the traditional version. These alterations are made for a variety of reasons—from clarifying a particular text to appealing to a newer audience. The phenomenon seems to have occurred largely in the late Second Temple period, between the third century BCE and 70 CE, and many such texts turned up among the Dead Sea Scrolls. But they would become widely known only long after Shapira's death.

Shapira may have come across one variety of rewritten Bible: the Samaritan Pentateuch. He was certainly familiar with the alphabet used by this ancient sect, and in some distinct ways his Deuteronomy resembled their unusual version of the Torah. When I first heard of this edition, its similarities to certain aspects of Shapira's scrolls had convinced me that his controversial Deuteronomy might have been an ancient forerunner of this text. Had I not found the sliced-up scroll in San Francisco, I might have continued to embrace this theory. The paleographical and orthographical arguments advanced by Ginsburg were strong, but a manuscript cannot be dismissed on such grounds alone. That's especially true when the manuscript in question has disappeared and modern scholars are forced to base their judgments on copies and transcriptions.

But now, suddenly, the Samaritan Pentateuch seemed to point in the opposite direction: if he was aware of the Samaritans' holy book, Shapira could have used it as his prototype. In a letter published in the *Athenaeum* after Ottoman gendarmes discovered the unbaked

"Moabite" idol in Salim al Kari's house, Shapira noted that the inscription on the idol seemed to be an "imitation of the Samaritan." Had he attempted something similar with his Deuteronomy scrolls?

Here it is difficult to resist the urge to psychoanalyze: If Shapira was going to forge a document, why would he choose as his guide something so offbeat as a Samaritan Pentateuch? Something so different from the traditional text that it was sure to raise suspicions among reverent scholars?

Then again, perhaps that was just the point. In forging the scrolls, maybe Shapira believed that scholars would be unlikely to dismiss them as fakes precisely because they were so quirky. Who, after all, would produce so daring a forgery? Why would someone take such a risk? Recall that when Shapira first displayed his scrolls for the savants gathered at the PEF headquarters, one man had exclaimed, "This is one of the few things which could not be a forgery or a fraud!" Perhaps this was just the sort of reaction Shapira was aiming for in summoning a vision of Deuteronomy that was too weird to fail.

The level of deception required to perpetrate this ruse would have been exhausting, carried on over the course of five long years—from creating the manuscript itself, to sending a faked transcription to Schlottmann, to writing Strack with word of a "curious manuscript," to performing for Besant, to inventing a story about Bedouin in hiding, to claiming the sheikh who connected him to the scrolls had suddenly died. It was all lies. Every time he recounted the discovery, he needed to keep his details straight—and, in fact, when I reviewed each version of the story Shapira told, I found a few small variations. The differences are subtle enough to be attributed to lapses in memory, but only assuming Shapira deserved the benefit of the doubt. The effort involved in such a years-long ruse would have been herculean; the letdown at being discovered, intense and demoralizing.

Today a large number of Semitic manuscripts appear on the

market each year, some real, some fake. The glut of forgeries represents a lucrative business and, says one well-known epigrapher, has "corrupted" the data set of inscriptions from the region and made the public skeptical about archaeology's ability to produce "reliable information." Shapira's scrolls were the first biblical manuscripts perceived as frauds and so, much as he has been credited with "forging a civilization" with his Moabitica, his scrolls have spawned an industry.

I am not alone in my appreciation for Shapira's role in the dark side of the antiquities trade. As I traveled around the world looking for his scrolls, I was amazed to find, in city after city, that his Moabite pottery was still part of numerous collections. The Palestine Exploration Fund displays several pieces behind glass in its London offices. In Jerusalem, Joe Zias, the former curator of archaeology and anthropology for the Israel Antiquities Authority, uses two Shapira heads as bookends in the entryway to his downtown apartment. The Hebrew University's Institute of Archaeology keeps its Shapira forgeries in a two-level storeroom on Mount Scopus. I examined several pieces of the Moabitica at the German Oriental Society in Halle, where the woman who ran the library's special collections department handed me a set of white gloves and asked that I refrain from taking photographs. One by one I removed each piece from its box: clay coins, an inscribed tablet, and two pots. Another box held a small clay figurine depicting a woman with enormous breasts dangling off to each side and holding what could only have been a dismembered penis. In the next box lay another, larger, woman with a crudely hacked vagina. It was, I will admit, extremely awkward handling such pieces in front of a woman I had only just met.

Later I traveled to Berlin for a meeting with Nadja Cholidis, a Middle East curator at Berlin's Pergamon museum. When I arrived, I caught the U-Bahn near my hotel and exited at Alexanderplatz. From there I headed northeast along Karl-Liebknecht-Strasse, passing the DDR Museum and crossing the River Spree before skirting the imposing green-domed Berlin Cathedral on my way to the museum's conservation department.

It was a warm day, and a group of Israeli tourists, sweatshirts cinched around their waists, was being led along the waterside by a Hebrew-speaking guide holding a red flag. Cholidis, a diminutive woman with shoulder-length hair and bangs, greeted me in the lobby. The room where preservation work is done was pristine: white walls met white floors, and large white tables balanced a host of ancient relics beneath fluorescent white lamps. A team of restorers labored methodically at these tables, performing minute repairs on the artifacts with the aid of binocular-like magnifying glasses anchored to movable arms—the sort endodontists use when drilling holes in patients' teeth.

More than a century ago, when it became clear that Shapira's pottery was fake, the museum removed the Moabitica from its galleries. But the material was never discarded, and today a number of pieces remain in storerooms—including five clay vessels and two figurines. Due to their fragility and the exigencies of storing them, Cholidis brought out only three of the pieces, and lay them on a table in their gray plastic crates: clay pots in various styles and varying degrees of degradation—chipped, cracked, dry, and peeling, the letters composing their invented inscriptions broken and missing their swoops and slashes.

As soon as Cholidis opened the crates, Sonja Radujkovic appeared and, hands in latex, removed the vessels. Radujkovic is a conservator for the Pergamon's Middle East Museum, which was in the throes of a massive renovation. Three years earlier, as the museum geared up for the project, staff began moving collections to a nearby facility for safekeeping. Before items were transferred, conservators stepped in to assess their condition, repairing those items in the worst shape to preclude damage during transport. Doing what she called "puzzle work," Radujkovic gathered broken pieces and identified where they belonged, filled holes, located weak spots and reinforced them.

Among these items, she told me, was the largest and most fragile of the Shapira vessels Cholidis had just set out. Wielding her acrylic glue with the skill of an orthopedic surgeon rebuilding a badly broken bone, Radujkovic had spent two or three weeks fortifying this single vessel for transport. I thought it remarkable that the museum would devote that kind of attention to a known sham. Of course, false as it might have been, it remained a bona fide relic from one of archaeology's liveliest scandals. The pottery had a famous backstory, and so, real or fake, had accrued a value of its own.

THE SAME IS true of Shapira himself. After years searching for his scrolls, what I'd managed to find instead was Shapira the man: vain, proud, intelligent, loving, deferential, industrious, entrepreneurial, greedy, fatherly, devious, chatty, maudlin, devout, sincere, insincere, grandiloquent, lucky, unlucky, hopeful, suicidal. In short, what I'd discovered tracking Shapira around the globe was a person who was complicated, contradictory, and human—perhaps too much so for one man to bear.

Shapira had bolted the shtetl for a backwater of the dissolving Ottoman Empire and, contending with the misgivings of Jews and Christians alike—all of whom found much about him troubling—built a life for himself as a husband, father, and businessman. He started with nothing and ended with nothing, but in between had fashioned himself a prime player in the revolutionary early days of biblical archaeology. While many people aim simply to survive, Shapira lived audaciously. He traveled where most other Westerners wouldn't dare, befriended men others would leave town to avoid, and negotiated with a Yemeni sultan for his release from captivity. He met the English prime minister, bought and sold manuscripts of unquestioned authenticity, and hobnobbed with Europe's leading intellectuals. He brokered deals no one else could broker, ran into difficulties, dreamed up new approaches, and tried them instead. He battled prejudice, his own ambition—and a French nemesis who saw it as his duty to cut Shapira down to size.

I felt now as though I knew Shapira. Knew him, at least, as well as any living person did. And whatever had been said about him at the time of his death, he was a human being—a son, husband, and father who had struggled to do right by his family. His suicide was not simply fodder for newspapers and books. It was a tragedy on a very human scale. When I found the cut-up scrolls, my wife was six months pregnant with our own daughter. Suddenly I started to see things through the eyes of my unborn girl. Shapira may not have been a great man, but he was a man. A troubled man who left behind a wife who never recovered from his death, and two daughters, one of whom hated Ganneau so much that she vowed to avenge her father's death. A man who never got to see his daughter shoot to literary fame. Who never met his grandchild.

Shapira's story resonates tangibly more than a century after his untimely death. That is due in large part to the fact that the story touches on a need that is fundamentally human: to search for truth, to hunt for that which is authentic. But why? When I put this question to longtime Noah's Ark hunter Bill Crouse, he told me a story.

"A man is traveling in the dead of winter on horseback, and he comes to a stream that's frozen," he said. "But he doesn't know if it is frozen enough to support him and his horse. Suddenly a team of horses gallops up behind him and runs across the river. So what's this guy do? He gets on his horse and rides it across the frozen river.

"What changed?" Crouse asked. "He had some facts."

But unlike the horseman of his story, who waited for someone else to show the way, Crouse has put his life in peril searching for such facts. On an expedition to Turkey in 1985, he was taken hostage by militants from the PKK—the Kurdistan Workers' Party—which at the time was calling for an independent Kurdish state. He escaped by sprinting down a mountain in the blindness of night. For him, such adventures are, in fact, theological fact-finding missions.

"Paul says in First Corinthians that if the Resurrection did not occur, then we are most foolish," Crouse said. Gathering information that would prove the Resurrection—and other biblical narratives—is both an affirmation of faith and an effort to demonstrate that religious Christians are no fools. "I believe, ultimately, that if we keep searching, we'll find out how all these things took place."

I asked the same question of Lawrence Schiffman, a Dead Sea Scrolls scholar at New York University, who cited "a kind of conspiracy theory."

"The assumption is that there is some hidden something that will radically transform our knowledge: art, a menorah, the Dead Sea Scrolls, something kept in the Vatican," he said. "The reason that people love these things is that they can't accept that there are certain things we know, and others that we don't know and we never will."

For his part, University of Iowa archaeologist Robert Cargill enumerated two primary reasons people search for biblical relics. The first, he told me, is money—"Religious relics are a *huge* business."

But these objects would not be so valuable if people didn't want to buy them. Searching for and owning them fills a void for believers, making the ethereal tangible.

"In a world increasingly reliant upon evidence and verifiable data, relics offer a form of spiritual 'evidence' that confirms one's beliefs," Cargill said. "Relics allow Christians to touch what they believe to be evidence of Jesus, thereby confirming their faith."

As the years went on, I often asked myself why I searched. Everywhere I turned, evidence had disappeared. Fire had destroyed scroll fragments and suitcases, sources refused to talk to me—and pressured others to do the same. There were moments of elation, but also moments of massive frustration. Perhaps most vexing of all was the constant presence of doubt: would I ever solve the question of the scrolls' authenticity? Every time I considered giving up, I was spurred on by one thought: *If you keep searching, you may find what you're looking for. If you stop, you certainly will not.*

I did not search for any of the reasons Crouse, Schiffman, and Cargill suggested. I searched because it was a great mystery. I searched because, on the good days, it was fun. I searched because I had grown up with biblical criticism at the core of my being—because the documentary hypothesis on the Torah's creation was paramount in my received wisdom. I searched because I hoped that finding Shapira's scrolls might shed light on all of this. Add further evidence to it. Complement my father's life's work.

And then I discovered that it had all been a fraud.

I have long been fascinated by the various types of genius—Mozart the musical genius, Bill Clinton the political genius, Woody Allen the comic genius. In Shapira, I came to realize, I had stumbled on another kind of genius, the situational genius. He was, to be sure, a virtuoso forger. In another era, he might have put his skills to work faking passports for dissidents and spies. He was also a nimble interpreter of the biblical scriptures, predicting one of the twentieth century's greatest archaeological discoveries seventy years before it happened. But perhaps more than all of that, he had demonstrated a genius for spotting historical forces at work, interpreting the mood of the public, identifying what it was they would want next, and giving it to them—real or fake.

With a new field of history being built all around him, Shapira had seen an opening and charged through it. England was Bible-crazed. Germany was beginning to approach the Bible critically. Archaeology was maturing. Advances in infrastructure were paving the way for Western believers to visit Palestine—their eyes, and wallets, suddenly open to what lay beneath its sands. Shapira's Jewish background had afforded him skills to create his "relic." His Christianity had led him to understand the desire for just such a thing among believers.

To pull off his deception, he had to walk a delicate tightrope, straddle multiple worlds. He was a dealer in authentic Hebrew manuscripts who lurked on less legitimate corners. He associated with scholars at some of Europe's best universities, and with wanted men unwilling to meet in the light of day. Historians talk of men and women born for the times and places in which they live. Would Shapira have been Shapira without the Bible critics? Without the steamships and consuls that pulled Europe toward the Ottomans? Without the chance discovery of an ancient stone pillar that spurred adventurous men to seek glory in the dunes that rose and fell east of the Dead Sea?

Shapira was a social climber. He could also be earnest. He was an actor—but could be modest in the presence of men of greater learning. He was a salesman, but was not too proud to point out when his wares raised problems. He had a temper, but could be tender with his children. He knew much of Jewish scripture, but had embraced Christ. He was a European who lived in the heart of the Near East. He was bold enough to forge his Deuteronomy and vain enough to think he would get away with it.

In short, he had the rare ability to shape-shift, to make the appropriate costume change, to put his interlocutors—whether an American debutante, a roomful of English scholars, or a Bedouin thief—at ease. Shapira was particularly well suited for an atmosphere as dynamic as that of nineteenth-century Jerusalem, where a constant stream of foreigners descended, visions of arks and tablets and resurrected messiahs dilating their eyes; where biblical archaeology's scramble from hobby to science was under way; and where the great powers were busy digging, in the words of one scholar, for God and for country.

Shapira claimed that he had put his scrolls away for several years after Schlottmann's early dismissal. Then, on encountering the work of Friedrich Bleek and the Bible critics, he had regained his confidence and headed off to England. It seems unlikely that Shapira, who traveled insatiably in scholarly circles, first came across biblical criticism in 1883. He must have encountered it, and its contention that the Pentateuch had originally consisted of several shorter documents, much earlier. Recognizing the excitement and controversy these theories were sparking in Germany and, even more so, in Britain—to say nothing of the desire for physical proof for all things biblical—he dreamed up a document that would prove these theories right. Then he took one further, ultimately deadly, step: he created the manuscript he'd imagined.

Shapira did his work well. So well that one of the world's leading historical institutions nearly shelled out one million pounds for what he'd produced. So well that for a few weeks in the summer of 1883, the proprietor of a small shop on a crowded Jerusalem street made himself a household name. So well that people are still talking about him today.

I have often imagined Annie Mason, sitting alone beneath the louvered light in her late husband's gallery, cataloging the contents of each display case as she prepares to sell them off, bird by stuffed bird, insect by mounted insect, leaf by dried-up leaf. Somewhere—in a wooden file cabinet, perhaps, wrapped in heavy paper, or shielded in the pages of a book on British coleoptera, she happens on a few crumbling leather strips that appear to be the severed spines of old books. She lifts one and searches for some indication of what it is, but there is nothing there—no visible words, no numbers, just some dark, oily residue. The Bass Museum, she thinks, wants the animal bones and the flintwork. The Burton Museum is after the birds. These strips are assuredly none of those things. Certainly no one has asked for them. And so she tosses them into a wastebasket, which she leaves out for the trash collectors. Later in the week, they arrive on their horse-drawn cart and remove Annie's rubbish—food scraps, coffee grounds, Shapira's scrolls. Along with the euphemistically named "night soil," they haul it eleven miles to the old cotton mill at Bond End that serves as Burton's dump. When they arrive, the collectors trot inside, saddle their horses, and empty the cart into the "destructor," a large incinerator that reduces the town's garbage to ash. And then they let the fire do its work. The food scraps—gone. The coffee grounds—dust. The night soil—smoke. And the scrolls, once valued at a million pounds sterling—they burn and burn and burn and then, simply, are no more.

The geographer David Lowenthal has said that by "revealing hidden assumptions about the past they claim to stem from, fakes advance our understanding no less than the truths which expose them." There is real value, then, in Shapira's scrolls. That is true, I tell myself on good days, despite the fact that they are gone. I watched the trailer for Sabo's film the other day. It's dramatic—dire music, lightning flashes, drenched English streets. "Is it a story about obsession?" he asks in his voice-over. "Absolutely."

Obsession. I think that's why, even after I discovered the scrolls were fake, I found myself back in Rotterdam, searching for Shapira.

After he died, his body had disappeared. Like his biblical namesake, no one knew where he was buried. I had found poetic justice in that, but suddenly couldn't let it lie. At his death, I discovered, Shapira had been classified as 5th Grade Civil Arms—the poorest of

Rotterdam's poor. He was buried in a pauper's plot in Crooswijk, just outside Rotterdam. As with all other such burials, Shapira's body would then have been exhumed and reburied in a mass grave ten years after his death.

When I arrived at Crooswijk's cemetery, a young couple gathered sticks and leaves from the base of a memorial, talking sweetly to their toddler, surely reminiscing about a grandparent they hoped the boy would not forget. Not far away, a woman was kneeling in the wet grass, clearing debris from a fresh grave. Approaching Shapira's final, anonymous resting place now, I found myself aching to make a similar gesture. A sign of respect, recognition, remembrance. I wanted, like Sabo, to place a rose on the mass grave and to inscribe a small note with the same biblical verse Shapira had written on his gift to Rosette: "I am a rose of Sharon, a lily of the valleys."

But I didn't have a flower, and couldn't clean a gravestone that did not exist, and, anyway, the sky was graying and my note would be soaked when the rain came. So I tried something else. In Jewish tradition, visitors leave stones on relatives' graves as a sign of respect. I picked up a pebble and set it down on a spot in the middle of the field. There it was, small and chalky beside a tangle of fallen leaves. But if I closed my eyes, I could just make out something else: my little rock grown to a grand headstone, polished and bright, bigger than any of those I'd seen when I first entered the cemetery. Because that's what Shapira would have wanted. There was even a single rose at its base, hovering over the neatly trimmed grass. And on the front, inscribed in clear black letters, this:

Moses Wilhelm Shapira
father, husband, agent to the British Museum

AUTHOR'S NOTE

A number of books proved particularly useful in my research. They include Richard Elliott Friedman's eminently readable *Who Wrote the Bible?*, from which I drew in my effort to lay out the history of biblical criticism. Yehoshua Ben-Arieh has published a number of excellent books on Palestine and Jerusalem in the time of Shapira, and I consulted *The Rediscovery of the Holy Land in the Nineteenth Century* and *Jerusalem in the 19th Century* for sections on Jerusalem's history. *Truly Fake: Moses Wilhelm Shapira, Master Forger* was the first document I read about Shapira, and the pamphlet's essays by Irit Salmon, Ya'akov Meshorer, and Haim Be'er proved an important early inspiration. Some biblical translations were taken from the Oxford University Press's *Jewish Study Bible*.

Although Moses Wilhelm Shapira kept a diary, apparently in Hebrew, it has, to my great regret, not survived. The vast majority of the written material he left behind—letters, articles, catalogs of manuscripts for sale—relates to his business affairs and offers little in the way of a glimpse at his personal life. For such insights, I had a novel, written by Shapira's daughter, on which to rely. Myriam Harry calls *The Little Daughter of Jerusalem* a "story of my childhood and my sorrows," and where other documentary evidence left blanks, the novel, though an imperfect guide, proved a useful aid.

Some time after I turned this book in to the publisher, I finally received a copy of Yoram Sabo's film in the mail. I was surprised to see that he, too, had ended "Shapira & I" by placing a stone on Shapira's burial site. Two parallel searches converging.

I spoke with hundreds of people along the way. Whenever possible, these conversations were recorded. In other instances I took notes during the conversations. Where either of these were not options, I relied on my memory, reconstructing the scenes and conversations as soon as was feasible after they ended.

Chanan Tigay
San Francisco

ACKNOWLEDGMENTS

I am indebted to a great many people who contributed to this book in ways large and small—from inviting me into their homes to assisting in the research, from translating old documents to sharing material, and from offering advice to reading early drafts. They include:

In Israel—Malachi Beit-Arie, Yehoshua Ben-Arieh, Aaron Eime, Shimon Gibson, Gila Hurvitz, Benyamin Lukin, Uri Melamed, Jordan Penkower, David Pileggi, Alexander Rofé, Rehav "Buni" Rubin, Irit Salmon, Yoram Sabo, Timna Seligman, Micha Shagrir, Daphna Tsoran, Lenny Wolfe, Joe Zias, the staff at Christ Church's Conrad Schick Library, and especially Emanuel Tov.

In France—Mahmoud Alassi, Sophie Bontemps, Marianne Cotty, Paul Fenton, Elisabeth Fontan, Cecile Gaudin, and Michel Moutot, who has long been my model of what a journalist should be.

In Jordan—Benjamin Porter and Bruce Routledge.

In Germany—Nadja Cholidis, Laila Guhlmann, Michael Ruprecht, and especially Annette Schwarz-Scheuls and her husband, Andreas, who welcomed me into their home and generously told me their story.

In the Netherlands—Hetty Berg, Caroline Dijckmeester-Bins, Adrian Bins, Rachel Boertjens, Theodore Dunkelgrün, P. A. van

Dam, Bart Wallet, and Anneke Barends, who was a wise guide and able researcher.

In England—Spencer Bailey, Ron Causer, Stephanie Clarke, Felicity Cobbing, Clyde Dissington, Margaret Duprey, Shane Lapsys, Brian Mole, Kate Savage, Denis Segal, Joanna Skeels, Richard Stone, Katherine Thorn, Robin Trotter, Julia Wheatcroft, Vanessa Winstone, and especially Ilana Tahan and Lynn Young at the British Library.

In Australia—Paul Beringer and Michael Turner. Matthew Hamilton's groundbreaking work on Shapira and his magnanimity in sharing his material were invaluable and came at just the right time.

In the U.S.—Jacob Appel, Lowell Bergman, Maxine Chernoff, James Davis, Mike Durrie, Barbara Eaton, Michael V. Fox, Nili Fox, Skip Horack, Eli Horowitz, Arthur Kiron, Diana Kohnke, Etty Lassman, Jerry Lippman, Catherine Lucas, Mike McGriff, Loria Mendoza, Arnold Mytelka, Paul Needham, Will Palmer, Tom Pitoniak, Gary Rendsburg, Adam Rosenthal, Ellie Schainker, D. Barry Sheldon, Ann Sherwin, Paul Sherwin, Richard Steiner, Justin St. Germain, Allan Webb, and Steve Zipperstein. Brad Sabin Hill was an extremely valued resource.

For additional support, thanks also to Lyn Sabin, Peter Sabin, San Francisco State University President Lester Wong, the Corporation of Yaddo, Blue Mountain Center, and The Mesa Refuge.

Lisa Bankoff, agent extraordinaire and indispensable sounding board, has been there from the beginning to see that this book got off the ground and made it to the finish line. So have her excellent assistants, Berni Barta and Dan Kirschen.

Hilary Redmon has been as smart, sensitive, and supportive an editor as one could ask for—and this book is so much better because of her wise input. Sonya Cheuse and Ashley Garland are the best publicity tag team in America. Ben Tomek is a marketing whiz and Emma Janaskie has gone above and beyond. Enormous thanks, too, to the rest of the wonderful team at Ecco, in particular Daniel Halpern and Miriam Parker—and Zack Wagman, for stepping in and so ably taking the reins.

Many thanks to my large and growing family of Tigays, Zubkoffs, Antopols, Moskins, Johnsons, Zuckermans, Joneses, Yinnones, and Hirsches. I'm particularly grateful to Marcia Antopol and Jeff Moskin for their constant enthusiasm and timely babysitting.

To my brothers Eytan, Hillel, and Yis, I had you in mind as I wrote this.

This book is dedicated to my parents, who have given me everything. Nothing I do can adequately express my endless gratitude to you. Still, given the values you instilled in us, a book—and one about the Bible no less—does seem an appropriate beginning.

And, finally, thanks to Nellie and to Rocky—and to Molly Antopol, who has been, and remains, my beloved partner in all that I do.

NOTES

PROLOGUE

1 calling her names, drunken German, missing sausages: Rotterdam Police Department incident log for March 9, 1884.

1 concerned dispatch: Ibid.

1 bloodied corpse: *De Tijd*, March 13, 1884, and *Leidsch Dagblad*, March 12, 1884.

2 stuffed with manuscripts: *De Tijd*, March 13, 1884.

2 business cards: *Leidsch Dagblad*, March 12, 1884.

3 reconsider their ways: *Autobiography of Sir Walter Besant*, p. 161.

3 eight pounds and change: draft letter of Consul Noel Temple Moore, Jerusalem, October 21, 1883.

3 most important purveyors: catalog of purchases made by British Museum's Department of Oriental Manuscripts between 1867 and 1878.

5 "good actor": *Autobiography of Sir Walter Besant*, p. 161.

6 "contemporary copy": Ibid.

6 Jack the Ripper: *Gloucester Citizen*, May 31, 2010.

7 midnight: Besant invitation to Ginsburg, July 23, 1883.

7 tossed them jauntily: memo of William Simpson, sketch artist, housed at the British Library.

8 snared the attention: P. Kyle McCarter Jr., Why All the Fuss?, *Biblical Archaeology Review*, May/June 1997.

10 could not be a forgery: *Autobiography of Sir Walter Besant*, p. 162.

10 He'd faced the same issue: Shapira letter to Hermann Strack, May 9, 1883.

10 poured it on the old leathers: Simpson memo.

11 "practiced in the time of Moses": *Autobiography of Sir Walter Besant*, p. 162.

CHAPTER ONE: FROM PHILADELPHIA TO JERUSALEM

15 Mar Athanasius Samuel: In its April 23, 1995, obituary for Mar
    Athanasius Samuel, the *New York Times* said that Kando became
    excited about the scrolls after "noticing that writing appeared on the
    skins when they were accidentally splashed with water." On the face of
    it, this seems to be yet another extraordinary parallel between the Dead
    Sea Scrolls and Shapira's Deuteronomy. Alas, the story is probably not
    true. The Dead Sea Scrolls scholar Weston Fields told me: "None of
    the first seven scrolls, only four of which came through Mar Samuel,
    was dark, with the possible exception of the Genesis Apocryphon,
    which changed hands in the middle of the first negotiations, and was
    unrolled only much later, after 1955 when [archaeologist Yigael] Yadin
    brought the 'Israeli' scrolls back to Israel after his 1954 purchase in
    NYC."
16 "My hands shook": as quoted in Weston Fields, *The Dead Sea Scrolls,
    A Full History*, p. 45.
18 "possibly a hoax": as quoted in the *New York Times*, March 4, 1949.
18 "the word of any Bedouin": Solomon Zeitlin, "The Antiquity of the
    Hebrew Scrolls and the Piltdown Hoax. A Parallel," *Jewish Quarterly
    Review* 45, No. 1 (July 1954): 1–29.
33 bought the scrolls: Sotheby's annotated auction catalog for July 16, 1885.
33 lent them out for display: Anglo-Jewish Historical Exhibition catalog,
    1887.

CHAPTER TWO: A BIBLE AND A SPADE

35 most popular writer: *Salt Lake Herald*, June 18, 1893; Dr. Andrzej
    Diniejko, "Walter Besant's Novels of East London," Victorian Web.
35 dispatched an invitation: *Cathedra*, April 1984, p. 185.
36 Kamenets-Podolsk: *The Yivo Encyclopedia of Jews in Eastern Europe*,
    article on Kam'ianets'-Podil's'kyi.
37 "my relationship with missionaries": Shapira appeal to German consulate.
37 putrid animal carcasses, Austrian Lloyd, loosened restrictions: Yehoshua
    Ben-Arieh, *The Rediscovery of the Holy Land in the Nineteenth Century*,
    pp. 191-92.
41 "ever so long": Bertha Spafford–Vester, *Our Jerusalem*, p. 137.
42 the committee voted: minutes of the London Jews Society Committee of
    Management, July 12, 1859. Where Shapira had received the position
    provisionally in May of that year, this vote made it official.
42 forty-five pounds a year: minutes of the London Jews Society Committee
    of Management, May 4, 1859.

42 Wednesday afternoons: minutes of the London Jews Society Committee of Management's Social Committee, February 9, 1861.

46 daily English lessons: minutes of the London Jews Society Committee of Management, August 7, 1860.

46 "men of business, nay, ladies": G. Rawlinson, "The Moabite Stone," *Contemporary Review*, August 1870, p. 97.

47 "fetishist passion": Haim Be'er, "Reflections on the Elusive Charm of the Shapira Affair," in *Truly Fake: Moses Wilhelm Shapira, Master Forger*, catalog of Shapira exhibit at Israel Museum, pp. 11–13.

48 a gathering place: Ibid.

48 Metal mice: Shimon Gibson, Jerusalem in Original Photographs, 1850–1920.

48 destroyed twice, besieged twenty-three times, attacked fifty-two times, and captured and recaptured forty-four times: Eric H. Cline, *Jerusalem Besieged*, p. 2.

49 church attendance lacking: minutes of the London Jews Society Committee of Management, March 11, 1862.

49 "best shop": Karl Baedeker's guide, *Palestine and Syria*, p. 145.

50 "the most pathetic spot": Jules Lemaître, in his preface to *The Little Daughter of Jerusalem*, p. xiii.

50 Ordnance Survey of Jerusalem: John James Moscrop, *Measuring Jerusalem*, pp. 74–75.

51 asked the mission's leaders: Minutes of London Jews Society Committee of Management's Social Committee, January 29, 1861.

51 applied now for protection: Shapira's appeal to German Consulate.

51 April 23, 1861: Shapira's marriage license.

52 sun-bright courtyard: *The Little Daughter of Jerusalem*, p. 6.

52 impressing his instructors: minutes of the London Jews Society Committee of Management, July 28, 1857; CMJ list of unmarried proselytes, 1858.

53 pretty women: *The Little Daughter of Jerusalem*, p. 64.

53 devoted himself so exclusively: op. cit., p. 65.

54 didn't make it home: op. cit., p. 66.

54 stroked his hair: op. cit., p. 173.

54 arguing bitterly: op. cit., p. 36.

54 her small hands: op. cit., p. 54.

55 she would wed her sheikh one day: op. cit., p. 49

55 worked late: op. cit., p. 135.

55 loneliness: op. cit., p. 254.

55 depression: op. cit., p. 104

55 imaginary heroes: op. cit., p. 7.

56 pride and love of display: op. cit., pp. 192–93.

CHAPTER THREE: LONDON

57 founder of at least six museums: Michael Turner, *50 Objects 50 Stories: Extraordinary Curiosities from the Nicholson Museum.*

57 "proved the truth": Baronness Hilda v. Deichmann (née de Bunsen), "Recollections of Sir Charles Nicholson," November 1903, p. 5, University of Sydney Archives.

58 four hundred ancient artifacts, a thousand antiquities: Turner, "Sir Charles Nicholson: Who Do You Think You Are?," in *50 Objects 50 Stories.*

58 began learning Hebrew: Nicholson's study notebook, University of Sydney library.

58 "most learned Hebraist": A. D. Crown, "The Fate of the Shapira Scroll," *Revue de Qumran* 8 (December 1970): 422.

58 "overtures were made": Shapira letter to Rev. Story of July 26, 1900, University of Sydney archives.

59 "considerable portion of the library": letter by Nicholson dated May 31 (no year, name of addressee illegible), University of Sydney archives.

59 "ask the acceptance": Shapira letter to Rev. Story of July 26, 1900, University of Sydney archives.

59 "most remarkable object": A. D. Crown, "The Fate of the Shapira Scroll," *Revue de Qumran* 8 (December 1970): 422.

59 "all carry his name": Turner, "Sir Charles Nicholson."

60 "fell into his hands, the contents lost": Crown, "The Fate of the Shapira Scroll," pp. 421–23.

62 "strangest books": Joan E. Taylor, *The Essenes, the Scrolls, and the Dead Sea,* p. 305.

64 "greatest of Oriental scholars": *Straits Times,* April 11, 1914.

75 Did Ginsburg consign them: Citing privacy issues, Sotheby's refused to tell me who consigned the scrolls to them for auction. I suggested that, 130 years later, whoever that person was had probably passed on. I thought the argument airtight. Sotheby's disagreed.

CHAPTER FOUR: AN EPIC BATTLE

The account of the discovery of the Moabite Stone presented in this chapter is compiled from several sources, including: F. A. Klein's own account of the find, published in the *Pall Mall Gazette* on April 19, 1870, and reprinted as "The Original Discovery of the Moabite Stone" in the *Palestine Exploration Fund Quarterly Statement* (*PEFQ*), March 31–June 30, 1870, p. 281; James King, *Moab's Patriarchal Stone: Being an Account of the Moabite Stone, Its Story and Teaching* (1878); the PEF's *21 Years Work in the Holy Land: A Record and A*

Summary, June 22, 1865–June 22, 1886; and a letter published by Ganneau in the *Athenaeum* on January 24, 1874, p. 127.

80 book-length account: *Moab's Patriarchal Stone.*

84 "A Bedouin compliment; perfectly free": Klein, "The Original Discovery of the Moabite Stone."

86 ethnic joke: Thanks to Professor Bruce Routledge of the University of Liverpool for his insights on Moabite–Israelite relations.

88 four hundred dollars: André Lemaire, "House of David Restored in Moabite Inscription," *Biblical Archaeology Review*, May/June 1994.

88 "young, clever Arab": Klein in the *Pall Mall Gazette.*

89 born in Paris: details of Ganneau's biography come from a number of sources, including two addresses about his life and work delivered following his death: L. H. Vincent's, "Clermont-Ganneau and Palestinian Archaeology," a speech delivered to the Palestine Oriental Society in 1923 and reprinted in the organization's journal; and André Dupont-Sommer's "An Investigator of Archeological Frauds: Charles Clermont-Ganneau (1846–1923)," printed in the report of the meetings of the Academy of Inscriptions and Literatures, 1974, pp. 591–609.

90 "no more possible doubt"; "an Arab of great intelligence": King, *Moab's Patriarchal Stone*, p. 27.

91 "the jabbering Arabs stood round": op. cit., p. 19.

92 "narrowly escaping": op. cit., p. 20.

92 "The aim of the expedition was then attained": op. cit., pp. 27–28.

92 "Burning with a desire": op. cit., p. 20.

92 "the master": Vincent, "Clermont-Ganneau and Palestinian Archaeology."

92 "hasty and precipitate action," "sanguine temperament": King, *Moab's Patriarchal Stone*, p. 39.

93 "paroxysms of terror": op. cit., p. 252.

95 considers renovating the stone: interview with Elisabeth Fontan, former chief curator for the Louvre's Department of Near Eastern Antiquities.

96 "I saw in the window": Ginsburg's journal of his travels in Jerusalem and Moab in 1872, held at the British Library.

96 "[I] rejoiced": Ibid.

97 Warren and Conder stayed at the hotel and Tyrwhitt-Drake died there: Shimon Gibson and Rupert L. Chapman, "The Mediterranean Hotel in Nineteenth-Century Jerusalem," *Palestine Exploration Quarterly* 127 (1995): 93.

98 "Ganneau did it": Ginsburg's journal.

99 "children of the Kingdom": Ibid.

100 "an extraordinary amount of imagination": Ibid.

101 "bags full of clay relics": The account of Shapira's Moabite pottery was compiled from numerous sources, including reports in the *PEFQ* from 1873, 1874, 1876, and 1878; Martin Heide, "The Moabitica and Their Aftermath: How to Handle a Forgery Affair with an International Impact," in *New Inscriptions and Seals Relating to the Biblical World*; letters held at the PEF to and from its members on the scene in Palestine and Moab; and others.

101 "the rage": Aloys Sprenger, *Academy*, March 11, 1876, reprinted as "The Shapira Pottery," *PEFQ*, April 1876.

101 "The talk of Jerusalem": "Lieutenant Claude R. Conder's Reports," *PEFQ*, July 1873, p. 88.

101 "grotesque uncouthness": Dunbar Heath, quoted by Ganneau in *PEFQ*, 1874, II, pp. 202–3.

102 Weser had studied: Heide, "The Moabitica and Their Aftermath," p. 194.

102 Weser made sketches: Ibid.

102 *shikutzim*: op. cit., p. 195.

102 other alphabets: op. cit., p. 196.

102 years after: op. cit., p. 207.

103 unknown Moabite script: op. cit., p. 196.

103 two different scripts: op. cit., pp. 206–7.

103 "No more valuable": Henry Lumley, letter, *Times* of London, January 26, 1872.

104 "no misunderstanding": *Academy* 3, no. 47 (May 1, 1872): 179–80.

105 "I have now the pleasure": *Academy* 3, no. 51 (July 1, 1872): 260.

106 "I regret": Ibid.

107 $235,000: Hershel Shanks, "Fakes! How Moses Shapira Forged an Entire Civilization," *Biblical Archaeology Review*, September/October 2002, p. 37.

107 Kaiser Wilhelm I: Heide, "The Moabitica and Their Aftermath," p. 198.

107 "Turkish in style", "delicately tinted clouds": *The Little Daughter of Jerusalem*, p. 177. In 1924, forty years after the Shapiras left it, the home would be purchased by the well-known Israeli artist Anna Ticho and her ophthalmologist husband, Dr. Avraham Albert Ticho, who ran a public eye clinic out of the first floor. Among other diseases, trachoma and other eye conditions ran rampant in the Jerusalem of that period and he had immigrated from Moravia in hopes of stanching these ailments, which had left scores of locals blind. Though Ticho served Jews and Arabs alike—including treating Emir Abdullah, the future king of Jordan—he was stabbed during the 1929 riots and left for dead in the streets, though ultimately he survived and lived until 1960. Today the villa houses an elegant restaurant on its first floor and spacious stone deck.

108 "labyrinth of alcoves," wooden terrace, stone divan: *The Little Daughter of Jerusalem*, p. 176.

108 "the ostrich broke free": Selah Merrill, *East of the Jordan*, p. 415.

CHAPTER FIVE: ROTTERDAM

111 the very institution: dateline of Ginsburg's letter to his daughter Ethel is "British Museum."

CHAPTER SIX: SCULPTING A CIVILIZATION

117 new Moabite stone: John James Moscrop, *Measuring Jerusalem*, p. 97.

118 "being a converted Jew": letter from Drake, June 19, 1872, held at PEF.

118 "as much as 1£ each": letter from Drake to Besant, August 21, 1862.

118 "not competent": Tyrwhitt-Drake letter to PEF, February 22, 1873.

118 "try to touch the sky," "silent and irritable," "gloomy silence": *The Little Daughter of Jerusalem*, p. 36.

119 "rock-cut repository": Claude Conder, "Lieutenant Claude R. Conder's Reports: Explorations in Jerusalem," in *PEFQ*, January 1873, p. 13.

119 "crowded Phoenician characters": op. cit., p. 14.

119 "late visit of Pastor Weser": Ibid.

120 into the paddock: *The Little Daughter of Jerusalem*, pp. 8–9.

121 "usually grave," "king of the desert": Ibid.

121 "My opinion is": *PEFQ*, 1874, p. 114.

121 "impossible to receive": op. cit., p. 115.

122 "white with anger": *The Little Daughter of Jerusalem*, p. 102.

122 "the ruin of you": op. cit., p. 104.

122 "hostile sentiment": *PEFQ*, 1874, p. 115.

123 "a certain Salim": op. cit., p. 117.

124 the exact narrative: Ibid.

125 "original trouvaille": Tyrwhitt-Drake letter to PEF, November 11, 1873.

126 "quite to yourself": Tyrwhitt-Drake letter to Besant, January 7, 1874.

127 "a piquant revelation": Schlottmann, "Chauvinism in Archaeology," *Norddeutsche Allgemeine Zeitung*, April 12, 1874.

128 taking credit for its discovery: Moscrop, *Measuring Jerusalem*, p. 106.

128 The Ottomans protested: Ibid.

128 sent specimens: Aloys Sprenger, *PEFQ*, 1876, p. 102.

129 "On that occasion": Baron von Münchhausen, *PEFQ*, 1878, p. 97.

129 questioning the process: Sprenger, *PEFQ*, 1876, p. 103.

129 abandoned efforts: Heide, "The Moabitica and Their Aftermath," p. 211.

130 the state of things was altered: Münchhausen letter to Shapira, printed in the *Athenaeum*, December 1, 1877.

131 great conjurer: Ibid.

133 "procured the unburnt idol": *Athenaeum*, January 26, 1878.

134 "advised not to purchase": Ibid.

134 "the example of Prof. Schlottmann": A. D. Neubauer, *Athenaeum*, Dec. 8, 1877.

134 "burst out crying": *The Little Daughter of Jerusalem*, p. 107.

CHAPTER SEVEN: PARIS

138 about 6 percent: correspondence with Mahmoud Alassi.

140 House of David: André Lemaire, "'House of David' Restored in Moabite Inscription," *Biblical Archaeology Review*, May/June 1994. Lemaire's discovery came on the heels of the sensational discovery in 1993–94 of the Tel Dan Stele, a similar-looking monument that also mentioned the House of David.

CHAPTER EIGHT: GERMANY

147 boxing tournament: That evening, super welterweight Ronny Gabel defeated Andy Thiele by TKO in the fourth of a scheduled six rounds.

CHAPTER NINE: THE ANTIQUARIAN AND THE MURDERER

173 "horrid man": *The Little Daughter of Jerusalem*, p. 105.

174 consigned two Torah scrolls: S. Baer, *Zwei alte Thora-Rollen aus Arabien und Palästina beschrieben von S. Baer ... gegenwärtig im Besitz von Johannes Alt ...* (Frankfurt: Verlag von Johannes Alt, 1870).

174 a sale: registers of purchases made by British Museum's Department of Oriental Manuscripts, held at British Library.

174 "exuberant spirits": *The Little Daughter of Jerusalem*, p. 167.

174 "the Bishop's wife," "even-tempered": op. cit., pp. 172–3.

000 "most important": registers of purchases made by Department of Oriental Manuscripts, held at British Library.

175 Shapira's telling: Shapira told his story of the scrolls' discovery on a number of occasions including, at greatest length, in a letter to the German orientalist Hermann Strack and a hand-written memo prepared as a "preface" to his Deuteronomy manuscript for the British Museum, and in other letters and articles. The account offered here is compiled from all these sources.

175 "steal his mother-in-law": Shapira's handwritten memo to British Museum as "preface" to offering his scrolls.

177 "Every Bedouin": Ibid.

178 "rob or steal": Shapira letter to Strack.

178 "various disguises": *The Little Daughter of Jerusalem*, p. 7.

180 five weeks: Shapira's handwritten memo to British Museum.

180 other scripts: *Athenaeum*, January 26, 1878, p. 123.

181 "only the case": Shapira letter to Strack.

186 the next month: Ibid.

186 "You'll never guess": *The Little Daughter of Jerusalem*, p. 213.

187 "speak at intervals": op. cit., p. 218.

187 September 24, 1878: Shapira letter to Strack.

187 "How I dare": Ibid.

CHAPTER 10: TERRA INCOGNITA

191 a second trek into Yemen: The account of Shapira's journey through Yemen is assembled from several sources including Chaim Goren, "Kiepert and Shapira's Journey in Yemen," *Ariel*, no. 120 (1996): 229–34; Paul B. Fenton, "Moses Shapira's Journey to the Yemen," *Mittuv Yosef*, 2011, pp. lxviii–lxxxi; and an article by Shapira in the *Athenauem*: "Arabia Felix," March 13, 1880.

191 handful of Europeans: Fenton, "Moses Shapira's Journey to the Yemen," p. xix.

194 "the following notes": Shapira in the *Athenaeum*, March 13, 1880, p. 346.

195 "unclean people": "Catalogue of M.S.S. brought over by Mr. M.W. Shapira from Yemen in the year 1879," p. 1.

195 "The amount of difficulties": op. cit., p. 5.

195 "lived among them," "Temanite Scroll," "nominal sum": Bertha Spafford Vester, *Our Jerusalem*, p. 138.

196 Nils Lind: Quoted in Helga Dudman and Ruth Kark, *The American Colony*, pp. 66–68.

197 "*Nevi'im*": *Nevi'im and Ketuvim* refer to the divisions of the Bible known in English as Prophets and Writings. A *Targum* is an Aramaic translation of a portion of the Hebrew Bible. *Mishnah* refers to the Jewish Oral Law, and *Seder Kodashim* is the fifth of six orders of this treatise. *Massekhet Middot* is a tractate from the order of *Kodashim*.

197 second manuscript sale, two further sales: registers of purchases made by British Museum's Department of Oriental Manuscripts, held at British Library.

198 "As the sellers": *Athenaeum*, July 15, 1882.

198 fundamental questions: My account of biblical criticism's emergence relies in part on Richard Elliott Friedman, *Who Wrote the Bible?*

199 received a copy: Shapira letter to Strack.

199 "report events": Friedman, *Who Wrote the Bible?*, pp. 17–18.

200 claim outright: op. cit., p. 20.

201 same story twice: op. cit., p. 22.

202 a style all its own: op. cit., p. 23.

203 "What a change": Shapira letter to Strack.

CHAPTER ELEVEN: SYDNEY

231 successful physician: Robert Bewick, *History of a Provincial Hospital, Burton Upon Trent.*

CHAPTER TWELVE: LONDON CALLING

236 William St. Chad Boscawen: minutes of the British Museum Board of Trustees, February 23, 1884.

236 informed the institution's trustees: minutes of the British Museum Board of Trustees, July 28, 1883.

237 "unspeakable interest": *Liverpool Daily Post*, August 9, 1883.

237 "antecedently improbable": *Saturday Review*, August 18, 1883.

238 "stranger than fiction": *Liverpool Daily Post*, August 9, 1883.

238 "found with a mummy": *Times*, August 21, 1883.

239 a large payment: John Marco Allegro, *The Shapira Affair*, p. 51.

240 "everyone bowed to them," "aigre-douce," "reckless extravagance," "German Banker," "whole of Judea": *The Little Daughter of Jerusalem*, p. 266.

242 "4th of August": Shapira may be mistakenly referring to an article that appeared in the *Times* on August 3, 1883.

242 "sad business": Shapira letter to Ginsburg, August 6, 1883.

244 "With some of [Ginsburg's] observations": *Record*, August 11, 1883.

244 once in Psalm 50: This is part of a broader phenomenon in the book of Psalms, which is divided into five sections. Book Two is known as the Elohistic Psalter, because in many psalms, where God's name, Jehovah (YHWH), was originally used, it had been revised to read Elohim, or God. This may have been an effort to avoid using God's holy name. Or, it could be for another reason that we don't know. Shapira claimed that the circles that produced his copy of Deuteronomy were Elohistic, which is to say that for one reason or another, they preferred to refer to God as Elohim and not Jehovah.

244 "greatest enemy": Shapira letter to Ginsburg, August 6, 1883.

244 "top expert": André Dupont-Sommer, "An Investigator of Archaeological Frauds: Charles Clermont-Ganneau (1846–1923), Member of the Academy of Inscriptions and Literatures."

245 "pitiless and irrefutable": D. Sidersky, "Several Portraits of Our Masters of Semitic Studies," 1937.

246 "sole fact": Charles Clermont-Ganneau, *Les Fraudes Archéologiques en Palestine*, p. 192.

CHAPTER THIRTEEN: FROM PARIS WITH DOUBTS

247 his great regret: *Times*, August 21, 1883.

248 a modern forger: Ibid.

240 on these strips; nothing is more easy: Ibid.

250 arriving at a figure: *Record*, August 24, 1883.

251 "Our only wonder": *Standard*, August 22, 1883.

251 eight days earlier: *Standard*, August 14, 1883.

252 first calling attention: *Times*, August 21, 1883.

252 very next day: *Times*, August 22, 1883.

252 underhanded efforts: *Standard*, August 22, 1883.

252 "Western credulity": *Academy*, August 18, 1883.

253 "flippant offer": *Echo*, Thursday August 23, 1883.

253 "a few minutes": *Times*, August 21, 1883.

253 "Dear Mr. Bond": Ginsburg's report, as published in the *Times*, August 27, 1883.

254 "was bought from": *Times*, August 27, 1883.

256 "first public exposer": *Times*, March 16, 1914.

256 "tried to anticipate": *Times*, March 17, 1914.

256 Dr. Ginsburg was drawn: *Times*, March 23, 1914.

257 "made a fool of me": Shapira letter to Ginsburg, August 23, 1883, held in the British Library.

257 "so disappointed": *Times*, August 27, 1883.

CHAPTER FOURTEEN: PLAYING DEFENSE

260 "excuse my troubling you": Shapira letter to Bond, August 25 or 28, 1883 (date is obscured).

263 "Who is the forger?": *Times*, Tuesday August 21, 1883.

265 "Deinard visited London": This story about Ephraim Deinard was brought to light by Brad Sabin Hill, who as the onetime head of the Hebrew

Section of the British Library has taken a keen interest in all things Shapira. The translation of Deinard's work cited here is his. Hill published the anecdote in his article, "Ephraim Deinard on the Shapira Affair," which appeared in *The Book Collector: A Special Number to Commemorate the 150th Anniversary of Bernard Quaritch LTD: 1997.*

268 "these monstrous figures": A. S. Yahuda, "The Story of a Forgery and the Mesa Inscription," *Jewish Quarterly Review* 35 (1944–45): 140.

268 "I swear by Allah": op. cit., p. 144.

CHAPTER FIFTEEN: IN LIGHT OF RECENT DISCOVERIES

275 "did not suffer": *Journal of Jewish Studies* 7 (1956): 187–93.

275 international Bible scholars: "The Case of Shapira's Dead Sea (Deuteronomy) Scrolls of 1883," *Transactions of the Wisconsin Academy of Science, Arts and Letters,* Vol. 47, 1958, p. 187.

275 "eminent scholars": Ibid.

275 "the benefit of new knowledge": J. L. Teicher, "The Genuineness of the Shapira Manuscripts," *Times Literary Supplement,* March 22, 1957, p. 184.

276 again went before: "The Case of Shapira's Dead Sea (Deuteronomy) Scrolls of 1883," *Transactions of the Wisconsin Academy of Science, Arts and Letters* 47 (1958): 187.

277 "prepared to condemn": op. cit., p. 215.

278 "private communication": op. cit., p. 200.

CHAPTER SIXTEEN: BURTON-ON-TRENT

281 "attack": *Burton Mail,* November 5, 1903.

281 "sterling qualities": *Lancet,* November 13, 1903.

281 "simple geniality": *Proceedings of the Linnean Society of London, From November 1903 to June 1904,* p. 35.

281 "one of the finest": *Burton Mail,* November 20, 1903.

281 "great loss": *Burton Mail,* November 6, 1903.

282 "most intriguing": Robert Bewick, *History of a Provincial Hospital, Burton Upon Trent.*

282 "Shells, birds, insects": C. F. Thornewill, "Obituary Notice of Philip Brookes Mason," *Journal of Conchology* 2, no. 4 (October 1904): 104–5.

282 "became the eventual possessor": Ibid.

293 "William Tate of London": "Burton-upon-Trent: Established Church," British History Online, http://www.british-history.ac.uk/vch/staffs/vol9/pp. 107-130.

293 lead carriage: *Burton Mail,* November 9, 1903.

CHAPTER SEVENTEEN: MR. SHARP-EYE-RA

301 "nearly fainted," "send us a telegram": *The Little Daughter of Jerusalem*, p. 267.
302 most of the servants: op. cit., p. 275.
302 "irreproachable record": op. cit., p. 273.
303 "Mr. Sharp-Eye-Ra": *Punch*, September 8, 1883, p. 118. The magazine did not end its fanciful parody with this cartoon. It also included the following unsigned poem, under the title, "How it was Done":

"The compiler of the Hebrew text was a Polish, Russian, or German Jew. ... There were no less than four or five persons engaged in the production of the forgery."—Dr. Ginsburg's *Report on* MR. SHAPIRA'S *Manuscript of Deuteronomy.*

SAYS AARON to MOSES, "Mankind is very dull;
A learned man may be a dupe, a scholar's oft a gull.
I think we might the *savants* sell,
Lead pundits by the noses.
I guess the game would pay us well."
"No doubt it would," says Moses.
SAYS AARON to MOSES, "A manuscript of, say

BC 800, is a thing that really *ought* to pay.
That Moabitish stone has filled
The world with wild 'supposes.'
How with *our* 'find' it would be thrilled!"
"Ah! wouldn't it!" says Moses.
SAYS AARON to MOSES, "The text of Deuteronomy,

Written on ancient leathern scrolls—skill matching with economy—
SHAPIRA—some invention quick,
(Romance on zeal imposes)—
I really think't would do the trick."
"Yes! Done with you!" says Moses.
SAYS AARON to MOSES, "That GINSBURG is a bore,

And CLERMONT-GANNEAU's far too fast with his linguistic lore.
That million will not come *this* way.
Learning our dodge discloses.
Archaic forgeries don't pay."
"No; hang it all!" says Moses.

303 "not worth his while": *Times*, August 31, 1883.

304 between there and Bloomendaal: *Leydsche Courant*, March 13, 1884.

304 "assortment of . . . Hebrew manuscripts": letters of Dr. Charles Rieu to trustees of the British Museum, October 15, 1883, and January 7, 1884.

305 "Dr. Rieu has the honour," "Rieu wrote again": Ibid.

306 "visible agitation," "the need to cast": Ganneau, *Les Fraudes Archéologiques en Palestine*, pp. 255–6.

308 Suspecting he was insane: *Leyds Courant*, March 13, 1884.

308 "The reason why": *Leydse Courant*, March 14, 1884.

309 Climbing quickly down: *The Little Daughter of Jerusalem*, p. 280.

310 "screaming and crying": Myriam Harry letter to Euting, dated October 20 (no year), held at the Bibliothèque Nationale et Universitaire in Strasbourg, France.

310 "his great misfortune": A second letter from Myriam Harry to Euting, dated February 2, 1889, held at the Bibliothèque Nationale et Universitaire in Strasbourg, France.

310 "in private correspondence": My thanks to Professor Paul Fenton of the Sorbonne, who discovered these letters by Myriam Harry, transcribed them, and generously agreed to share them with me.

310 bankruptcy proceedings: letter from German Imperial Consul Reitz to W. Duisberg, August 16, 1884, Israel National Archives.

311 inventory: letter from Imperial Consul by Proxy J. Boness to W. Duisberg, August 23, 1884, Israel National Archives.

CHAPTER EIGHTEEN: SAN FRANCISCO

314 "act of providence": *San Francisco Call*, May 9, 1913.

322 "corrupted," "reliable information": Christopher A. Rollston, "The Crisis of Modern Epigraphic Forgeries and the Antiquities Market: A Palaeographer Reflects on the Problem and Proposes Protocols for the Field," *SBL Forum*, March 2005.

323 "forging a civilization": Hershel Shanks, "Fakes! How Moses Shapira Forged an Entire Civilization," *Biblical Archaeology Review*, September/ October 2002, p. 37.

327 "hidden assumptions": as quoted by Neil Asher Silberman in "On Relics, Forgeries, and Biblical Archaeology," *SBL Forum*, February 2006.

330 "for God and for country": Neil Asher Silberman, Digging for God and Country: Exploration, Archeology, and the Secret Struggle for the Holy Land, 1799–1917.

SELECTED BIBLIOGRAPHY

Allegro, John Marco, *The Shapira Affair* (New York: Doubleday, 1965).

Baedeker, Karl, ed., *Palestine and Syria: Handbook for Travellers* (Leipzig: Karl Baedeker, 1876).

Baer, S., *Zwei alte Thora-Rollen aus Arabien und Palästina* (Frankfurt: Verlag von Johannes Alt, 1870).

Ben-Arieh, Yehoshua, *Jerusalem in the 19th Century: The Old City* (London: Palgrave Macmillan, 1985).

Ben-Arieh, Yehoshua, *The Rediscovery of the Holy Land in the Nineteenth Century* (Detroit: Wayne State University Press, 1979).

Besant, Walter, *Autobiography of Sir Walter Besant* (New York: Dodd, Mead and Company, 1902).

Bewick, Robert, *History of a Provincial Hospital, Burton Upon Trent* (Burton-upon-Trent: David Whitehead Ltd., 1974).

Clermont-Ganneau, Charles, *Les Fraudes Archéologiques en Palestine* (Paris: Ernest Leroux, 1885).

Cline, Eric H., *Jerusalem Besieged: From Ancient Canaan to Modern Israel* (Ann Arbor: University of Michigan Press, 2004).

Dudman, Helga and Ruth Kark, *The American Colony: Scenes from a Jerusalem Saga* (Jerusalem: Carta, 1998).

Fields, Weston W., *The Dead Sea Scrolls: A Full History* (Boston: Brill, 2009).

Friedman, Richard Elliott, *Who Wrote the Bible?* (New York: Harper & Row, 1987).

Gibson, Shimon, *Jerusalem in Original Photographs: 1850–1920* (London: Stacey International, 2011).

Harry, Myriam, *The Little Daughter of Jerusalem* (New York: E. P. Dutton and Company, 1919).

King, James, *Moab's Patriarchal Stone: Being an Account of the Moabite Stone, Its Story and Teaching* (London: Bickers and Son, 1878).

Merrill, Selah, *East of the Jordan: A Record of Travel and Observation in the Countries of Moab, Gilead and Bashan* (London: Richard Bentley and Son, 1881).

Moscrop, John James, *Measuring Jerusalem: The Palestine Exploration Fund and British Interests in the Holy Land* (New York: Leicester University Press, 2000).

Palestine Exploration Fund, preface by Walter Besant, *21 Years Work in the Holy Land: A Record and A Summary, June 22, 1865–June 22, 1886* (London: Richard Bentley and Son, 1886).

Salmon, Irit, curator, *Truly Fake: Moses Wilhelm Shapira, Master Forger* (Jerusalem: The Israel Museum, 2000).

Silberman, Neil Asher, *Digging for God and Country: Exploration, Archeology, and the Secret Struggle for the Holy Land, 1799–1917* (New York: Anchor, 1990).

Taylor, Joan E., *The Essenes, the Scrolls, and the Dead Sea* (Oxford, England: Oxford University Press, 2012).

Turner, Michael, *50 Objects 50 Stories: Extraordinary Curiosities from the Nicholson Museum* (Sydney: Nicholson Museum, 2012).

Vester, Bertha Spafford, *Our Jerusalem* (New York: Doubleday, 1950).

ABOUT THE AUTHOR

Chanan Tigay is an award-winning journalist who has covered the Middle East, 9/11, and the United Nations for numerous magazines, newspapers, and wires. Born in Jerusalem, Tigay holds degrees from Columbia University and the University of Pennsylvania and was a recent Investigative Reporting Fellow at the University of California, Berkeley. He is a professor of Creative Writing at San Francisco State University.